John
t
An

John Jacob Astor and the First Great American Fortune

Alexander Emmerich

McFarland & Company, Inc., Publishers
Jefferson, North Carolina, and London

A shorter version of this book was published in German as
John Jacob Astor: Der enfolgreichste deutsche Auswanderer (Stuttgart: Konrad-Theiss-Verlag, 2009).

LIBRARY OF CONGRESS CATALOGUING-IN-PUBLICATION DATA

Emmerich, Alexander.
 John Jacob Astor and the first great American fortune /
Alexander Emmerich.
  p.   cm.
 Includes bibliographical references and index.

 ISBN 978-0-7864-7213-0
 softcover : acid free paper ∞

 1. Astor, John Jacob, 1763–1848. 2. Businesspeople —
United States — Biography. 3. German Americans —
Biography. 4. Millionaires — United States — Biography.
I. Title.
 HC102.5.A76E458 2013
 381.092 — dc23
 [B]   2013023694

BRITISH LIBRARY CATALOGUING DATA ARE AVAILABLE

© 2013 Alexander Emmerich. All rights reserved

No part of this book may be reproduced or transmitted in any form or by any means, electronic or mechanical, including photocopying or recording, or by any information storage and retrieval system, without permission in writing from the publisher.

On the cover: Oil painting of John Jacob Astor by Gilbert Stuart, 1794; engraving by William Faden, 1777 (Library of Congress)

Manufactured in the United States of America

McFarland & Company, Inc., Publishers
 Box 611, Jefferson, North Carolina 28640
 www.mcfarlandpub.com

In Memory of Jürgen Herrmann

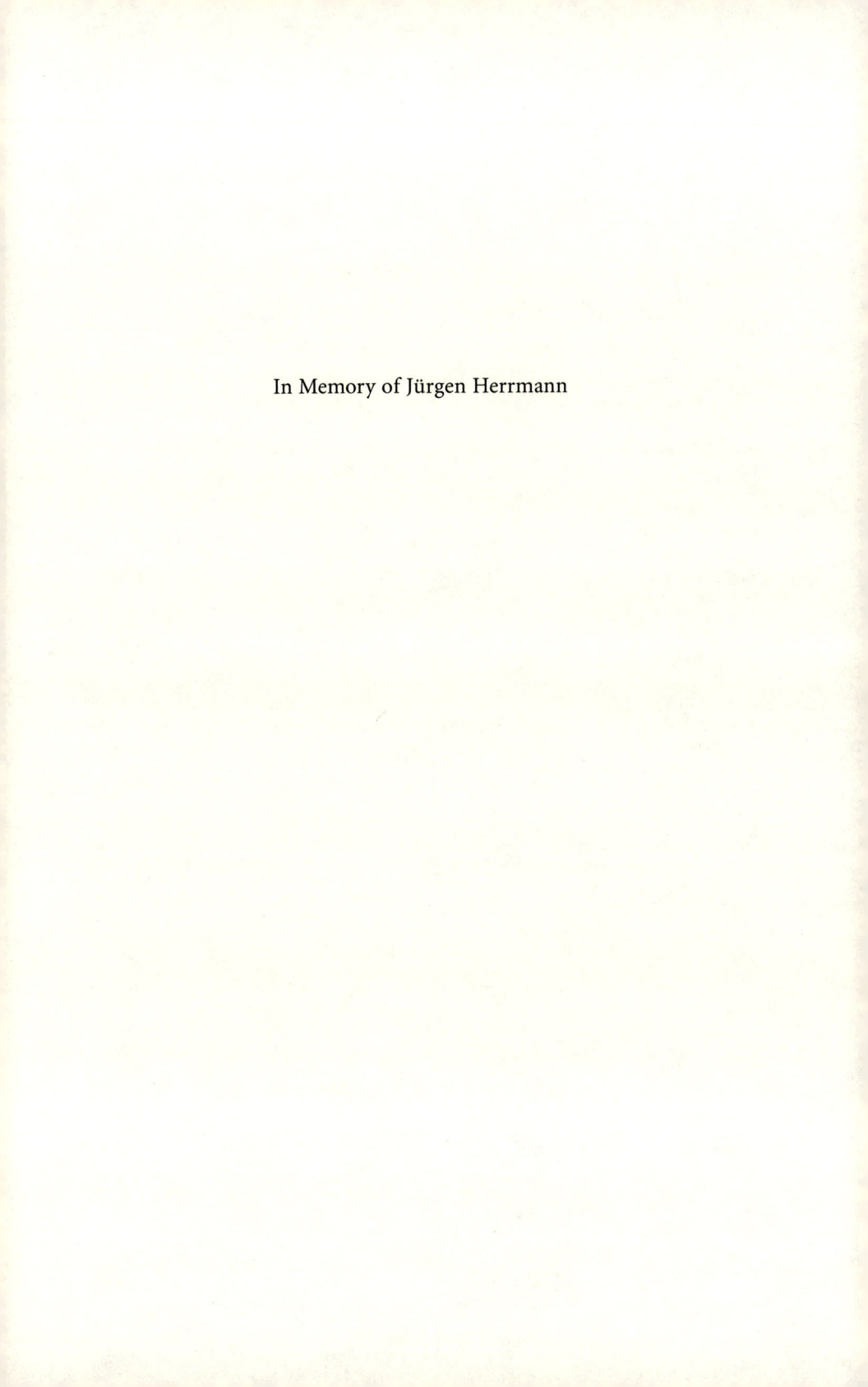

Table of Contents

Preface 1
Introduction 3

1. Origins, 1763–1780 17
    Family Background 19
    Astor's Youth 22
    The Decision to Leave Germany 24

2. Apprentice, 1780–1784 30
    First Professional Steps 31
    Crossing the Atlantic Ocean 33

3. Immigrant, 1784–1800 39
    Arriving in New York 41
    Following Native American Paths 49
    Family and Social Network 54

4. Visionary, 1800–1815 60
    Enter the China Trade 61
    Real Estate on the Rise 66
    Founding the American Fur Company 69
    Astoria, Oregon 74
    The War of 1812 and the Loss of Astoria 85
    Astor and the Peace Treaty of Ghent 91

5. Global Player, 1815–1834 97
    The Formation of the Second Bank of the United States 98
    Business Genius 100
    Returning to Europe 105
    Trade on the Frontier 113
    Retreat from Business 119

6. New Yorker, 1834–1848 124
    The Astor House 126
    Washington Irving's *Astoria* 131
    Economic Crisis and Immigration Waves 137
    Age and Death 140
    Astor's Last Will — Founding a Dynasty 143
    Astor's Public Image and Legacy 150

7. Astor Revisited — Afterthoughts 167

Notes 173
Bibliography 189
Index 195

Preface

The name "Astor" evokes many associations. It stands for luxury, hotels, ships, cities, wealth in general, and for a New York dynasty. Movie lovers might remember Astor Pictures, a production company that existed up to 1956, or maybe even the German-American actress Lucile Langhanke, whose career only took off after she started to perform under the name Mary Astor. Then there is Margret Astor, the famous line of cosmetic products, or Astor cigarettes, the ones with the elegant red packaging.

New Yorkers, on the other hand, run into Astor all over the city. There they encounter Astor Place, Astor Boulevard, Astor Court, Astor District, Astor Row (Harlem), Astoria (Queens), and the former Astor Library, now part of the New York Public Library. The name Astor rings everywhere. The most Google hits are produced by the Waldorf-Astoria, the famous hotel that inspired generations with its glamour, splendor and famous visitors, and the setting of TV series and movies. There are copycat hotels in all corners of the world that seek a part of this aura of the rich and famous so closely connected to the name Astor. Not to mention the first American settlement on the Pacific Ocean is still called "Astoria" and was founded in 1811 by a group of trappers. They were called the "Astorians" and were fur traders on the coast of Oregon at the mouth of the Columbia River.

In addition, there are cities and townships all over the United States which are named Astor, Astoria or even Waldorf. Furthermore, the name does not seem to be exclusively in use within the United States. One can find hotels named Astoria all over the world. Eventually, some who have visited Heidelberg and Mannheim in southwestern Germany might have come by the city of Walldorf in its vicinity. So what does Walldorf have in common with New York? Not much on a first glance, though visitors to Walldorf run into the Astorhaus, the Johann-Jakob-Astor-Straße, Astor Garten, Astorhalle, and FC Astoria-Walldorf, the local soccer club. Even the Lions Club is called Walldorf-Astoria. In Heidelberg one can find the Astorstraße as part of a settlement of the U.S. Army, as well as the small but beautiful Hotel Astoria Heidelberg.

The Astors were one of the leading New York families over the last 250 years. Together with the Rockefellers, Vanderbilts, Morgans and Carnegies, they were among the wealthiest families in New York during the Gilded Age at the end of the 19th century. They enjoyed a life that Europeans previously had only seen at royal courts and palaces. The Astors, moreover, behaved like royals themselves by enjoying their wealth, making "big business," and spending on philanthropy and social care. But the Astors were more than that. They were the first family to reach the legendary super status that is nowadays reserved for people like Donald Trump and Bill Gates.

But not only that: the founder of that dynasty, John Jacob Astor, was the first man in history who had climbed the social ladder from bitter poverty to immense wealth. Nowadays not everybody knows his life story anymore, although it was published in many newspapers and magazines over the last 150 years. If you ask someone what comes to your mind if you hear the name "John Jacob Astor,"[1] the answers are manifold: Wasn't John Jacob Astor the founder of that famous hotel in New York, the Waldorf-Astoria? Wasn't John Jacob Astor the name of the richest passenger on the *Titanic* when she sank in 1912? Some reports might also tell that a certain John Jacob Astor was the greediest man of the 19th century. But what is true about it? And who was this person who gave his name to so many things?

Introduction

Penniless, John Jacob Astor (1763–1848) had left his hometown Walldorf, close to Heidelberg and Mannheim in the German southwest, for America. When he died on March 29, 1848,[1] in New York, he left not only stocks, two hotels, a theater and a large amount of real estate in Manhattan, but also 20 million U.S. dollars, a sum that seemed too hard to even imagine for his contemporaries. The *New York Times* estimated that now his fortune would cash in at 116 billion U.S. dollars.[2] Therefore Astor can be counted the third richest American of all times, worth twice as much as Bill Gates in his time.

Never before had his fellow New York contemporaries seen an immigrant rise from rags to riches like he did. Never before had someone accumulated such a large amount of money. Nobody had ever pictured wealth like Astor accumulated. Therefore, he did not have any role models and could stand no comparison because nobody before him ever achieved what he did. He was the first who rose from extreme poverty to extraordinary wealth. Neither the idea nor the term "American Dream"[3] existed, and the future "land of the unlimited opportunities"[4] was still an undiscovered country. Horatio Alger would describe the social upward mobility of the kind Astor experienced as a "dishwasher-to-millionaire-career" in the 1860s, more than 20 years after Astor's death. Even the first usage of the French word *millionaire* is only documented for the United States in the 1840s,[5] when Astor had already become a multimillionaire. He had realized his personal American dream of rising from poverty and gaining economic freedom before others, Americans and Europeans alike, started to dream of it.

Being the influential businessman he was, John Jacob Astor had of course become a person of interest for his contemporaries. Although he was cautious about his reputation, Astor did not always receive positive feedback. His wealth that amounted to such a previously unheard-of sum provoked Astor's opponents.

After his death, defamatory remarks dominated the press coverage of his passing. While he was still alive, authors mostly praised Astor's success story in rising from a poor immigrant to one of the leading personalities in North American economy, and named him an example of the greatness of the new nation. Among the examples of this positive take on Astor are the short biography by David Jacques from 1844 in *Hunt's Merchant Magazine*, one of the most widely read magazines of its time, and the portrait by Moses Yale Beach in *Wealth and Biography of the Citizens of the City of New York* in 1845. Soon afterwards public opinion dramatically changed. Now we encounter the image of an avaricious old millionaire, who reminds us of Ebenezer Scrooge in Charles Dickens's *A Christmas Carol*. A coincidence, or more? Was old Ebenezer modeled after Astor?

When Charles Dickens visited the United States in 1842, the city of New York was on his itinerary.[6] New York's elite were happy to give him a warm reception. A big ball was organized in his honor, and weeks with one dinner after the other followed. On February 19, 1842, Dickens and Astor met during one of these dinners at Astor's first hotel, the City Hotel.[7] During his stay in the United States, Dickens always commented positively about the American way of life. However, once back home he started to revise his view and publicly uttered his dislike of New York City, its upper class, and the United States of America in general. In the months after his return, he published several anti-American newspaper articles, along with his soon famous *A Christmas Carol*, which would become one of the most famous pieces of its time. Taking into account the rumors surrounding Astor and his wealth, it is easy to see how contemporaries and later writers thought that Dickens was inspired by Astor. For many he symbolized the old, avaricious man who needed to be brought back to sympathy and helping others.

Popular documentaries, collective biographies and similar types of information often describe Astor in this way. It is interesting to discuss how the originally positive image of Astor became more and more gloomy over the years. Why was it literally reversed after his death in March 1848? Which image prevails in public today? What did historians find out about John Jacob Astor?

New York dailies were full of articles about Astor after his death. Even months afterwards, papers continued to discuss the stories of his life and death. Astor was still headline news, and every hearsay, rumor, and anecdotes were printed. His will, which was published on March 30, 1848, in the *New York True Sun*,[8] created an even higher public curiosity. The *New York Tribune* wrote: "As to the Will of Mr. Astor, there are a thousand rumors afloat."[9] The will started an intense debate about Astor's life and the acquisition of his wealth after the New Yorkers found out how much he was worth. Nobody had ever earned nor left 20 million dollars[10] in those days, and before the public could accept that someone could actually inherit this much, there were ethical and legal issues to discuss. For the first time in the new republic, the ideals of republicanism were confronted with the consequences of economic liberalism. In a series of newspaper articles, Astor was featured as example of the evil, greedy capitalist and "un-republican" Scrooge: "[He was] industrious in the accumulation of riches, he was like wise very penurious and niggardly in money matters. What he saved he kept, and looked up to the day of his death."[11] In a lead article on April 5, 1848, the attacks on Astor culminated in the demand to return the larger part of his property and cash to the people of New York because Astor had made a good deal of his profits from speculating in New York real estate. Therefore his gains should be returned to the New Yorkers.[12]

Even after the articles had stopped a few weeks later, Astor was still on everybody's lips. A year after his death, Horace Mann, the so-called "father of American education," used him as an example of the negative effects of wealth in his speech, at the 29th anniversary of the Boston Mercantile Library Association, warning the audience of the dangers of hoarding millions: "[Astor was] the most notorious, the most wealthy, and, considering his vast means, the most miserly of his class in this country. Nothing but absolute insanity can be pleaded in palliation of the conduct of a man who was worth nearly or quite twenty millions of dollars, but gave only some half million of it for any public object."[13]

Research Interest and Relevance

A biography of John Jacob Astor must therefore raise questions about how to judge Astor's memory and public image. His contemporaries, the journalist James Gordon Bennett,[14] the "father of American education" Horace Mann,[15] and other critics drew his picture as a greedy old man who was nothing but the true personification of Ebenezer Scrooge from Charles Dickens's *A Christmas Carol*. Others saw in him a true model because of his spectacular social uprise. To them he was the ideal American success story of the sort that was popularized by Horatio Alger's many novels in the 1860s.[16] Alger's stories always featured the rise of a young man from a humble background who finds success through hard work, courage, ambition and acting on behalf of his fellow man.

In order to understand Astor's life it is equally important to analyze the popular anecdotes that entwine his life and legacy. Many of them were taken at face value by historians and have been copied and pasted from book to book without any questioning. This book analyzes those popular stories for the first time in relation to their origin and effect. This book finally traces how these Astor stories found their way into the collective memory of his adopted home.

Without any doubt, Astor's career is a clear fulfillment of the American myth of success.[17] After his arrival in the United States as a poor German immigrant in the summer of 1784, he managed to rise as no one had done before. He became a millionaire before this term even entered the American language. So John Jacob Astor already lived the American Dream while others—Americans and Europeans alike—only dreamt of it.

Astor's life is part of the American success story that is so closely connected with the American self-image. In cultural studies as well as in economic analyses we find entries like *success*—but never failure. As Max Weber illustrated in his work *The Protestant Ethic and the Spirit of Capitalism*, the secularization of the Puritan faith created an ethic that made the pursuit of material and social success a moral obligation.[18] This secularization was the basis for their specific American myth of success. Weber names Benjamin Franklin as his example for both the secularization of Puritanism and the career of a "self-made man"[19] that is shaped by virtue and success. Franklin was the fifteenth of sixteen siblings in a Puritan family. Coming from an underprivileged background, he soon rose to become an inventor and internationally renowned diplomat. Weber was convinced Franklin's success was the result of his virtuous life.[20]

In the course of the 19th century, this originally religiously motivated virtue developed into a social function that guaranteed social recognition. In some cases it was enough only to appear virtuous.[21] The beginning of the American republic gave rise to successful business entrepreneurship.

John Jacob Astor was the first of those businessmen. Only the self-made men of the Gilded Age, like Jay Gould, J.P. Morgan, Andrew Carnegie, and John D. Rockefeller, would surpass him in terms of wealth. All of them were aware of Astor's success story, even if they did not consciously follow his example.[22] The basic idea of the American myth of success remained the same through the decades, though: Every individual had the opportunity to rise to a higher position through his own capabilities and talent.

It is the goal of this thesis to analyze Astor's successful immigration and social rise in the early republic of the United States of America. I aim to answer those leading questions: How did Astor acculturate to his host culture? What role did his personal process of acculturation play in his career and social rise? What networks he was part of in New York's plutocracy? How did he develop his business ideas? And what was his impact on the American society and culture?

Methods and Theoretical Premises

Astor's motives to leave Germany certainly were neither political nor religious, but socio-economic. He left Walldorf shortly after the Revolutionary War ended and about 50 years before the big waves of immigrants streamed into the United States.[23] He came to the United States at a time when the national identity took shape in the early republic.[24] This period is usually considered to stretch from the Declaration of Independence to the end of the War of 1812.[25] Following this period American society developed into the world's most egalitarian, most individualistic and most commercially active society, as Gordon S. Wood described it.[26] These years are commonly referred to as time of the *market revolution*.[27] The period was characterized by economic and geographic expansion and a boom of traffic and transportation, in all of which Astor not only took part but was also the driving force, as shown in this biography. After all, he managed to become the leading businessman of his age, which was shaped by the tensions between republican and liberal values.[28] He established himself as a multimillionaire who took advantage of the social and economic changes of his time to protect and increase his wealth.

Astor's personal lifelong driving force was to become an accepted member of American society. His personal acculturation[29] constituted a decisive impulse at the beginning of his career. In general, the process of acculturation explains the cultural and psychological changes that result from the meeting of two different cultures. Both cultures start to influence each other, so that the effects can be seen in multiple levels within both cultures. Those effects take place at first in changes of culture, customs, and social institutions. These often include changes in food, clothing, and language. At the individual level, differences in the way individuals acculturate have been shown to be associated not just with changes in daily behavior and mentality, but with numerous measures of psychological and physical well-being. The acculturation of an individual might develop faster because the individual is not bound to a group's internal culture and rituals. Also, in the case of marriage, an individual tended to marry someone from another culture, rather than somebody who migrated within his own ethnic group. Generally, acculturation can be considered as second-culture learning.

However, the acculturation model described by Milton Gordon in the 1960s was never used to analyze the acculturation of an individual. According to Gordon, acculturation is the first part of assimilation. It is the first stage through which an individual must pass. For him, acculturation means behavioral assimilation. It is followed by structural assimilation (social assimilation), and marital assimilation of the individuals of the minority society and individuals of the dominant society. Although this proposal has been criticized, it does indicate that there is a continuum through which individuals pass, beginning with acculturation and ending with complete assimilation.[30]

Furthermore, Astor's way to success can also be explained by his drive to gain wealth and to climb the social ladder. He meets Max Weber's characteristics of a modern new-world capitalist in terms of a strictly rational organization of his business, the separation of private life and business, and rational accounting.[31] In order to provide an explanation of his success as a businessman, capital must be understood not only in the traditional, material sense but also as having a cultural, symbolic and social component.[32] Pierre Bourdieu stressed that many social phenomena and processes cannot be adequately explained if only the material capital is taken into account. He considers the other sorts of capital[33] — with a special focus on social, symbolic and cultural capital — as central to the explanation of social phenomena. Social capital results from the use of the networks of which one is part by birth, heritage or steady efforts to rise.[34] There is a seamless transition to symbolic capital. Bourdieu gives prestige, honor or good reputation as examples of symbolic capital.[35] In order to gain social or symbolic capital, wealth and property are not enough. According to Bourdieu, the key to social rise and full acceptance lies in cultural capital. He segments the cultural capital into three subcategories: objective cultural capital, which consists of the possession of luxury goods like artworks, elegant furniture and expensive instruments; incorporated capital, which consists of the opportunity to invest time in education, esthetics and good taste; and lastly, institutionalized cultural capital, which consists of titles, offices and honors. Bourdieu himself warned against reducing these mechanisms to an individual because gaining these different sorts of capital cannot be achieved by employing rational planning.[36]

The writing of historical biographies was controversial during recent years. In the 1970s the historic social sciences, then at the height of their influence and reputation, challenged the writing of historical biographies to justify itself. Therefore authors of historical biographies started to add pages and pages of justifications in their introductions. In 1971 the German historian Hans-Ulrich Wehler detected the crisis of the political biography in relation to this. However, in the end the historical biography not only recovered from this crisis but also gained new impulses and directions out of it. During the last couple of years the criticism of biographies as a historical genre has mostly stopped, and the voices critical of the theories of writing historical biographies have ebbed.

The "linguistic turn" had a direct impact on biography's development, determining the collapse of clear theoretical notions of "subject," "subjectivity," conceptions of self, levels of textualization, and definite historical contexts. It questioned the borders between author and subject and denied the possibility of existence of "truth" as a historical account.

Later historians, such as Elizabeth Colwill, confronted the limits of postmodern theories by inquiring about the possibilities of writing historical biographies in a time of blurred conceptual borders, without losing sight of the subject and his narrative, however circumstantial and problematic: "How might historians recount the public lives of distinguished and self-actualizing agents in an age that problematized the singularity, intentionality, and autonomy of the individual? How could scholars steeped in debates over the shifting meanings of public and private, the powers of the unconscious, and the pitfalls of positivism write linear narratives about transparent and transcendent individuals?"[37] The answer came in the form of many "alternative" biographical forms, which threatened to put an end to the biography as a genre. The last phase, in Hähner's vision, starts in 1980s, with the New Historicism and the role of context and contextualization for biography writing.

Germany, however, experienced a strong desynchronization in terms of participation in the biographical discourse after 1945. Klein explained the German skepticism and mistrust in biography first through the debilitating effects of National Socialism. After 1945 German public discourse aimed to reconstruct a sense of stability, of coherence. Questions about the constructed essence of truth and identity were not welcomed. After the complete breakdown of such a rigid political and social system, people were not willing to engage into a postmodern debate. Thus, biographical productions of the time mostly followed a conventional pattern of thought.

Another explanation for the German delay in taking part in biographical discourse was a false understanding of postmodernist theories. Taking into account that Roland Barthes's text concerning the "death of the author" was translated and published in Germany only in 2000, with a delay of 40 years since its first publication, misunderstandings could occur easily. A last explanation, in Klein's view, is the fact that the German society, after 1945, was unable for a while to think in historical or psychoanalytical terms.[38]

These factors generated the "biography crisis," which determined historian Hans-Ulrich Wehler to point out, in a study published in 1969, that the biography as a genre was a lost cause for academia. Wehler questioned biography's relevance for the study of history, sociology and political studies, in the context of the "death of the subject," the multiplication of narrative perspectives and diversification of focus.[39] However, biography not only survived, but the crisis pushed its development. Moreover, it adapted to the demands of the recent theoretical debates by inaugurating new branches. One could talk of "pathography,"[40] of biography as a spin job, as feminist tract, as deconstructionist exercise, or as philosophical exercise.[41]

Historiographical Findings

At first glance it seems as if life and career of John Jacob Astor were the topic of many books. However, this view is misleading. There is no academic and source-based analysis of Astor's life. Within the last 200 years, only a few historians wrote about John Jacob Astor and analyzed the origins of his business, or the story of his success or immigration. Moreover, many journalists and other writers based their books uncritically on the anecdotes about Astor.[42] In the end all these writings are to be understood as products of the time in which they originated.

All of the previous biographies only took a closer look at Astor the successful businessman. How he made it to the top and how he was acculturated into American society was of only minor interest. However, it is hard to explain Astor's career and life without a thorough analysis of his economic and social rise. Therefore it is of utmost importance to understand Astor in the context of his role as an immigrant. This study broadens the general view of Astor, and the focus on Astor as an immigrant allows a more vivid picture of his personality and success than ever before.

In the second half of the 19th century, many biographical sketches were published before and in the immediate aftermath of Astor's death. David Jacques was one of the first to publish his Astor story in *Hunt's Merchant Magazine* in 1844.[43] *Harper's New Monthly Magazine* published James Parton's 15-page article on Astor.[44] German authors found in him the perfect example of the successful immigrant. In many German pamphlets, emigration magazines and newspapers of the 19th century, Astor was looked at from a positive point of view.[45] They all published a short life story, focusing on his motivations to emigrate as well as a positive conclusion of his career.

At the beginning of the 20th century Astor's life was a topic in World War I propaganda and socialist scenarios featuring the evil capitalists. The German-American Gustavus Myers was a particularly outspoken opponent of Astor. Myers understood himself as a social reformer. In 1911 he published his *History of the Great American Fortunes* in order to gain support for a more socialist approach in American commerce. It was not in his interest to give an adequate image of Astor's life, but to use him as a parable for his contemporaries, who should see how the unimpeded drive for more money corrupted a person.[46] Therefore he based his research only on a few public documents and many rumors and anecdotes. According to Myers, who was also a German-American, Astor's German origins were to blame for his ruthless behavior. Nevertheless, his book became influential and was translated into German in 1916.

Only a few years afterwards, Elizabeth Gebhard argued against Myers's portrait. In her view Astor brought many good abilities to the United States, and due to his German heritage he was able to rise much above the average immigrant.[47] Both views can count as examples of different images that were held in the public about German-Americans in the wake of World War I. After the war Astor's story was usually mentioned in books on the Westward expansion, fur trade or American businessmen.[48]

During the Great Depression and the world economic crises, Astor was again a topic for historians and other social scientists.[49] Kenneth Wiggins Porter published the first biography of Astor based on research from a business point of view in 1931.[50] His huge two-volume work did not focus on Astor as person but on the business practices and business models he employed in his companies.[51] However, his facts were backed up by an intensive study of the sources available to him. He used business papers, plus correspondence files from Astor, his family, and members of Astor's trademark business, the American Fur Company. Porter dissects each and every business move and clearly identifies successes and failures. But his portrait lacks a clear central question, and therefore his line of argumentation is hard to follow. Without any doubt, he presented a thoroughly researched analysis of Astor's business, but it is also hard to read, irritating in parts, and without much background on the man himself.

Following Porter's publication, Astor was in popular discussions again. This led to the case in which several descendants of a fur trader named Johann Nicolas Emerick sued the Astor descendants in 1928. They called for one-third of the Astor fortune, because it was said that Emerick would have received one-third of his income if they had become partners. The claimants showed several sources in an effort to prove their claim. But those sources provided no real evidence, and the claimants lost. Nevertheless, their attorney, Calvin I. Hoy, published a book purporting to tell the real story behind Astor and Emerick. The sources he used to prove the supposed connection was just the product of popular rumors and writings of third persons, which were in no way contemporary writings proving a partnership. Eventually, they could not even demonstrate that Astor and Emerick had ever met.[52] While Astor might have met Emerick on his voyage to North America, it is highly improbable that he and Emerick became business partners. The existing sources and business papers do not show any proof for that connection.

Over the following decades other stories about Astor followed in the United States. This time the Astor family was at the center of attention and their dynasty was the topic.[53]

The National Socialist historians also discovered Astor as a focus of their research. In the *Handwörterbuch des Grenz—und Auslanddeutschtums* he was portrayed as a "pioneer of success and wealth seeking enthusiasm with unleashed individuality."[54] However, Astor was seen as a traitor to the German nation: "The German observer watches witch fear and sadness at the life of this man ... there is no connection between the German people and this man."[55] There was no room in the Third Reich for any appreciation of Astor's individualism, which was in sharp contrast to the goals of the National Socialist Party. Emil Bode characterized Astor in his National Socialist propaganda as a "German, who gave up his 'German-ness.'"[56] While other expatriate Germans were celebrated as shining examples of German-ness, Astor was reduced to the status of un-German, American capitalist.[57] Suddenly he was too acculturated by German standards. In the war propaganda, Astor was the German who had been seduced by U.S. decadence and was therefore an example of everything that was wrong with the United States of America.

Only in 1991 was a second academic publication focused on Astor. John D. Haeger analyzed Astor's fur trade and real estate business. He argued for Astor's role as the first modern American venture capitalist.[58] He more or less continued Porter's economic evaluation of Astor's business practices and modernized the former view of his business activities. He concentrated on Astor only insofar as it was business-relevant. Recently another two biographies were published in the United States: a journalistic one, and one in the field economic history again. Bestseller author Axel Madsen published an easy-to-read biography of Astor that does not include any new sources and is purely based on anecdotes and secondary sources. Madsen tries to make up for the lack of original research by including lengthy descriptions of Astor's contemporaries that again do not contain any new findings.[59]

In 1993, James P. Ronda published his well-researched work *Astoria & Empire*. He concentrates only on the establishment of the outpost of Astoria and the strategies behind that idea. Astor's person, life and career play only a minor role. Ronda focuses more on the people who were actively traveling to the Pacific Northwest and building the trading outpost.[60]

All in all, a proper analysis of Astor's life is still missing. The public view is still torn. On the one hand, James Parton, Gustavus Myers, and Arthur Howden-Smith portrayed Astor as an avaricious and selfish Mr. Scrooge, while Elizabeth Gebhard und Wilhelm Oertel von Horn, on the other hand, saw the honest immigrant who worked hard and earned much in return. Among historians, these images have not played any important role so far. The perspective of economic history was purely business-oriented. Nobody before has analyzed Astor's life story from the perspective of immigration and his impact on culture.

Sources

This book uses sources from state, church and public archives. The most important sources are the letters between Astor and his contemporaries, as well as newspaper articles. For the first time American and German sources are analyzed to the same extent. Therefore a more balanced view of Astor's life has been attempted. I also added many new archival sources that had not been available to Kenneth Wiggins Porter from other archives and American editions.

The largest volume of unpublished sources can be found in the Astor Business Records at Baker Library (Harvard University). Three manuscript books as well as 29 volumes of private letters and business papers are available for researchers. Porter only made use of the business papers and completely ignored the private letters.[61] Other relevant archives that were used are Beinecke Library (Yale University)[62] as well as the New York Public Library,[63] and the archives of the New York Historical Society[64] and the German Society of the City of New York.[65]

Published material became more and more available through the years, and in 1991 the Astor Business Letters were published.[66] However, relevant references concerning Astor can also be found in the published editions of presidential papers from James Monroe,[67] James Madison,[68] and Thomas Jefferson,[69] letters from Henry Clay,[70] and the First Lady of the early republic, Dolley Madison.[71] It is important to also include the advertisements in newspapers and newspaper articles themselves among the published sources. They are previously overlooked sources of Astor's perception by the American public. I also analyzed contemporary accounts of Astor and his projects. The first and foremost of these is Washington Irving's novel *Astoria; or, Anecdotes of an Enterprise Beyond the Rocky Mountains*, which tells the story of Astor's fur company and the founding of the trading post Astoria.[72] Irving was offered a handsome payment if he wrote a piece on the actual events in Astoria. Astor finally wanted to read his own view of the endeavor and let Irving work with all the original documents and files. Therefore even this novel has a right to be placed among the factual accounts on Astor.

Furthermore, diaries like Philip Hone's, the former New York mayor, and other written accounts of Astor's contemporaries were researched.[73] Philip Hone kept a diary from 1828 to 1851 and commented on each and every event in New York's upper class. In this account, Astor plays a major role.[74] Another important diary was written by James Gallatin, the son of Astor's friend Albert Gallatin, who quite in the contrary to his father was no big fan of the multimillionaire.[75] Members of the Astor family, like his great-grandson William Waldorf Astor, themselves gave their own accounts of the forefather's life and business.[76] Also Astor's favorite daughter Eliza Astor Rumpff left her memoir. Her account in particular has been completely ignored by historians up to now.[77] Joseph A. Scovilles gives a vivid picture of the merchants in early New York.[78] Scoville's source can only be interpreted with great care and in comparison with other sources. His volumes reveal him as credulous, gossipy, careless, and consequently inaccurate.

Other noteworthy sources are the annals of priest Carl Stocker.[79] He wrote the histories of Walldorf and many other surrounding cities in 1888. His comments on Astor cannot be considered sources of high value. Nevertheless, Stocker provided his readers with a vivid description of life in Walldorf. The first major German biography on Astor was written by Wilhelm Oertel von Horn. It was published in 1854.[80] In his small book Horn praised Astor's career and gave his readers the most detailed view of Astor's youth in Walldorf. Unfortunately, he does not provide us with a list of sources he used. But he must have done some research on Astor and claimed that he spoke with classmates and childhood friends. As proof, he names Valentin Christoph Kamm,[81] who went to school with the young multimillionaire, as his source. Although his book presents a glorified and transfigured image of Astor, the general environment and atmosphere of Astor's youth can be considered trustworthy. Furthermore, I used the Walldorf church records of the reformed church to find the true dates of birth and other information relevant to the Astor family.[82]

On the first glimpse it looks like John Jacob Astor's life and career were the objects of many historical studies. But most accounts of his life are neither well researched nor do they follow a modern method of research. The authors of those studies were for the most part journalists, who copied the mistakes, fake information and rumors of earlier writings.

Structure

Chronologically, this study spans all of Astor's lifetime. Every single chapter cuts down Astor's life into phases. Chapter 1 takes a new look at his origins and his family background, analyzing the framework of Astor's life in the old Palatinate as well as his family situation in particular. Both the unfortunate situation in the palatine region and his broken family provide enough reasons for young Astor to eventually emigrate. The death of his mother and the fact that he grew up with a stepmother play an especially prominent role, because he lost his real mother early. Furthermore, he had to deal with the emigration of two older brothers, as well as with the drinking problems of his father.

The short Chapter 2 describes and analyzes Astor's time in London. There, he lived with his older brother George and made his first steps into acculturation. Also, he learned the principles of the dealings of a merchant as well as the English language. Therefore, when he arrived on American shores, he had a big advantage most of the other immigrants never had: he could already speak the language.

The next chapter deals with Astor's arrival in the New World. The focus lies on his next steps of acculturation. In particular I analyze his marriage to his Scotish-American wife Sarah Todd Astor and the founding of their family. The advantages he gained through the marriage with his wife is a further cornerstone for his later success. Parallel to that process, Astor got connected to the German-American society in New York. This chapter also features his professional beginnings.

Chapter 4 deals with his first successes as a merchant and visionary. Step by step he left the surrounding atmosphere of his fellow German-Americans and became more and more American. He no longer attended gatherings and social circles of his ethnicity, but shared the visions of Americans of that time and finally became an American citizen himself. He was bold enough to get in touch with President Thomas Jefferson and become a public figure.

Chapter 5 follows Astor's rise to an American entrepreneur in international commerce. At first, he observed more experienced traders of the China trade. Later he followed in their footsteps and engaged himself into the business trade with China. He provided China with American furs on the one hand, and brought Chinese goods to the United States on the other hand. But President Jefferson's embargo interrupted his successful enterprise and Astor had to stop his overseas trade. Therefore, Astor applied his ideas westwards—far earlier than many others. He followed Jefferson's idea of an "empire of liberty" in the west and founded, with the president's support, the American Fur Company. The company's goal was to develop trading routes all over the west and to establish outposts along these routes. The first outpost Astor founded was Astoria at the mouth of the Columbia River, the first American settlement on the Pacific Coast.

Chapter 6 analyzes Astor's life as an established multimillionaire. Here, I describe how Astor expanded his operations after the War of 1812 and how he reorganized the management of the American Fur Company. He began to be involved in other business activities, such as the establishment of the Second Bank of the United States and the beginnings of the Mohawk & Hudson Railroad Company. Through most of the 1820s, however, Astor spent his time in Europe, mostly in Paris and at Lake Geneva. In that period, he saw himself as an American observer who reported from Europe about social and political tensions of the Old World to American politicians like Henry Clay and President James Monroe.

Chapter 7 describes Astor's last years after his last return from Europe and his resignation as chairman of the American Fur Company until his death in 1848. During this time, Astor operated on one side as a patron and sponsor. On the other hand, he enjoyed finally being anchored in New York's upper class. He founded the first hotel of the Astor Family, asked the famous American writer Washington Irving to write the novel *Astoria*, and retired to his estate Hellgate outside of Manhattan, where he died in March of 1848.

In the last chapter, I examine the public perception of John Jacob Astor's personality. For this purpose, I analyze the origins of this public image, which was established by the New York yellow press right after Astor's death, and how this image finally got into the collective memory of the United States. In addition, this chapter provides an overview of the development of places of memory and the cultural remembrance of Astor.

1

Origins, 1763–1780

John Jacob Astor was born in Walldorf, in southwestern Germany. Walldorf is close to the French border, south of the cities of Mannheim and Heidelberg in the heart of the old Palatinate.[1] Sharing a border with France guaranteed the Palatinate a vital role in medieval Germany when the Holy Roman Empire was ruling most of West and Central Europe. The Palatine Prince Electors, who resided in the famous castle of Heidelberg and later in the castle of Mannheim, not only secured the western borders of the Empire, but they also received in return the honor of being among the four nonclerical rulers who elected the German king and emperor.

The times had changed in the years right before Astor's birth. Heidelberg's castle, with its famous Renaissance gardens, was largely destroyed by the French during the so-called Palatinate War of Succession (1688–97), which is also known as King William's War. After the destruction, the castle was never rebuilt, leaving the former residence behind as a tourist attraction for generations to come. However, the period of peace that followed allowed the Palatinate to prosper. From 1742 to 1799 Carl Theodor,[2] was the new Palatine Prince Elector, indulged in the fine arts and sciences.[3] He invited famous thinkers and artists in music, philosophy, literature and the sciences to his court in Mannheim. Voltaire and Lessing discussed their thoughts on enlightenment with the Palatinate ruler.[4] However, due to dynastic developments, the palatinate was soon unified with Bavaria, and Prince Elector Carl Theodor moved his court to Munich and let Mannheim's short-lived reputation as a refuge for the avant-garde artists fade away.[5] The Palatinate never regained its former glory either politically nor culturally.

The number of Palatinate residents dramatically increased during the period of peace following the Palatinate War of Succession. However, extreme weather conditions like floods, frosts and heat waves caused harvest after harvest to fail and led to famines and plagues. These affected the rural population the most and many of them decided to immigrate to North America. They crossed the Atlantic Ocean, settled down in Pennsylvania, as well as along the

Walldorf in the 18th century (Vereinigung Walldorfer Heimatfreunde).

Hudson River Valley in the state of New York,[6] and became a big part of the Pennsylvania-Germans.

This wave of immigration was mainly motivated by religious and social-economic reasons: Palatinate inheritance laws guaranteed each son a part of the family farm.[7] This system also meant that the individual fields became smaller and smaller with each generation. During periods of bad weather this meant the fields were simply too small to either carry enough crops to feed the families or to pay the taxes to the court. In other regions of Germany this was compensated by new agricultural methods like innovations in fertilizing and feeding inside the stables.

With the Prince Elector in Munich, the Palatinate was nothing more than an unimportant border state. Innovations were introduced in Bavaria rather than in the Palatinate. Therefore the population in the German southwest looked further west in order to improve their living conditions. The situation on the other side of the Atlantic seemed tempting to them. People who were deeply rooted in agriculture and traditional German crafts saw the only way to safety for the lives of their loved ones in taking a step into the unknown: they boarded a ship, and spent months seasick on crowded decks with only a vague idea of what to expect from these North America colonies that somehow belonged to the British Empire but allowed private individuals to gain their own land and elect their representatives in the colonial parliaments.[8]

The censuses of that time show that there were more and more people living in the Palatinate, contributing to the pressure to emigrate. The number of inhabitants rose from 264,000 in 1773 to 323,000 inhabitants in 1791.[9] Leaving behind the densely populated areas in central Europe, the many royal laws and taxes, and the lack of any hope for improving their situation seemed the only way out.

From the end of the 17th century Carl Theodor, a Catholic, was the ruler of a primarily Protestant Palatinate. Before the Religious Peace of Augsburg (1555) ruled differently, it would have meant the Palatinates would automatically turn Catholic. After Augsburg the subjects were entitled to their faith, but this also meant even more religious or cultural borders for those who chose to keep their old religion. Most of the villages established two, some three or more schools. Each school served only children of one belief. However, it would be wrong to assume that children enjoyed anything like a general education. While the rulers devoted themselves to their roles as benefactors of the fine arts and sciences, the common man only enjoyed the education he could afford in time and cost. There was nothing like a teachers' education, and many times the village teachers were those who could read and write a little bit better than the other villagers, but had not necessarily had any proper training or experience in education.

What counted for the Palatinate counted also for Astor's hometown Walldorf. By the middle of the 18th century, there lived about 250 families in 200 houses with nearly 800 persons altogether in Walldorf. Therefore the village was bigger than many of its neighboring villages. It could look back on a long tradition of being a trade center because it was so conveniently located on an important north-south passage that had been used in ancient times by Germanic tribes as well as the Romans as an important trading route. In the 1750s the town of Walldorf had three churches (a Catholic, a Lutheran, and a Reformed one) as well as a synagogue. The strong agriculture encouraged the settlement of secondary crafts, like bakers, butchers and other producers.[10]

Family Background

Walldorf's Reformed Church registers the birth of a certain Johann Jacob Astor on July 17, 1763.[11] He was the sixth child of Maria Magdalena vom Berg and Johann Jakob Astor, the elder.[12] Father Astor was a butcher. His profession heavily depended on the prospering agriculture and the wealth of his fellow villagers. An animal could only be spared for butchering if it was not needed elsewhere to produce milk, pull a plow, or transport crops. Meat was a luxury item, as was the service of a butcher, who would perform a service that could be done by other people on a farm in-house. Therefore father Astor made a good profit when his fellow villagers were in a festive mood, celebrated births, weddings or funerals, but he lacked income whenever people cut back on meat due to economic distress. Astor the senior would go from door to door to offer his services and would find most work before Christmas and Easter. Therefore the family hardly had enough to eat in the other months of the year.[13] As some biographers suggested, father Astor never had the leading butchery of the village.[14]

The Astors had married on April 15, 1749,[15] in the newly built Reformed Church of Walldorf.[16] Their first child, Peter Astor, was born in March 1750 but died soon afterwards.[17] Two years later the second child was born and baptized Georg Peter in memory of the first child. Heinrich (1754), Catherina (1757) and Melchior (1759) followed, till Johann Jacob Astor was born in 1763. As the youngest son he got the name of his father.[18]

However, his birth was followed by a family tragedy. Maria Magdalena Astor died at the age of 33 on May 1, 1764, when Astor was not even a year old.[19] Women and toddlers had extremely high death rates.[20]

Astor's father (Vereinigung Walldorfer Heimatfreunde).

For craftsmen the choice of spouse was no longer made by the parents alone in the second half of the 18th century. However, romantic notions of love and passion played no special role in finding partners; more important were issues of property, efficiency, utility and at least a bit of sympathy for each other. A second marriage after the death of a spouse was usual. Furthermore, the relationship with the children was unemotional, brief, stern and aloof. The relationship between children and their parents was marked by certain discipline and obedience, as well as by beatings.[21] Astor's family life was by no means exceptional. Two years after Maria Magdalena's death, his father married again on July 8, 1766. His bride was Christina Barbara

Seybold, a 24-year-old.[22] The new couple had six more children, and the family had big problems fitting all the children in their little house. They spent many evenings around the only fireplace in the house, waiting for the father to bring back something to eat from work. Christina's first child, who was named after Maria Magdalena, died shortly after birth. Her second child was again named Maria Magdalena, but this time she survived. Anna Eva, Elisabetha, Sebastian and Maria Barbara followed.[23]

Soon it was obvious that there was no room for the older children of Astor's first marriage. Heinrich was the first of Astor's brothers to leave the family home.[24] In 1775 he became a Hessian

Astor's mother (Vereinigung Walldorfer Heimatfreunde).

mercenary to finance his passage to North America by fighting for the British against the American revolutionaries.[25] Soon Heinrich became Henry, and once on the North American side of the Atlantic, he left the military and became a butcher in New York.[26] Georg Peter, Astor's oldest brother, immigrated to England in 1777. He established himself in London and started to build wooden musical instruments.[27] The same year, Melchior also left, though he only moved to the neighboring village of Oftersheim, where he became the village butcher.[28] Within 14 years Astor had lost his brothers and his real mother. Only his sister Catherina remained with him in Walldorf in their father's house together with his new family. These losses significantly influenced his character. Shaped by these experiences, Astor found it hard to establish connections to other people. He was never strongly emotionally bound to any group of persons. There was nobody that he could not leave behind.

Later Astor's sister Catherina married Georg Ehninger and migrated to the United States sometime between the arrival of John Jacob in 1784 and the birth of her first child George in 1792. In his famous account of *The Old Merchants of New York*, Scoville wrote: "Old Mr. Ehninger was a cordial distiller, and he died from the effects of an accident caused by burning spirits."[29] Ehninger had one son with Astor's sister Catherina: George Ehninger, born in 1792 in New York. After the tragic death of her husband, Catherina tried to run the distillery on her own. Later she married again, to a man called Michel Miller. After the wedding both were running the distillery.[30] As Elizabeth Gebhard argued, Catherina believed in the business of distilling alcohol. She deeply thought that she had found a place in the business world, like her brother did later within the fur trade.[31]

Astor's Youth

The Astor children enjoyed the general education available to children who did not have to work in the fields and family farms.[32] All of the Astor children went to the church school of the Reformed Church in Walldorf.[33]

Some historians claim that Astor enjoyed a much above average education thanks to the school reforms in the dukedom of Baden.[34] Indeed, there was a big school reform in Baden under Duke Karl Friedrich in 1771. However, Walldorf did not belong to Baden before the reorganization of German territories in 1803.[35] Therefore the reforms did not influence Astor's education in any way. Also there might be a misconception among some authors concerning the so-called Reformed school, which was nothing but the school of Walldorf's Reformed congregation or the Protestant-Calvinistic church. Calvinism had a strong tradition in the Palatinate. The Reformed school was established in 1737 in Walldorf.[36] It was merely a one-room, one-class school, but it was open to all children of the Reformed congregation. About one in ten of Walldorf's children actually learned how to read and write. However, hardly any of the children of the farmers actually attended school.

Between 1740 and 1783 the head teacher of the Reformed school was Johann Valentine Jeune, a descendent of a French Huguenot.[37] He shared the teaching load with the Reformed priest, Johann Philip Steiner.[38] Both were educated men.

Steiner and Jeune became important persons for young Astor. They supported him wholeheartedly. Both of them were fond of Astor, who was talented and easy to motivate. Being a curious child, he soon surpassed many of the older children.[39] However, being the oldest remaining child, Astor soon had to step into his brothers' shoes and help his father. Therefore his education was sketchy at best. What he was missing at school when he helped

Astor's home (Vereinigung Walldorfer Heimatfreunde).

his father, he learned from Jeune after school. Jeune introduced Astor to the Calvinist ideas and explained to him how these ideas caused a controversy in France that had led his father to flee. Diligence and engagement would be the key to wealth, and in return wealth would be the sign of being chosen by God. Jeune asked Astor to always be modest and decent in order to please the Lord.[40]

When Astor was confirmed in the Reformed Church on Easter Sunday 1777,[41] his childhood came to an end. He was now at the age where one either would become an apprentice or start working directly. But for Astor, there was no time for any further education. His classmates would go on to be apprentices of a craftsman or they simply stayed on their family farms. Few had other options.

With all of his older brothers away, father Astor demanded that he stay in Walldorf to help him. Astor's brothers had left and therefore his father was more than one hand short. Obviously, he had to work for his father. What was an occasional occupation as long as he was at school, turned into something permanent as soon as he was out of school. Astor could not see himself working as a butcher to make a living, but there was nothing he could do instead. He was afraid to end as an agricultural worker helping the farmers in the stable as well as on the field.[42]

Astor's home (Vereinigung Walldorfer Heimatfreunde).

According to Horn, young Astor's teachers Jeune and Steiner did not have any doubts that Astor would make his way and improve his situation. But his reality in 1777 looked different. Astor argued often with his father. Their relationship was far from being a good one. In 1854 William Oertel von Horn published a biography of Astor that included accounts from Astor's childhood friends. Valentin Kamm, who received confirmation into the church the same day Astor did, talked about how Astor often slept in the stables, away from his family house, only to avoid confrontation with his father. When Astor had not gone home for days and did not have any food, his school friends fed him. Elizabeth Gebhard suggested that those years were a period of loneliness for young Astor: "During these years, he formed the habit of absenting himself from the social gatherings of friends, and in his hours of leisure he went away to brood by himself."[43]

The Decision to Leave Germany

Astor's decision to leave Germany was neither politically nor religiously motivated. His primary goal was to leave his old life, the poverty and financial insecurity behind and start anew. He was rather pushed away than pulled to America. Therefore his migration was motivated by *push-factors* rather than by *pull-factors*.[44] He was lacking any kind of connection to his stepmother, after his mother had died before he was a year old.[45] He and his siblings were the second family for his father and they had less and less room in his father's life.[46] So they left, one by one. Why should he have stayed behind? Wasn't self-preservation man's first duty? His brothers' letters, Henry's in particular, seemed to ask him to take his fate into his own hands. Henry must have talked about the unlimited opportunities in North America, and George must have talked about the trade in the exciting metropolis of London.[47] Anything seemed more attractive to Astor than remaining in Walldorf. He feared experiencing a fate similar to his father's. After the older Astor sons had left, his father turned bitter and seemed to have lost all joy.[48] Astor senior turned to alcohol to forget his sorrows. There was nothing left for Astor to do in Walldorf. He had to make a move and leave.

Henry had left the Hessian regiment and settled in New York, which grew into the commercial center in the newly founded United States. It was a relief for Astor to hear that the brother he admired so much was not fighting anymore. Now his brother was settled as butcher in New York. George had taken a less violent path and started building and trading musical instruments in London, the center of the British Empire. London was the place to be for merchants. Even though the brothers ended up on opposite sides of the Atlantic, both agreed: leaving Germany improved their lives. While George enjoyed being part of the exciting British Empire with its important trading companies and global network of trading routes, Henry was fascinated by the changes in North America and the ideas of independence that had succeeded in the American Revolution.[49] From a European perspective it was an outrageous thought for most of the people to dare to declare independence from a worldly ruler. Could the population be trusted to make the right decisions? Why should the population agree to pay taxes, if there was no authority but the one voluntarily granted by the people for the people?

Soon George asked for Astor's help in London. His instruments were highly popular and he needed someone to help him in selling the pieces. George took it upon himself to convince his father that it would be in Johann Jakob's best interests if he could leave Walldorf. However, father Astor was not ready to let another of his children leave, especially since his other children were still too young to help him in the butchering business. So Astor was in a bind and turned to his mentors Jeune and Steiner for help.[50] Both happily promised to talk to his father. They knew Walldorf would not be the place where Astor could fulfill his ambitions and grow into the person they saw in him. In the end his father gave in and let his and Maria Magdalena's

Reformed Church of Walldorf (Vereinigung Walldorfer Heimatfreunde).

youngest son go to London to learn some English and how to build instruments.

When American newspapers reported Astor's death in 1848, they mentioned the year 1780 as his year of departure from Walldorf.[51] According to them, he only brought a humble bundle of clothes and a couple of coins when he started his way to success. His family and friends waved goodbye and many tears were shed when the boy left. His classmates and teachers missed him. For his father it was a great loss because he was now relying on his second wife to fill in for his son in his business. A last deep breath when Astor looked back, and the familiar houses soon vanished beyond the horizon, with only the church towers the last reminder of his previous life. Jeune is supposed to have comforted those who stayed behind: "He'll get through the world. He has a clear head and everything right behind the ears [sic]."[52] With the last reminders of Walldorf in sight, Astor sat down on a little sandy hill to clear his mind. What would he find away from Walldorf? What was really behind all the praises he had read from Henry and George? He decided to follow his teachers' advice: "To be honest, to be industrious, and not to gamble."[53]

Parton published his 15 pages on Astor's life in 1864. In his text appears for the first time within the Astor historiography this explicit pledge, which the author probably borrowed from Horn's book. Nevertheless, Horn never mentioned explicitly an oath, but he described how Astor imposed rules for his future life. Horn's sources are not revealed. Maybe he was inspired by articles and short biographies of Astor published after his death. Six years before Horn published his small book, the German journal *Germania. Archiv zur Kenntniß des deutschen Elements in allen Ländern der Erde* published a short entry on Astor, in which is written: "When Astor was about to leave for the distance, he decided always to be righteous and to be busy as well and in particular never to gamble."[54]

Astor's decision to leave was motivated first and foremost neither by religious reasons—like many German immigrants in the 18th century—nor political ones, but socio-economically. Among all the factors that brought Astor to the radical act to emigrate were primarily the family and social circumstances in which he grew up. Due to the fact that his siblings had shared the same experience and had emigrated as well, it is safe to say that the conditions of his childhood and his early youth were essential arguments for his decision to leave his old life behind him.

What Parton tried to describe is a called a rite of passage. Those rituals are often ceremonies or events such as confirmation, marriage or baptism. Especially the rite of confirmation demonstrates the transition to the world of adulthood. Astor's confirmation neither brought any changes for

Vereinigung Walldorfer Heimatfreunde. Astor leaving home.

the young man, nor was he now accepted as an adult, but had still to work as an errand boy for his father. So the moment he left could be considered his rite of passage into the world of adulthood. He had left not only his hometown, but the circle of his father's influence, and was about to act independently. However, his first task was to leave his poverty and his difficult childhood behind.

2

Apprentice, 1780–1784

Most of the time those leaving their home to start over again followed the examples set by friends or family, written in letters or in immigration magazines. A great many immigrants followed people they knew who had gone before. So in this sense Astor followed the path and example set out by his brothers. The capital of the British Empire was the largest and most densely populated city in Europe. Ships from all parts of the known world landed and cleared their freight: spices, food, animals and people from the colonies, crown colonies and trading posts far, far away. London grew from 575,000 inhabitants in 1700 to 900,000 at the end of the 18th century. When Astor arrived, London was bigger than Paris, which had been the commercial capital as long as most of the trade was primarily done on land trading routes across Europe. Now London was the big switchboard, where long as well as short-distance trading routes met and goods were sent to their new locations after the taxes were deducted.[1]

London's new wealth showed. The medieval city gates of the city of London soon made room for the expansion of settlement towards the London harbor. All people wanted to have free access to the city, not only authorized traders and registered merchants. These measures opened a new dimension of business in the city. Many new shops opened and the transport of goods reached a previously unknown speed due to the innovative infrastructure, where wide streets allowed many carriages to travel at the same time into the same direction.

As the center of the British Empire and therefore the world in the mid–18th century, London was the heart of a global network of traders, merchants and the colonial economy. The English metropolis was the core of the British mercantilism. Every trading good had to be brought from the colonies to London through the custom. Although Liverpool and Whitehaven became important harbors within the Empire, London kept the leading role. Over 69 percent of all overseas business was brought to England through the harbor of London.[2]

Other clear signs of the dominance and prosperity of the city were the structural improvements in the British capital since the mid–18th century. In addition to several sanitary cleanups, some parts of the city were removed, especially the gates to the city of London. This happened to give all residents free and direct access to the heart and commercial center of the British capital. This measure liberated the market. With this arrangement, the speed and efficiency of trade within the city increased and ensured an unobstructed circulation of goods and products.[3]

The economy was booming in London when Astor arrived. The contrast to his small village could not have been bigger, and Astor soon realized that London was providing the first chance for him to observe, learn and make the best out of all this.

First Professional Steps

In order to get to London, Astor wanted to take one of the ships that commuted between the Dutch North Sea and southern Germany on the River Rhine. He did not have any money, so the fastest way to make his plan come true was to walk to Speyer, which was about 30 miles from Walldorf and was one of the stops for the ships on the Rhine. Some raftsmen who transported wood from the Black Forest to the Netherlands and always needed an additional hand hired him.[4] Within two weeks he had made it to a Dutch harbor. There are no sources which prove where Astor headed, but considering the time and circumstances, he may have traveled to Rotterdam, the big Dutch merchant city. There he bought with the money he earned with the raftsmen a ticket for his passage to London. He made it! His only preparation consisted of reading George's letters. He still knew neither English nor Dutch but arrived safely in London three weeks after leaving home.[5]

When he arrived, his brother and his young wife welcomed him. George had already established himself successfully as a shop owner and instrument builder. He was skilled in music and crafts. That was George's dream come true. On November 9, 1779, he married 17-year-old Elizabeth Wright from London. Her father had to agree to this, because Elizabeth was still underage. Wright was only too happy to give his daughter to George. The German boy had made a great impression on him. George was diligent, efficient, and he took good care of Wright's daughter. Both Elizabeth and George were fond of Astor. He did not have to start from scratch but could rely on their help. Elizabeth, who was about his age, taught Astor to speak, read and write English.[6]

When a journalist tried to find out more about the instrument business of the Astors, almost 100 years later he contacted the company Shudi & Broadwood, because he assumed that the Astor brothers might have worked at this company. He got the answer: "Messr. John Broadwood & Sons writing with reference to the statement that the original John Jacob Astor joined an elder brother in London who was employed in the factory of his uncle, the senior partner of that firm, remark: There was no firm of Astor & Broadwood. The original John Jacob Astor did a large business with us, but he was not a partner in our firm, which was at first Shudi, then Shudi & Broadwood, and during the present century John Broadwood & Sons."[7] However, the sources do not demonstrate that the two brothers were following in the footsteps of an uncle. Moreover, the Walldorf Churchbook shows that all the brothers of their father died in Germany, and there is no remark of a possible emigration of one of the uncles to London.[8]

In any case, George worked as an instrument maker. He specialized in flutes, but later he produced pianofortes. When his younger brother arrived in London, George started to train John Jacob in the ways of an instrument maker and how to keep the books. Soon enough the brothers opened a larger instrument shop in Wych Street 26 and called it George & John Astor. It became clear that George would be the builder and Astor the salesmen. George built flutes, clarinets, and all kind of keyboard instruments. Astor had the opportunity to learn how to talk to customers, what it took to sell, and all the administration necessary to run a business successfully.[9]

Thus, Astor's subsequent acculturation in the United States was significantly facilitated by his years in London. These years were to some extent an unusual and successful preparation for his later life and career in the United States.

His migration can be called a *chain migration*. This is a form of a follow-up migration, based on personal information such as letters, reports and success stories from trusted persons. Immigrants from a certain settlement follow others to a particular neighborhood in an immigrant-receiving country. In general, migrants perceive this form of migration as less risky and stressful.

In London, John Jacob Astor learned not only the English language; he also learned English behavior, and came to understand much about how to behave in a foreign country and how to accept a foreign host culture. Unfortunately, there is very little information about his time in London. Therefore, it is hard to find out in which social circles Astor participated.

In this period Astor changed his name from "Johann Jacob" to the English pronunciation "John Jacob." This was a clear sign of his willingness to be a part of the Anglo-Saxon culture and a proof that his acculturation had begun. The losses he had suffered in his youth made it easier for him not only to disconnect with his former home in Germany but also to be more open to a new culture and all traditions of a foreign country.

Crossing the Atlantic Ocean

The life in the capital and commercial center of the British Empire was just what Astor had been waiting for. It was so different from his home and it opened many new opportunities for him. Young John Jacob jumped right at it and seemed to be willing to acculturate rapidly.

But after more than three years, John Jacob was looking for a new challenge. Whether he planned to move on to the United States from the very beginning of his migration or if it was a new idea he developed in England, cannot be known for sure. In any case, after successfully establishing their shop the Astor brothers soon went separate ways, at least in terms of where they lived. While John Jacob first brought his business skills to good use, France had entered the Revolutionary War on the side of the newly declared United States of America and supported the former British colonies against the English crown. Finally, in 1781, the British General Lord Cornwallis[10] surrendered the British force in Yorktown and peace negotiations could start. On September 3, 1783, the Peace Treaty of Paris officially sanctioned American independence.[11]

Many had run away from battles and fighting and had left their houses and land behind them. After the signing of the peace treaty it was the time to rebuild the houses, farms and cities. After an interruption of eight years it was obvious that there was much need for new products, new buildings, and new clothes in a newly founded republic.[12] Luxury items, such as furs and instruments, were in high demand, because they suggested peace and wealth. In addition, they demonstrated normality after the war.

Astor had seen in London a booming economy and realized what chances for the individual came with it. He felt that it was time for him to travel over the Atlantic Ocean and see with his own eyes what his brother Henry had been writing about America for years. In London, Astor had enjoyed a taste of a new and vivid world, but New York offered him the chance to actually contribute to the rebuilding of the city and the establishment of business as he had seen it in London. The young salesman thought that, the moment the war was over, the demand for everything coming through the London harbor — luxury items, art and instruments — had to skyrocket. The former colonists were always dependent on the deliveries from London, and during the war many goods had not been allowed to leave London for North America. However, now that regular trade could commence again, it was the hour of

Astor on board the *North Carolina* (Vereinigung Walldörfer Heimatfreunde).

the Astor brothers. George would continue to produce instruments in London. John Jacob would then import them and sell them in New York. There was an upper class ready to invest in high-quality luxury products.

John Jacob Astor was so impatient that he did not even want to wait for the next spring to cross the Atlantic. The opportunity was too big to miss. His only previous experience on sea was the 20 miles crossing the Channel, so he might have underestimated a little just how rough the Atlantic could be over the winter months. In November 1783, only two months after the War of Independence officially ended, Astor boarded the *North Carolina* in Southampton.[13] He was then 20 years old and ready for his next adventure.

The *North Carolina* was supposed to land in Baltimore, a little south of New York, in order to avoid the icebergs and pack ice further north on the Atlantic Ocean. When John Jacob's great-grandson John Jacob Astor IV died on board the *Titanic* in 1912, the *New York Times* traveled back in time and published a report about the two Astors crossing the Atlantic Ocean. Both voyages suffered from bad weather and storms, but while the original John Jacob Astor reached his destination in 1784, his descendant was not that lucky, and died while crossing the Atlantic Ocean.[14] As the *New York Times* and many other sources reported, John Jacob invested five pounds sterling in the passage[15] on the middle deck. Many different writers have reported that Astor's luggage consisted of seven flutes, two clarinets, some money, and his best suit. There is no source for that, but it became a popular theme. Probably Moses Yale Beach was the origin of that myth, but it remains unclear from whom he had that information.[16] If Astor had known that it would take him five months to reach the other side of the Atlantic on this vessel, he might have waited some more time. The voyage proved to be long and tempestuous. November gales and December storms pushed the little craft to its limit, and gave John Jacob Astor many sleepless nights and uncomfortable days while the *North Carolina* was shaking between the rough waves of the ocean.[17]

Later reports of his passage gave a vivid picture of the unconventional and pragmatic nature of Astor's thoughts, which were interpreted as purely materialistic and capitalist by many of his biographers.[18] Taking into account his Reformed education and rural upbringing, it seems more likely that pragmatism was a character trait Astor simply had from early on. The winter of 1783 was hard and severely cold. The Atlantic was rough, the weather was stormy, and the *North Carolina* did not make many sea miles per day. It rather seemed she was stuck in the middle of the Atlantic. On a particularly stormy day the *North Carolina* came so close to the pack ice that the passengers feared the ship would collide with an iceberg and sink any minute. This was the moment when Astor appeared on deck wearing his best suit. When he was asked why, he insisted he wished to still possess his best pieces of clothing in case he was rescued.[19]

The unfortunate highlight of the journey was still ahead of them. One day before the *North Carolina* reached Baltimore at the end of January 1784, she was suddenly caught in the icy waters of the Chesapeake Bay close to the Virginia coastline. The first couple of days were not much of a change for the passengers. It was as cold as always and as narrow as always, only the ship was no longer shaken around, which might even have been a benefit for many of them. The captain was responsible for feeding his travelers, so Astor and his fellow passengers remained on board at first and shared their hopes and experiences about North America.[20]

One of the biggest legends or myths about Astor concerns something that supposedly happened on board the *North Carolina*. There he is said to have made an encounter which, it is commonly said, changed his life for the better. However, there are almost no sources which would prove that the following story actually happened, as it is believed by many people. Especially in Germany, rumors of that legend are still active.

When the *North Carolina* could not continue her voyage, Astor spent much time with another German on the ship. It is commonly said that the name of this German was John Nicholas Emerick, although there is no proof either for the existence or the name of that foreigner in the primary sources. Ever since Astor's death, many people have researched Emerick's person and origins. Due to the lack of sources, it is hard to demonstrate that a person with that name and of that age was actually on board the *North Carolina*. Usually, the public tends to believe in a belated source: just because Emerick's name was printed in a newspaper in 1929 in connection with Astor, Emerick must have met him in 1784.[21]

Nevertheless, according to the myth, Astor and Emerick were the only Germans on board and their common language bound the two men together. Most sources report only that Astor met a German 10 to 12 years older on board the *North Carolina*. Emerick had already spent some time in North America, and during those days at sea, he supposedly confided in Astor the secrets of the fur trade. He told Astor story after story about the furs that were traded in upstate New York. He claimed to be on his way back from Europe, where he had sold furs and made a good profit on them. Emerick was thrilled that he could buy the furs so cheaply from the Native Americans and sell them so expensively to the Europeans. Moreover, according to the legend, he described to Astor where to buy the furs, and how to pack, transport and preserve the skins. Furthermore, he confided into him all the names of the principal dealers in New York, Montreal, and London. Wouldn't this be a profession for the young Astor? He had already established himself in one

2. Apprentice, 1780–1784

craft. Emerick suggested Astor to become a furrier himself. By that he would enjoy the highest profits from his furs. Moreover, it is said that he made John Jacob Astor a one-third partner.[22]

Nevertheless, what role Emerick played, if he ever existed or not, and if he was on board the *North Carolina*, analysis of Astor's business papers shows no hint that would prove a connection between the two.

However, Astor had seen how successful the fur trade was in London and the idea seemed appealing to him. He would keep that in mind. After days when the *North Carolina* was still not moving, Astor began to think about how to get on shore himself. Weeks later he packed his bag and stepped onto the ice. It was dangerous to walk to shore. The ice was slowly breaking. But Astor made it safely to the beach and finally he took his first steps on North American soil. The rest of his fellow travelers waited on board till the *North Carolina* finally made it to Baltimore on March 24, 1784.[23]

The article published in the *New York Times* in April 1912 described not only John Jacob Astor's voyage to North America. It also suggested that the ice on the North Atlantic played a key role in gathering all his fortune. On the one hand, the ice took the life of John Jacob Astor IV while he was traveling on the *Titanic*. On the other hand, the ice on the Atlantic Ocean caused a "break" through which the original John Jacob Astor was able to make his fortune. Without the advice of the unknown German, according to the *New York Times*, the Astor family would have remained poor: "That Col John Jacob Astor should perish in the sea, by shipwreck, seems fatally malign. It is as though the sea, which had done so so much for the prosperity of the Astors, hat at last exacted its inexorable toll, but only after more than a century of waiting. The original John Jacob Astor twice escaped shipwreck, and it was left for his great-grandson to pay the price."[24]

John Jacob Astor arrived in Baltimore some days prior to the *North Carolina*. Once again arriving in a new city, he took a close look at the brick buildings around him that reminded him very much of London. When he was searching for a place to spend the night on Market Street, a short man approached him. The stranger had heard Astor's German accent and introduced himself as Nicolaus Tuschdy, a German-Swiss immigrant. The two of them had a good chat, as Astor described 50 years later in a letter: "I took a walk to see the town, getting up Market Street. While standing and looking about, a little man came out of his shop. This was Nicholas Tuschdy. He addressed my saying — young man I believe you are a stranger [...] Then he says we are near countrymen. I am Swiss. We are glad to see people coming to this country from Europe."[25]

Right after the talk, Tuschdy invited Astor home to dine with him and his wife. The couple enjoyed the company of the young German who had so much to tell about the situation on the other side of the Atlantic. They were highly impressed with his business skills and offered to let him sell his instruments in Tuschdy's shop without paying any commission. Astor stayed for three weeks, and in the end he left with all instruments sold and a good profit made that allowed him to conveniently travel to New York in mid–April.[26]

3

Immigrant, 1784–1800

Towards the end of the 18th century it was hard to imagine that there would be a time when all of Manhattan would be settled and the city of New York would be famous for buildings as high as the sky. In Astor's time New York looked very different: the city was nothing more than a small settlement on the southern tip of Manhattan. Furthermore, by the end of the War of Independence, most of this city had been destroyed. On Broadway, the British burned down New York's previously highest building, the Trinity Church. Many of the houses had war scars and much rebuilding and reconstruction were needed. During the war, most citizens of New York had fled to the countryside while the city was under British attack and occupation. Now that peace had been negotiated, the New Yorkers returned. However, not only the old New Yorkers returned. Between 1783 and 1785 about 12,000 so-called "new" New Yorkers[1] doubled the population to 24,000. Nevertheless, New York was still more of a small town than a real city. Only a few streets connected the harbor and the settlements in the very south of Manhattan Island. Most of Manhattan was still used for agriculture or not used at all. Doubling the number of inhabitants, and more or less the number of houses and apartments, therefore still did not mean a major expansion of the city to the north, but it showed the level of interest in settling there.

In 1784 the Second Continental Congress made New York, already the commercial center of the former colonies, the capital of the newly founded United States of America. Now the new federal administrators, politicians, civil servants and their families also settled in New York. The city was on the move and everyone felt it. Broadway was at the heart of "new" New York. Known to be the broadest street, Broadway was the infrastructural lifeline of the city. To be on Broadway also meant to be seen by and to meet other New Yorkers. Therefore securing a house on Broadway was also a question of public exposure. The rich and famous New Yorkers, merchants and politicians alike, lived south on Broadway and were buried close to Trinity Church. Wall Street was still a little street close to the city wall and housed many merchants and ship owners from the old Anglo-Saxon and Dutch families. They enjoyed the short commute to their offices and ships in the harbor. The well-paved streets were full of carriages, carts, horses, stalls and people on foot who transported goods. They sold their products and bought what was offered, from food to the most luxurious trading goods from abroad. New York Harbor was literarily surrounding the city. Freight was cleared wherever there was an opportunity to land, and the port authority was making sure trade was proceeding without interference. After the war, the first ships to anchor in New York came from the Caribbean and overseas.[2]

Germans settled in New York from the early 18th century onward. Their numbers speedily increased, and in 1748 the German-Lutheran Church of New York was established.[3] Soon the German Reformed Church of New York followed, as well as the German Society of the City of New York, which was founded in 1784.[4] Though Germans were not a very visible group in the public life of the city, most of them were successful merchants and belonged to New York's upper class. With the increasing numbers of immigrants in the mid–19th century, Germans started to settle on the Lower East Side in a part of the city that was mostly settled by Germans: Little Germany, the first "ethnic neighborhood" of the United States. Here one could find all–German bars, shops, restaurants, and theaters. The street signs were in German, and German traditions were respected, although there were also other immigrants living among the German-Americans. The Germans were doctors, workers, merchants, journalists, artisans and farmers, and they came from different German states, from French Alsace, German-speaking Switzerland, Prussia and Austria; they spoke different dialects, belonged to different faiths, and brought various customs and traditions to the New World. In addition, some kept their German identity in North America, while others accepted at least a new hyphenated identity. But after the third generation of immigrants and under pressure during World War I, all German-Americans had to adopt the host culture quickly. They left Little Germany. Now Chinatown and Little Italy occupy the spot.

As early as the Revolutionary War, the Founding Fathers heatedly debated how New York should further develop economically. Ninety per cent of the population still lived off agriculture. However, Alexander Hamilton,[5] first Secretary of the Treasury and close friend of George Washington, had more farsighted plans. To him it was obvious that banking and paper money and stock-based trade were the future, not the exchange of goods. Taxes were instrumental in his plans. They did not serve as a security for the nation's public reserve, but as a reinvestment in order to further the interests of the state. His vision collided with Thomas Jefferson's plans. The future third president of the United States favored a focus on rural life and agriculture as the most important industry in the new nation. In his view the vast natural resources in soil and water across the continent predestined a concentration on building the United States as an agricultural community. He was intensely influenced by the ideals of the classical Roman republic, where senators would be called from their countryside estates to serve the public. Without being paid by the federal administration to serve, politicians with a strong personal connection to their land and independent income seemed a perfect match to secure the stability of the political system in the new nation. Thomas Jefferson fully trusted the *common man* to work hard and serve the community.[6]

Hamiltonians and Jeffersonians only settled their differences in the Compromise of 1790. New York would henceforth be the nation's most important city in commerce and culture, but would "be lighted of the load of politics," as historians later wrote. Jeffersonians insisted on moving the political capital further south so politicians would be closer to the countryside where many of them had their permanent residences. They also hoped to secure their influence and the dominance of the rural economy from a new capital on the Potomac River. Located between the Southern and the Northern states and named after George Washington, the first president, a new political center was built. Till all the offices of the president, the Senate and the House of Representatives were completed, Philadelphia was chosen as the second capital of the United States of America.[7]

In New York there was no need to imitate European capital architecture anymore and the city could go back to what it was best at: trading. And New York traded hard. Ships arrived from the Old World as well as the newly discovered overseas territories. John Jacob Astor arrived at the right time. New York offered him opportunities much beyond what London had to offer. Trade was rapidly expanding, new niches opened with every ship that arrived and every new immigrant. New York was in the center of the free play of economic powers and Astor was right in the middle of it. He saw successful business strategies in action when he was in London, where he had developed the necessary social and language skills to find success within a short amount of time. New York was the city that never slept, even then. Nowhere else he could have made a better use of his talents.

Arriving in New York

John Jacob Astor did not move on to Philadelphia or the Pennsylvania countryside, as many of his fellow German immigrants did during those days. In Pennsylvania he could have settled in a German community and would have had a head start within an established group of German immigrants. He would not have had to improve his English or adapt to a new English-speaking environment with English tradition and culture in order to start his business. He could have enjoyed the coziness of familiar voices, rituals and habits. But he did not. Astor's goal was New York, not a possible "New Walldorf, Pennsylvania." John Jacob was determined to dive into the lively atmosphere of that growing city that was to rise like a Phoenix from the ashes. The entire town seemed to be starting anew and Astor wanted to be a part of that. His brother Henry had written so much about what was happening there in New York, and now John Jacob had the chance to see it with his own eyes. He assumed the new New Yorkers would be ideal customers for his instruments. They had the time and money to occupy themselves with music and surround themselves with precious, expensive craftsmanship. Astor also hoped his brother Henry would be of similar help to him as his brother George was in London.

In spring 1784 Astor reached New York, and he was happy to see Henry again after 9 years of separation.[8] The sources do not deliver an exact date of his arrival in New York. According to Astor's letter to Washington Irving, he arrived in Baltimore by March 24, 1784. Afterwards he spent some time with the Tuschdy family, and it must have taken a while to travel to New York.[9] It is safe to assume that John Jacob Astor arrived at his new home in June or July 1784.

Since Henry had arrived in North America, he had dropped his German name of "Heinrich" and Americanized it. After Henry's departure from Walldorf he had led an exciting life. He had enlisted as a mercenary in the British army and fought on their side in the Revolutionary War. His regiment became famous under the name "Hessians" because many, though not all of his fellow mercenaries came from the Hesse region, a little north of Henry's own home. Enlisting for the British secured him passage to the North American colonies in exchange for his participation in fighting the American revolutionaries. However, shortly after his arrival he left the troops and carried on his family's traditional profession by becoming a butcher in New York. After the Peace of Paris he was officially naturalized an American citizen in 1783, as were all inhabitants of the former colonies. Some weeks earlier, Henry had married Dorothy Pessenger, the stepdaughter of John Pessenger, who was also a butcher of German origin. Her stepfather's family had lived in upstate New York, 50 miles away from Albany, until a Native American tribe attacked their settlement. While running away, the family was protected by another tribe and brought to safety. In 1742, John was born during the time his family lived with the Native Americans. Later the family moved to New York, where John married Dorothy's mother while she was still a child.[10] The family stayed in New York, where Dorothy met Henry Astor eventually.

During that time, Henry was by far not as successful as George has been in London. But nevertheless, Henry had a better life than he would have had if he had stayed in Walldorf. As was common during those times, Henry sold his meat at the market stalls at Bull's Head. Each morning he displayed his produce there and sold freshly butchered meat. With his wife's help he soon managed to get a bigger stall at the Fly Market on the East River in Lower Manhattan.[11] There it was easier to earn more. During the course of time, Henry Astor was making a good fortune with his businesses. He started off with a little hand-pulled carriage and humble display and was then able to afford not only a proper carriage but also a horse to pull it. Henry and his wife combined hard work and economic thinking.[12] However, when John Jacob arrived in New York, Henry was still far from the wealth George had accumulated in London. He and his wife had rented a little house at the corner of First and Fischer Streets on the Lower East Side, which only offered space for two people.[13] Only much later had they saved enough money to actually buy a house in Bowery Lane[14] in the part of New York that was later known as Little Germany and today as Chinatown.

Since space was limited, Henry had asked his friend George Dieterich to let his brother stay with him. John Jacob was not only welcome to live with George Dieterich, his also worked as delivery boy for Dieterich's bakery. This was a great job for John Jacob because this way he was soon very familiar with New York and many of its inhabitants and businesses. Each day he was on the street and delivered Dieterich's German bread. With the help of his landlord, Astor soon was well connected in the German-American community of New York.[15] Of course, Henry and his wife also did what they could to support the young Astor. John Jacob had a big advantage over his fellow German immigrants: he was already fluent in English when he reached American shores. Therefore he was never limited to the network of German-Americans but also made fast contact with English-speaking Americans. Henry introduced his younger brother to the congregation of the German Reformed Church of New York. John Jacob soon became an active member of the congregation. Not only did he regularly attend church there, but from 1791 to 1797 he was the treasurer of the congregation and managed all of its finances.[16]

When the German Society of the City of New York was founded in 1784 it soon became another hot spot for the German-American community. New York's German Society was modeled after the German Society of Philadelphia. Its goal was to provide help for German immigrants and produce information about the chances and dangers of immigration for those in Germany thinking about coming to America. Henry Astor joined the German Society in 1785.[17] Following Henry's example, John Jacob joined in 1787.[18] However, in contrast to his commitment in church, John Jacob did not participate in activities like the annual convention of the German Society before the 1830s.[19] He was simply not as interested in German-American issues as in connecting with the established American society in New York.[20]

John Jacob was eager to start his own business in New York. With the vibrant start-up atmosphere around him, there were multiple chances for him to work and rise. Religion did not make any difference in defining one's social status or the professions one chose. This was so different from what Astor had experienced during his childhood in Walldorf. Also his working-class background was not a problem here. And Astor kept the words of the Declaration of Independence very dearly to his heart: the rights to life, liberty and the pursuit of happiness. That was what Astor had chosen as his credo and path in the new nation. The chances to make one's own living and economic success were there. Everyone had the same chances to grab these and make the most of them. This is what Astor had already promised himself when he left Walldorf.

After a few months John Jacob Astor left Dieterich's bakery. He was driven by his own ambition. The wages from the bakery provided him with enough means to go back to importing instruments made by George. Also, he wanted to look into the fur trade, which was supposedly recommended to him by Emerick before he had reached America. So he watched closely the few small fur traders in New York. Who were their customers? What did they offer? How did they make their profits? Where did the furs come from? The best way to learn about this was to actually work for one of the successful fur traders.

The Quaker Robert Bowne, an aged and experienced fur trader, was looking for a clerk at that time. Astor applied for this position, and Bowne finally considered him. Astor got two dollars a week, and like before, he found a home in the family of his employer.[21] The old fur trader liked young Astor's ambition and diligence. Readily he shared his experience with the young German. In Bowne's shop Astor prepared the furs for retail and also kept the books. He also learned how to treat the furs, where to get them, and who would buy them in New York. Astor did well and sold many furs for Bowne. The young man was ambitious in selling furs as well as in learning the business. Elizabeth Gebhard attested of him: "He was moral, temperate and industrious, and to these foundational qualities, he added incessant activity in acquiring knowledge of furs, fur-bearing animals, fur-gathering Indians, fur-abounding sections, fur-dealers and fur-markets."[22] In many ways Astor followed his legendary oath, which he swore when he left his hometown Waldorf for America.

William Armstrong and Joseph A. Scoville reported in their 19th century writings from two other fur traders, for whom Astor might have worked in

1785 before Robert Bowne engaged him. Looking at the sources, it is hard to say if this really happened or not. Nevertheless, it would show that Astor had in no way any difficulties getting in contact with the host culture.

As a clerk for a fur trader, John Jacob Astor proved once more that the new language was no obstacle for him. Due to his London experience he could easily work with Americans, he could negotiate with American dealers, and he could sell his goods to American customers. His knowledge of English made it easier for him to import or export goods and build a business network which would extend from New York to England and Canada. In that way, John Jacob Astor was significantly different from most of the Germans immigrating to the United States. While others stayed within the bounds of their ethnic group, his acculturation had already started. Thus, he could become part of the American host culture more quickly.

His first steps in the fur trade business are hard to reconstruct. Astor was at least working for one established fur trader in 1784–85. Several authors have suggested in this context different names for the merchant who initially employed young John Jacob. Nineteenth-century writer William Armstrong associated young Astor with a fur trader named Wilson in his book about New York society.[23] But Armstrong fails to mention Astor's first months in New York and his work for George Dieterich, as well as his business with musical instruments. Thus, his account is not complete enough to be trustworthy. Furthermore, Scoville reported that Astor learned the fur business from Hayman Levy.[24] However, this is the only mention of Hayman Levy in the writings about Astor. Therefore, due to the lack of credible sources, it is hard to reconstruct Astor's professional life within this period.

In the meantime George had sent the first deliveries of instruments from London. Astor kept them in his new little room that he had rented from Sarah Todd, a rich widow. In order to reach potential customers, he started, on September 20, 1784, to put ads into the most important New York daily, the *New York Packet*. His ads read: "German Flutes— Extraordinary Quality— to buy at the publishing house."[25] He published these ads during the start-up phase till March 10, 1785. Because his room only provided limited space, he sold the flutes for a small fee right at the publishing house of the *New York Packet*. The trade was enough of a success that George and John Jacob risked the cost of shipping more and bigger instruments from London to New York. Shortly after New Year's the next shipment arrived in New York. With his increased income, Astor was now able to publish longer ads from January 27, 1785, onward. Also the instruments he imported got bigger. He had an organ shipped from London: "Just to be imported ... and to be sold ... 1 Chamber Organ with Diapason Stops, German Flutes, tipt with silver and common, [etc.]"[26] Working for others like Bowne was obviously not enough for John

Jacob. Importing instruments from Europe was successful and paid well from the very beginning, and he could manage the imports on the side while working for Bowne. Only months after his arrival in America he had established himself — admittedly still as a small player, but nevertheless — in the transatlantic trade.

Soon, the demand for Astor's instruments was so high that George was unable to produce enough instruments in time. Therefore, John Jacob contacted the London company which was mentioned before, Shudi & Broadwood. This is the reason why some writers saw a connection between Astor and this company. In the same letter, which the company wrote to a journalist 100 years later, they wrote and praised the business relation with John Jacob: "Whatever Astor ordered — and he ordered largely — he paid for, the invoices being sent to his brother, George Astor, a flute maker."[27] To prove their business connection, but also that Astor was a customer and not a partner, they included a letter:

> The following copy of a letter is in proof of our assertion: "March 14, 1785. Messers. Broadwood & Sons — Gentlemen — Please to make me one of the best grant pianofortes you can. I rely on your honor to let it be good one. I wish to have it plain in every respect, and the case of handsome wood. The belly may be screwed fast. When done call on Mr. George Astor for payment. I shall wish to have it shipped in July or August next by the ship Hope for New York [...] to be sent Mr. J. Astor.[28]

This letter also proves how the Astor brothers did the business. John Jacob was still in charge of selling the instruments as he had been before in their London shop. George was acting as an agent for his brothers to supervise the financial affairs.

However, not only was John Jacob's business prospering, there were also some changes in his private life. Not long after he moved into his new room in a building which belonged to an older lady, John Jacob found himself dating his landlady's daughter, Sarah Todd, who had the same first name as her mother. Her father had died 15 years before, and her mother was happy when she found out that Sarah was romantically involved with the young, aspiring German. Sarah was of Scottish descent and her family had long lived in America. Therefore she was well connected in New York and knew merchants and ship owners everywhere. She was a perfect match for Astor. Even though he was just at the beginning of his career, his ambition and diligence made a huge impression on Sarah.[29] The two fell in love and after some months the decision to marry was made. When asked by one of his granddaughters why he had married Sarah, Astor is said to have answered with a sigh: "Because she was so pretty, my dear."[30] This sentence is remarkable, because it is one of the rare lines in all of the sources I analyzed where John Jacob Astor showed emotion.

After Astor had courted Sarah and asked for permission to take her as his wife, they finally married on September 19, 1785, at the German Reformed Church of New York.[31] As in many other ways, Astor did not really fit in with the average immigrant when it came to his choice of his wife. First-generation immigrants mostly married within their ethnic group, not outside of it. His brother Henry, for example, had married a German, as did his brother George. However, John Jacob's wife was part of the established, English-speaking New York society. So John Jacob not only got a wife, but also a place in the established families in New York, leaving his German-American heritage behind. After the wedding he would only speak English. This was an extraordinary step within his acculturation. The marriage with Sarah Todd showed once more his willingness to become part of his American host culture. This was even noted back home in Walldorf. In 1888 the local priest, Ludwig Stocker, made an entry about this seemingly unusual attitude in the chronicles of Walldorf. To Stocker, Astor was not a German immigrant anymore, but a true American, because Astor "married an American and therefore became American himself."[32]

Sarah Todd Astor (Vereinigung Walldörfer Heimatfreunde).

Sarah also brought money and property into the marriage. Now the young family had their own house in Queen Street 81 with showrooms in the basement.[33] This wedding brought not only personal happiness to Astor, but also economic independence. Soon after the wedding Astor left Bowne's fur trade and established his own business together with his wife. The pious and business-minded Sarah was not only a loving wife for Astor; she also ran the fur store in the house.[34] When he would be traveling, she would take care of the business and customers at home. After the wedding John Jacob moved to Sarah and her mother to the house in Queen Street.[35]

Much more important than Sarah's money and the house was her social network. Her connection with New York's upper class was a decisive factor in Astor's success. Furthermore, Sarah's brother Adam, a captain at sea, was a great asset to Astor's import trade because he was well connected to many of the captains and ship owners who delivered cargo to New York. Also Sarah's stepsister, from a first marriage of Sarah's father, would establish many useful contacts among New York's merchants. Sarah's nephew, John Whetten, was an officer at sea and also added valuable contacts to ship owners. Astor would work with him many times during his active time and also gave him command over his ships on multiple occasions. Sarah Todd's social and economic network was the basis for the trade empire to be established by Astor.

Nevertheless, it was not just unusual for that time that an immigrant married a woman of the host culture, it was also unusual that a daughter of a higher-class family was allowed to marry a rather poor young immigrant man. Due to the lack of sources, the reasons why that marriage was allowed to proceed stay in the dark.

After the wedding, Astor's time as an independent merchant had begun. If there were no instruments in stock he bought German toys and other goods fabricated in Germany. As he had foreseen, New York's upper class longed for luxurious goods from Europe after the end of the Revolutionary War. This conflict had long interrupted the regular trading routes and had let the desire grow for a better time. Astor had a good sense for those developments and increased his instrument imports as an ad in the *New York Packet* from May 22, 1786, shows: "Just imported from London, an elegant assortment of Musical Instruments, such as piano fortes, spinets, piano-forte guitar, the best of violins, German flutes, clarinets ... and all other kinds of strings, music books and paper ... which he will dispose of on very low terms for cash."[36] He repeated this ad over the next two months. Similar ads also appeared during the following year in the *New York Packet*.[37] Astor had managed to get a class of people interested in his goods who were both wealthy enough to buy the products and traditional enough to appreciate what was fabricated in Old Europe. According to the Pierce Piano Atlas, among Astor's customers were the United States presidents Thomas Jefferson, James Monroe and James K. Polk. All of them owned an Astor piano.[38] John Jacob also broadened his access to New York's upper class and cultivated his ardent wish to be a part of it.

John Jacob Astor was always ambitious. He was satisfied with the successful instrument trade, but his drive for a better life brought him directly to new business ideas. He had a feeling that there was a longing for more luxurious items, namely furs, among his customers. New Yorkers were ready to pay large sums for furs. Now Astor wanted to make use from the insights into this business he gained during his time at Bowne's.

The British trading companies in Canada dominated the fur trade during these years. The entire North American market was firmly under their control. Due to this strong competition from the North and their efficient organization, only a few American traders had tried to get their foot into the fur trade. Hardly any of the American merchants had ever been to Montreal in Canada, where the most furs were sold during this time. Furs that were bought there to be traded in the United States had to be shipped to London first, where they were taxed and returned over the Atlantic. Only then were these goods allowed to be imported to the United States. Astor had imported enough goods from London to feel he was experienced enough to engage in this risky endeavor. Also he could count on the support of his brother George in London, who would supervise the taxing of the furs and ship them to New York.

On April 29, 1788, John Jacob published his first ad in the *New York Packet* that not only advertised the instruments imported from London, but also the furs imported from there. He had added the following to the usual ads: "[I] also buy and sell for Cash all kinds of furs."[39] Importing instruments provided Astor with his starting capital, financial independence, and the economic freedom to engage further into the fur trade. Astor saw his chances in the fur trade because other merchants hesitated to engage in it. Slowly he filled this niche. His great-grandson, Viscount William Waldorf Astor, described the importance of the fur trade for the Astors retrospectively at the end of the 19th century: "The lucrative results of the fur trade bear comparison with the later products of Californian gold mines. Each was the El Dorado of its day, each gave employment direct or indirect to many thousands, and each was the object of intense competition."[40]

Following Native American Paths

Americans still settled only on the Eastern shores of the continent, close to the Atlantic. None of the states of the new nation reached beyond the Appalachians. Where Native Americans lived, hunted or settled, Americans saw nothing more than a beautiful but dangerous wilderness. Therefore only a few Americans had settled in those wild regions, beyond the established state borders on the so-called frontier.

It was tiring to travel to these regions because no roads had been built there and only a few people knew their way around. The easiest way was to travel in a canoe, as most of the trappers, peddlers and fur traders did. For most Americans, their world ended at the Appalachian Mountains. In spring 1788, Astor would join these adventurers and explorers in order to get into the backcountry of the state of New York.[41] But what inspired him to take that risk and what reasons were behind it? Why did he leave his successful business to go on the dangerous trip to the frontier?

For three years John Jacob Astor ran his New York shop, buying and selling furs and peltries. He was right: the fur business brought him some money. Additionally, with the cold winter of 1787–88 the demand for furs increased. Astor could have sold many more if he only had them in stock. At this time he remembered what he had learned from Bowne about hunting and trading with Native Americans.[42]

Finally, young Astor decided to take the risk and hunt on his own. He planned to start a voyage of discovery, which would change his later life. He bought what he needed for this in New York and walked off to the unexplored parts of the state of New York towards the Canadian border, close to the Great Lakes, where he intended to work as a trapper. He targeted beavers and raccoons. Their furs would later be made into fur coats, caps and gloves. First he followed Native American trails, but he soon bought a canoe to move north more quickly. He slept outside and ate fish or meat from the animals he hunted. Day after day he waited in the woods for the animals to be trapped.[43]

After a couple of weeks, he returned from the first of his trips with many furs. Sarah was relieved to see him safe and sound. The both of them went on to make proper furs from the animal skins and sold them in their shop. Astor was right: his profits increased significantly and the success only fueled his ambition. He was thinking about his next steps. What if he not only set his own traps, but also bought more furs directly from the Native American hunters? Would it be possible for him to get in touch on his own with Native Americans?

Elizabeth Gebhardt reported, that "Nothing escaped young Astor's eyes or ears." Furthermore, she stated that "he was familiar with the handicap of an unknown tongue in a strange land, and he set himself in his leisure hours, to studying the Indian languages." This sounds like the pattern Astor acted upon all his business life. Also, Gebhardt was sure that "he could converse intelligently in the languages of the Mohawk, Seneca, and Oneida tribes," and that "he was the first fur trader to win this advantage."[44]

John Jacob Astor prepared himself for trade with Native Americans. Before he left for his next trip he packed beads, clothing and wooden toys to trade for furs. Aware that he was not able to communicate other than with signs, he also packed a flute in order to let the music speak to gain the trust of the Native Americans, as some writers suggested.[45]

In fact, Astor succeeded in establishing his first contact with the Native Americans of upstate New York. Astor was now able to trade furs for the goods he brought. These trips made Astor familiar with the fur trade and how to buy furs from Native Americans. He learned a lot about where to trade furs, how to get there, and who needed to be traded with. He understood how to peacefully approach the Native Americans, communicate with them, and establish a personal relationship with them. This was what made him different from many other American fur traders. The region that Astor got to know as unexplored wilderness would not long remain uncivilized. Other merchants followed Astor's example, and the routes Astor had used for his travels soon became official trading routes on which even trains would later travel. Among them were the routes to Long Island; the routes through the valley of the Hudson River to Lake Champlain, to the Niagara Falls and to Montreal; the route from Albany to Buffalo; and a couple of paths in New Jersey and Pennsylvania. Buffalo and Rochester would originate where Astor had founded trading posts with Native Americans. On his trips, he had followed Native American trails that had been used for centuries before.[46]

Astor's lonely trips through the wilderness that laid the foundation of his increased profits and therefore his later wealth were enough to develop into stories and anecdotes among his contemporaries. One that is particularly revealing about the public view of Astor dates back to the 1860s. James Parton published in *Harper's Monthly Magazine* a story about how Astor met James Wadsworth, the father of James S. Wadsworth,[47] the Civil War general, on one of these trips. Wadsworth had met Astor when the young fur trader had got stuck with his carriage in a swamp on his way back to New York after Astor had traded with the Native Americans. Desperately trying to pull the carriage out of the slough, Astor nearly lost his life in the attempt to save the gold that was loaded on the carriage. Only after giving in to losing his carriage and the gold was Astor safe. This story shows how closely Astor was susceptible to the traditional temptations of gold and wealth. Even his early trips were later used in order to moralize how to reasonably deal with a large fortune. [48]

Towards the end of the 19th century Astor's trips also received some positive acknowledgment. William Waldorf Astor wrote a small portrait of his great grandfather's life. A few years prior to this, Frederick Jackson Turner published his famous essay "The Significance of the Frontier in American History." In his essay Turner argues that only the cultivation of the wilderness and permanent confrontation with nature at the frontier transformed the European settlers into Americans who left the Old World behind them. This thesis was not only discussed among historians but also by the general public. Therefore, William Waldorf Astor shared the experiences and adventures John Jacob Astor had at the frontier in the June edition of the *Pall Mall Magazine* in 1899. He gave a picture of his great-grandfather as a European immigrant who wandered through the wilderness at the North American frontier. His great-grandfather lived there and traded as an honorable man with the chiefs of the Native American tribes: "Wherever he went he dealt with the chiefs, bargaining with them in a spirit of fairness and humanity, and forbidding his agents ever to sell liquor to the savages."[49] William Waldorf Astor described how John Jacob became a true American in the wilderness and tried to place him right into the tradition of American pioneers.

The way in which Astor's walks through the American wilderness were described points out two different, almost opposite reports. The more critical came from Gustavus Myers. Adopting a very harsh standpoint, he transforms Astor into a greedy trader ready to corrupt the helpless natives. Without citing any source, he is sure that Astor was able to get the best furs and pelts just for some cheap bottles of rum.[50] The corruption of the Indians by alcohol, however, fits into the argumentation of the German-American Myers. He was a supporter of the Socialist movement and argued in his publication of 1911 against the richest Americans of his time. Not only his compatriot John Jacob Astor, but also many other American millionaires of the 19th century were accused in this book.[51]

On the other hand, Axel Madsen painted a romantic picture of Astor's first contact with the Natives: "He took out a flute and tootled a few Baden-Baden folk tunes."[52] Supposedly, Madsen thought that the term "Baden-Baden" would describe Astor's home country. But Baden-Baden is a city with which Astor had nothing to do. As I mentioned before, Walldorf did not belong to the German region of Baden during that time. In this way, both terms are wrong, because Astor grew up neither in the city of Baden-Baden nor in the former Duchy of Baden, but in the old Palatinate. Furthermore, the author does not mention any source for his statement. Axel Madsen's book from 2001 is full of such imaginative details which are at best fabrications. Nevertheless, he is a popular author of many novels and fictionalized biographies, and he had never claimed to write an academic study based on research.

After 1788 John Jacob no longer went on these trips himself. He sent agents to buy from the Native Americans. Astor had decided to go to Montreal himself to trade there and ship the furs via London to New York. He would be a real competitor for the British and Canadians. In Montreal he learned about the general conditions of the international fur trade. He found out where to buy cheap and was able to establish a network of agents who traded on his behalf when he returned to New York. In the end he supervised the buys and the shipping to London. Until 1808, he left for Canada sometime between June and August and returned to New York City between October and November each year. [53]

Astor quickly became part of the Montreal business world. He sometimes brought his family on these journeys, and he got invitations to all important

3. Immigrant, 1784–1800

business meetings and social gatherings. There he met the important members of the big Canadian companies.[54] The business contacts and experience Astor made in Canada were essential to his later success. He could not have come to a better place for his intentions.[55]

Many early biographers believe that while Astor was away for business, his wife Sarah was in charge of the New York shop. They also point out that the couple was acting a good team, modest and with a similar understanding of business. Scoville wrote about her: "It was a curious fact that Mrs. Astor knew more of the value of the furs than he did.... When they became very affluent she used to make him pay her $500 an hour for using her judgement and knowledge of furs to promote his commercial plans. He paid whatever she asked."[56] Astor had hired Alexander Henry in Montreal to take care of the trading while he was back in New York. Henry was well connected and very experienced so that he was an ideal agent for Astor. Furthermore, Astor rented a warehouse in Montreal where he and Henry were able to stock the furs before shipping.

Astor's Canadian fur trade also made it into his ads in New York, where he explicitly offered high-quality furs from Canada. He also introduced a discount for customers who bought in large amounts. From October 28, 1788, he announced: "[...] for sale a quantity of Canada Furs, such as beaver ... which he sells by large or small quantities — a considerable allowance will be made to every person who buys a quantity."[57]

Astor managed to steadily increase his trading network and developed his business into a large-scale trading empire with offices not only in New York but also in Albany and Montreal. However, New York remained the center of his enterprise. It was in New York where most of his customers lived and so he only advertised his products here. Albany soon became a major trading post for the furs from the Great Lakes. Astor's longtime friend and business partner, Peter Smith, managed the fur trade with the Native Americans and trappers there.

Albany became an important transportation hub between New York and the fur areas around the Great Lakes. Therefore, Astor hired Peter Smith as an agent for the Albany office. Smith worked closely with the New Yorker, especially in the 1780s and 1790s. He was also an immigrant, and like Astor had come to American shores in 1784. On behalf of Astor, he organized the fur trade with the Indians and trappers from Albany. Over time, Smith's activities expanded along the Mohawk River toward Lake Ontario. In order to control his business and to discuss further steps, Astor visited Smith and Albany each year on his way to Montreal.[58]

Up to 1796, importing from Canada remained a tiring venture. Because Canada was still under British rule, all goods needed to go on a detour via

London on their way to New York. This only changed after the Jay Treaty. This treaty between the United States and Great Britain was named after the American negotiator, politician, Founding Father, and first Chief of Justice of the United States John Jay. It took effect on February 29, 1796, and regulated unresolved issues between both nations, which were yet not settled after the Revolutionary War.[59]

Now, Astor was finally able to transport the furs directly from Montreal to New York. The provisions of the Jay Treaty not only facilitated trade but also meant that the cities Mackinac and Detroit at the Canadian and American border now belonged to the United States. This opened a whole new access to the resources in the region around the Great Lakes in the Midwestern United States that were under British influence up to then. After he had received news about the ratification of the Jay Treaty, Astor is said to have burst out in joy and have exclaimed: "Now I will make my fortune in the fur-trade."[60] However, the facilitation of the imports also meant more competition for Astor. More and more American merchants tried to trade in fur. Astor had a head start and could already look back on ten years of experience in the fur trade.

Family and Social Network

The years 1788 and 1789 were important milestones in Astor's life. He had focused on trading in luxury items and therefore reached out early beyond his ethnic origins and German-American networks. He had realized that his success was to be found among the established upper class, and he had secured his place in this class with marrying Sarah Todd.

After three years of marriage John Jacob and Sarah expected their first child. In 1788 Sarah was pregnant and gave birth to a daughter who was named after John Jacob's mother Magdalen. The couple would have eight children in total. However, three of them died as infants: Sarah, born 1790; Henry, born 1797; and also their last son, born November 13, 1802, did not survive. He must have died shortly after his birth, since his name is not recorded. Altogether, five children of the Astor family survived.

In 1791 Sarah gave birth to the couple's first son, who was called John Jacob II. Though his own father had been Johann Jakob Astor, John Jacob did not count him as the first John Jacob. He had left behind his Walldorf origins and apparently did not want to suggest any connection with the Old World or reverence for his father. He considered himself the first John Jacob, and naming his first son John Jacob Astor II underlined his desire to built a dynasty of Astors in the New World. However, John Jacob II did not become the successor John Jacob had hoped for. The child was mentally impaired and needed constant care all throughout his life.[61] In 1792 another son was born: William Backhouse Astor. He was named after one of Astor's business partners and was to become the heir to the business. Two more daughters followed. In 1795 Dorothea was born. She was named after Dorothea Astor, the wife of his brother Henry. The last child of the couple was Eliza, who was born in 1801. She was the youngest and Astor's favorite. She was the one who would accompany him when he traveled to Europe.[62] Like her siblings, Eliza spent her childhood at her parents' home. Astor's financial success made it possible for his children to be educated by private teachers. However, he also sent them to institutes of higher education, including a girls' school in Philadelphia and the most important college for young women in Middletown, Connecticut.[63]

Over the previous years the Astors had become rich fast. Their modest living led to a steady increase of their fortune. Even though Astor lived like a nobleman compared to his humble childhood in Walldorf, he never was a big spender. He wanted to nurture his wealth. He was constantly looking for ways to keep his fortune safe. His brother Henry recommended investing in real estate, which was still relatively cheap on Manhattan Island. Astor soon owned a rental apartment that created steady income. Both of the Astor brothers were convinced that the prices for real estate had to rise due to the high number of immigrants from Europe. Henry had seen the city double in size since his arrival and there was no end in sight to the expansion. John Jacob liked Henry's thinking and bought his first real estate in Manhattan in 1789, adding yet another industry with a high turnover to his portfolio that already consisted of trading in instruments and furs.[64]

John Jacob's steps were cautious at first. On May 18, 1789, he bought the corner of Bowery Lane and Elizabeth Street. He bought the neighboring real estate from James Bolmer, who owned a restaurant nearby, in the same year.[65] However, Astor soon increased his efforts and bought more real estate.[66] He must have been fascinated by the opportunity to buy land and own it. This was a prerogative of the rich and royal where he had come from in Germany. His father, a butcher, had not been allowed to buy and have property of his own. Ten years had passed since John Jacob had left Walldorf, and he had not only successfully achieved his economic freedom but had also gained property. None of this had been possible for him in the Old World. With the expansion of his trade, the shop in Queen Street, where he still lived with his wife, had served its purpose and had to be swapped for a larger one. Astor had enough savings to easily rent new and bigger shop space in Little Dock Street 40, which is now Water Street in Manhattan.[67]

It was also in 1789 that Astor was finally naturalized in the United States.

The legal framework of the time provided that all white male immigrants could become American citizens five years after their arrival. They had to promise to recant their former citizenship two years afterwards and pledge their allegiance to the American Constitution. This was the moment John Jacob had waited for. On February 28, 1789 — almost exactly five years after his arrival — he became a citizen of the United States of America. However, the official papers formally recognizing this were little more than the documentation of what had already happened. Astor had made the best use of his time after his arrival and established himself as a successful self-made businessman. He was an integral part of the thriving business community in New York. From 1790 onward he was listed among the merchants in the *New York Directory and Register*. [68]

During these years Astor drastically expanded his business. When British, French and American vessels repeatedly had unfriendly encounters on the Atlantic, Astor saw his opportunity to add yet another trading good to his portfolio: weapons. As advertised in the *New York Gazette and General Advertiser* on August 4, 1797, Astor offered 14.000 pounds of English cannon powder of best quality and cannons to equip American ships.[69] The advertisements of 1798 show the entire range of Astor's merchandise. In addition to the gunpowder mentioned above, he offered in June 1798 for the first time: "A few casks of water colours for paper ... some elegant looking glass plates ... refined salt petre."[70] Throughout November he offered guns and weapons in the *New York Gazette and General Advertiser*: "24 Cannons, 4 pounders ... round shot, 20 Barrels Cannon Powder, 600 quarter casks fine Musket ... 12 Muskets with Bayonets, 14 Swords...."[71] However, apparently trading in weaponry was not rewarding, and from 1800 onward Astor reduced his investments in cannons and munitions again. Soon Astor stopped selling weapons and ammunition and concentrated more on the China trade. The import of foreign spices, silk and tea looked more promising.

Other branches of Astor's business blossomed and Astor had to move to bigger office space again. In the mid–1790s he would move to New York's hot spot, the place all businessmen of his standing needed to be: Broadway. This time Astor did not hesitate. His wife and he bought 149 Broadway in 1794, right in the commercial center of the city, for their family and business. Astor had made it to the most prestigious spot in New York. He lived among the rich and famous.[72]

As with many of his influential and powerful contemporaries in the early republic, Astor was involved in Freemasonry. On June 24, 1717, the four lodges had formed the Great Lodge in London and laid the foundation of modern Freemasonry. In the following years it had spread all over Europe. The first lodges in America formed in the 1730s. Many influential politicians of Astor's time were members of North American lodges like Henry Clay, DeWitt Clinton, and Benjamin Franklin, as well as the presidents George Washington, Thomas Jefferson, James Monroe, James Madison and Andrew Jackson. Many values of the Freemasons originated in the enlightenment. All members of the lodges—irrespective of their class or status—were expected to live the ideals of freedom, equality, brotherhood, tolerance and humanity. The Old World did not receive Freemasonry as favorably. The Catholic regions in particular saw Freemasons in sharp opposition to church dogmas, and they were therefore viewed very critically. On April 28, 1738, Pope Clement XII published a Papal Bull titled *In eminenti*. This tractate forbade Catholics to be members in secret societies like the Freemasons, because they "act evil" or else "they would not avoid the light of the world."[73] In public, Freemasons were not tolerated in America either. Many Americans deemed it as revolutionary, or worse, as a threat to religion.

After Astor had attended some public events held by New York's Freemasons in 1790, he became more and more interested in this secret society. Only months later he was officially accepted as member of Holland Lodge No. 8[74] that belonged to the Grand Lodge of the State of New York. On May 30, 1787, a group of eight Masons of Dutch descent living in New York City had established a new lodge that would conduct its proceedings in the Low Dutch language. After some negotiation, and after conceding that minutes would be maintained in English for the benefit of Grand Lodge inspectors, a warrant was issued on September 20, 1787. The Holland Lodge was formally consecrated in ceremonies held on October 1, 1787.[75]

From its very beginnings, Holland Lodge has had a distinguished membership, including honorary membership conferred in 1789 on President George Washington while the nation's capital was in New York City. Distinguished members included Baron Von Steuben, the Revolutionary War general, and Samuel Fraunces, the famous tavern keeper, who joined in 1789 just prior to his service as steward to President Washington. Other notable early members included future New York City Mayor and New York State Governor DeWitt Clinton. He went on to have as distinguished a career in Masonry as he did in public office, rising to become Grand Master of Masons in the State of New York, among other high offices in related bodies.[76]

Astor now added a new network to his already well-connected public relationships. He enjoyed the regular meetings with many of his fellow businessmen and other high-powered New Yorkers. Freemasonry really echoed in Astor what his teacher Jeune had taught him at the reformed school in Walldorf. Freemasonry was an ideal vehicle to channel the enlightened spirit in the New World. By becoming a member, Astor moved further away from his fellow German-Americans towards an environment that was dominated by Americans. Seven years later, Astor became Senior Warden and later ended his career among the Freemasons as a Master of the Holland Lodge.[77] Since both were Freemasons, Astor must have met DeWitt Clinton at some Freemasonry meetings. DeWitt Clinton, once in office as governor, initiated the building of the Erie Canal. It was not that Astor would not have had a career without being a Freemason. But the connection to DeWitt Clinton made it easier for him to approach President Jefferson in 1808. Besides that, it does not seem that becoming a Freemason was boosting his career, as the usual conspiracy theorists might argue. Nevertheless, joining a Freemasons' lodge was a clear sign that Astor was accepting the habits of his host culture.

Furthermore, John Jacob Astor joined other circles of his host culture that were more business like than Freemasonry. The beginnings of the New York Stock Exchange also lay in that period, and Astor was interested in this new business opportunity. From July 1791 on, New York's merchants traded stocks three times a week on a closed auction in the Long Room of the Merchant's Coffee House. After the market was repeatedly shaken, they formed an alliance on May 17, 1792, and signed the Buttonwood Agreement. This agreement regulated how stocks were traded and exchanged in New York. The following year the stock exchange was moved to the upper rooms of the Tontine Coffee House on Wall Street.[78] Even though Astor was not among the original signers of the Buttonwood Agreement, he often visited the Tontine Coffee House and bought stocks for his himself and his daughter Magdalen, who was only four at the time, and met with fellow businessmen.[79] Astor was as often at the Tontine Coffee House as he was at Mrs. Keese's Boardinghouse, located on the corner of Broadway and Wall Street.[80] Both locations were frequented by New York's political and commercial high society. It was easy for him to expand his network there.

Because of his friendship with DeWitt Clinton, Astor was once again the reason for a certain speculation among his contemporaries. This rumor was first printed in Scoville's book about the *Old Merchants of New York*. He wrote that when Astor was asked what was the biggest gain he had missed out on, he replied: Buying Louisiana.[81] There were rumors that Gouverneur Morris, DeWitt Clinton, and Astor had lined up to make their move before President Jefferson could buy the vast territory that stretched from the Mississippi Delta to the Rocky Mountains from the French for $15 million. The three New Yorkers are said to have planned to buy the territory and sell it to the president themselves to make a decent profit in the resale.[82]

Nevertheless, Scoville's account is the only work mentioning that episode. There are no other sources which prove Astor had any such intention. Furthermore, Scoville contradicts himself by arguing on the one hand that Astor wanted to make a profit of 2.5%. On the other hand, he says that Astor and the other investors wanted to sell the Louisiana land to the United States for the same price for which they planned to buy it.

It is safe to say that not even all three of them together would have been able to spend $15 million in 1803. However, the fact that their contemporaries feared they could do so makes it obvious what kind of an exceptional status the three of them enjoyed in New York. As for Astor, the story also shows how much his contemporaries feared him. Being a Freemason was something the public was very skeptical of. Forming an alliance with Clinton and Morris, who were leading Freemasons themselves, would not have been received well among the New Yorkers. This would have stirred their fears of secret societies. In the context of these speculations about the Louisiana Purchase, Astor was portrayed as highly unpatriotic for the first time. It was voiced that his intention to buy the territory was nothing more than the first step to form his own "nation" or to make a profit from selling it to the United States. Again Astor was criticized as an avaricious and unscrupulous capitalist.[83]

4

Visionary, 1800–1815

Astor rose during a time when America's economy was largely influenced by the ideals of economic freedom almost without any restrictions.[1] America's public, however, was still largely influenced by the ideas of republicanism from the pre-revolutionary time that had an anti-capitalistic tenor. Republicanism meant more to the revolutionaries than the Declaration of Independence and resisting the British crown.[2] It was a utopia that was built upon the moral integrity of a self-governing people. The virtuous citizens were the foundation of the young nation. The governing body did not understand itself as a ruler but as the mediator between citizens and their interests. Therefore the top governing body of the United States even today is mostly referred to as the administration and to a much lesser extent as the government. The first duty of the U.S. administration is to serve the people—not vice versa, as in Old Europe during Astor's times. The people's first duty, on the other hand, is to serve the republic. Therefore the economic success of an individual was to benefit the people rather than to accumulate as private fortune.[3]

During the course of Astor's career, liberal ideas gained more and more influence among the Americans. The first steps of democratization and the transformation of public opinion supported this. A society formed that was more and more individualistic, egalitarian, but thriving for economic success. Republican ideals were less and less important to the businessmen who made the best of the chances offered in the early republic. A capitalistic culture evolved that was cultivated by a new, rising class to which Astor belonged. The republican ideas that lay at the heart of the movement towards independence slowly faded in the generation that followed the revolutionaries in the leading positions of society, politics and economies. This new generation demanded a new America that would not imitate the traditional ways of the Old World, but would establish a "brave new world" that would develop into a prospering community driven by the business-mindedness of the people.[4]

The ideas of liberalism protected the individual liberties of the citizen from the intervention of the state and other citizens. To Astor the opportunity to trade without limitations was essential, of course. According to John Locke the central thought of liberalism was the idea of private property.[5] In Locke's terms private property meant the irrevocable, inalienable and natural right to life, liberty and property.[6] Thomas Jefferson used these thoughts for his Declaration of Independence and swapped the right to property with the pursuit of happiness, which was more abstract and therefore much less legally binding.[7]

After the Federalists George Washington and John Adams, Jefferson struck during his tenure a new political course. He favored a decentralized republic with strong individual states and an agricultural character. Furthermore, the third president demanded that the republican state would leave no further debt to the next generation, and thus stood in opposition to Alexander Hamilton's claims of a liberal economic policy. In Jefferson's vision the individual citizen should therefore be virtuous citizen, who followed the common good for the "pursuit of happiness."

Enter the China Trade

The fur trade was a successful business for Astor. But as a restless and ambitious businessman he was not satisfied with it. He was constantly looking for new markets. The Pacific Ocean offered him a space where he could trade on routes away from English and French warships.[8] China seemed to be a promising trading site. It seemed equally attractive as the fur trade had been 15 years earlier. Astor had watched the cautious steps taken by fellow merchants in the Chinese market. Now 37 years old, Astor thought it was time to take up this business himself. From 1800 onward he traded with China.

As with the fur trade, Astor was not the first American to enter the China trade. He had observed it for some years. In 1784 several merchants from Philadelphia under the leadership of financier Robert Morris sent the first American vessel to China. This ship was the *Empress of China*. Two years earlier, the emperor of China had allowed an association of merchants in Canton to trade with non–Chinese. The *Independent Gazette* reported on the importance of her first voyage: "The first ship from this new nation, to that rich and distant part of the world [...] The gentlemen, whose ambition to discover new resources of wealth, by forming new channels for the extensions of our commerce had thus prompted them to risque their property."[9] The *Empress of China* took the lead in what would soon become a great fleet of American ships heading to Canton in China. Goods from China became an American rage.

An endeavor like this was unheard of before the Revolutionary War.

Many markets and ports of the British were closed for American merchants. In a way similar to the fur trade, the British East India Company enjoyed a monopoly on the transpacific trade.[10] The British property in the West Indies was a major market for retail and a source for raw materials before the American Revolution. Afterwards China slowly replaced them as a port. Astor was aware of this shift in the market dynamics and saw that the time had come to invest in the China trade.[11]

After careful research and meetings with other ship owners and merchants, Astor decided to ship furs and Hawaiian sandalwood to China and intended to buy Asian goods there. According to his announcements in the *New York Gazette and General Advertiser*, Astor offered for the first time goods from Asia in 1799.[12] He continued with the China trade for the next few decades. Up to 1812 Astor sent one, sometimes two vessels per year to Canton. His cargoes consisted of furs, ginseng, spices, cochineal to produce red colorant, quicksilver, cotton, iron, and blackwood. His ships brought back black and green tea, nankeens, silk, sugar, cassia and several minor articles.[13] In this way the Chinese market would get what was of high demand there, and New Yorkers would be able to enjoy the Asian specialties that were sought after by many. Astor's ships would be best used on both passages. It was a further advantage of the China trade that the Pacific did not suffer from the rising tensions between England and France in the Napoleonic Wars that impeded shipping on the Atlantic routes. Ships and goods were equally safe on the Pacific compared to the Atlantic.[14]

As in many instances before, the origin of Astor's China trade also found its way into the popular image of Astor. His contemporaries were not ready to believe that Astor's success was a result of his modesty and business-mindedness. Many contemporary writers voiced their doubts about Astor's success. Due to the fact that he was the first person in history rising from poverty to immense wealth, nobody could believe that this career was a result of hard work, daring visions and maybe a bit of luck. Or at least not pure luck, as, for example, Joseph A. Scoville insisted. He published a multi-volume edition of *The Old Merchants of New York City* in which he expressed doubt that Astor's business skills made him successful. Among many facts about Astor and other merchants, he includes episodes about Astor that are far from true. In this context he declares the beginning of Astor's success in the China trade was just a stroke of luck. Other writers, like Parton, Gebhard and even W.J. Ghent, who wrote the short biography of Astor in the *Dictionary of American Biography*, also mention this anecdote. Arthur Howden-Smith expresses some doubts about the truth of the story, but still believes that it has happened. Only Porter has doubts.[15]

Scoville insinuates Astor had traveled to London himself in 1795 in order to sell furs there. Allegedly, after he had finished trading, he had to stay a couple of days before returning to New York, and he used this time to collect news and information about his business. When he visited the British East India House, Scoville suggests that Astor realized one of the directors had the same name as one of his former classmates from Walldorf. This person turned out to be a "Wilhelm from Germany," as Scoville reports. The writer continues with the revelation that Wilhelm indeed was an old friend from Walldorf. Happy to see this old friend again, Scoville claims that Wilhelm issued a Permit No. 68 for Astor. This, he says, permitted Astor to trade in all the ports in which the British East India Company traded. Back in New York City, Astor was supposed to have decided with his business partner, James Livermore, to send a ship full of goods to Canton (China) where the goods could be traded due to the permit that had been received in London. Scoville even asserts that Astor and his partner had a turnover of $55,000 from this first ship to China.[16] According to Scoville, the first ship sent by Astor to China left North America in 1795.[17] But this is four years too early, due to the fact that Astor published his first advertising to promote goods from the China trade in 1799.[18]

The story, in its complete form, seems like the work of a single imagination. Its first appearance in print was in Scoville's *Old Merchants of New York*. There it is said that the story was told by Astor to a business acquaintance who had asked him to what fortunate occurrence he ascribed his early success. Porter argues that it is unlikely that Scoville invented the story on his own. However, he thinks that there is the possibility that Astor was the origin of the story: "It is at least a possibility that Astor was himself responsible for the tale. He was much given to practical joking, and to tell such a tale to an inquisitive acquaintance and make him believe it would doubtless have had a strong appeal to Astor."[19] Nevertheless, the existing sources which have survived until today show hardly any humor on Astor's part.

As with so many other anecdotes, this makes no difference. Scoville's claims don't have any grounds. Historically a Permit No. 68 existed, but it was only valid in the time prior to the American Revolution, when trading with China was an exclusive prerogative of the British East India Company. When Astor started trading with China, there was no need for permission of that kind any more, and the permit was no longer issued.[20]

The first ship that carried Astor's goods to China was the *Severn*.[21] Astor had secured a share in the ship despite his doubts. He had hesitated because sending a ship was a dangerous endeavor. It could sink, or could be robbed or destroyed by pirates. There were many security issues. In the end Astor's business mind kicked in and his longing for the profits outweighed his doubts. So he was ready to take the risk. If all had gone according to his wishes, he would have sailed on the ship himself. However, he could not afford to lose that much time in the course of the voyage. Therefore he sent a person he really trusted: Captain Steward Dean. Dean was the husband of one of Sarah Astor's nieces. After years of research, observation and planning, the *Severn* left for China on April 29, 1800.[22]

It was a long and dangerous trip. First the *Severn* followed the American coastline south around Cape Horn. Then it reached Hawaii before it crossed the Pacific towards Asia. Full of impatience, Astor remained in New York and waited for the *Severn* to return with the luxurious goods he hoped to acquire in China in order to make a nice profit on them. The *Severn* left Canton at the end of December of 1800[23] and reached New York after 130 days on May 11, 1801.[24] A little more than a year after the *Severn* had left for China, Astor was able to enjoy the fruits of his success. All the furs had been sold. The ship brought back a loading deck full of spices, tea and silk. She also brought back the turnover Astor had hoped for. He had had the right gut feeling! Full of joy about the successful expedition, Astor increased his trade with China. The *Severn* repeatedly traveled the Pacific to China till Astor finally bought all of the shares that were available for the *Severn* on May 25, 1804,[25] and owned the ship afterwards. He invested the turnover in another ship and bought the *Beaver*, a ship specially manufactured to travel the Pacific.[26] She was built by the firm of Eckford & Beebee in New York City and registered on May 7, 1805. Her weight was 427 tons and she could hold a cargo of 1100 tons.[27]

With this small fleet and the connections of his wife Sarah to various New York shipping companies, Astor rose within the first decade of the 19th century to become an influential shipowner. In 1805, he finally invested in newly built ships that were specially equipped for trade with China.[28]

Writing about Astor's trading activities in the Pacific region, Scoville mentions that by the turn of the century one of Astor's ships was on its way to Canton. During the trip, this ship dropped anchor at the Sandwich Islands to get water, food and firewood. As the ship arrived at Canton, an administration official inspected the cargo. He discovered the firewood and, as Scoville reports, completely lost interest in all the other goods. He agitatedly inquired about the price. The captain of the ship did not immediately understand the interest of the Chinese in the wood, until the Chinese officials offered an unexpectedly high price for the timber. Only then did the captain realize the value of the ship's cargo. It was sandalwood — highly in demand in China in those days. Without any hesitation he sold the timber to the Chinese officials. Scoville writes further that Astor held from that day onwards for 17 years the sole right to trade the highly sought-after sandalwood in China.[29] This account of Scoville paints the same image as the aforementioned "Astor legends," the Louisiana Purchase and the cart full of gold which was about to sink in the swamps of New York State. In all three anecdotes, Astor does not gain his wealth because he was a smart and skillful trader and a foresightful merchant. Scoville and other writers try to demonstrate that Astor was always helped by luck more than by business acumen. In every case his fortune was only gained by accident or a blind strike of luck, and not by hard work and honest labor.

With his two ships Astor intensified the trade with China.[30] However, this was a short-lived success. On December 22, 1807, President Jefferson issued the Embargo Act that forbade any further trading by American ships at foreign ports. Therefore Astor could no longer trade at Canton. Jefferson's incentive for this act was the fact that European ships attacked American ships on a regular basis. So the Embargo Act simply ruled out trading between American ships and any of the European powers or their respective allies that were engaged in the Napoleonic Wars.[31] As a consequence the American ships and their crews were safer, but America's official trade with foreign powers completely ceased and piracy boomed. This was nothing short of a catastrophe for Astor. Suddenly he could neither trade with China nor London on official channels. Astor's carefully established import business with instruments and other goods from London abruptly stopped, and his business with his brother George had to end along with it. When Astor received a shipment of pianos on December 2, 1807, just three weeks before the Embargo Act was ratified, it marked the end of 20 years of successful imports of instruments from London.[32]

But the end of their trade relations, which stretched over almost 25 years, did not mean that Astor and his brother George grew distant from each other. Until George's death in December 1813 they continued their correspondence regularly.[33] The embargo eventually led Astor to focus more on the American fur trade from 1808 onwards. He also strengthened his activities in the China trade the following year.[34]

Astor did make the most out of this situation. He looked and found ways around the embargo. Together with Albert Gallatin,[35] an immigrant from the German Swiss, who was secretary of the treasury in Thomas Jefferson's administration, Astor found a way to send a ship with goods to China. Gallatin and Astor became friends, but there is no source left that documents their first contact. The earliest letter which shows a connection between the Swiss-born politician and the German-born merchant dates back to August 3, 1808. This letter is written by Gallatin and addressed to Thomas Jefferson. Gallatin mentions that he knows a certain John Jacob Astor of New York.[36]

However, in Astor's plan to send a ship to China during the embargo, a certain Mandarin with the name Punqua Wingchong played an important part. Punqua Wingchong was a Chinese merchant and administrative officer, a mandarin. Some of Astor's contemporaries voiced the opinion that Punqua Wingchong was no merchant at all. They suggested Astor only had him on his payroll to get in touch with President Jefferson in order to get a special permit to send a ship to China. Whatever Punqua Wingchong's plans had been, he was able to gain Jefferson's trust and had a vivid exchange of letters with him.[37] Jefferson was under the impression that it was a diplomatic advantage to respect Punqua Wingchong's wishes and let a ship travel to China, even with the embargo in place. Gallatin was asked to issue a special permit for the Chinese merchant that would allow him to ship a large amount of furs and other goods to China.[38]

Gallatin did not have to search long before he found the right person to do the actual shipping on behalf of the Chinese diplomat. Astor was the man he was looking for. The two immigrants with a German-speaking background immediately liked each other. Both shared the same mother tongue, came from a similar background and had similar stories to tell. Gallatin and Astor became friends for life. Eventually, Gallatin gave Astor permission to ship both Punqua Wingchong and the goods back to China.[39] This was a unique and exceptional opportunity for Astor to move goods with the embargo still active. Gratefully Astor accepted.

However, his fellow merchants were less than impressed. None of them received a similar official blessing, and so they felt this special treatment for Astor only made it obvious how unjustly they were treated. All of them envied Astor for his opportunity and protests soon formed, though the departure of the *Beaver* was not to be stopped. Astor's ship left New York's harbor on August 17, 1808, on its government mission to China. Punqua Wingchong was on board along with his goods that were cleared for export. Additionally, Astor managed to ship the finest furs that sold for over $200,000 in Canton.[40]

Real Estate on the Rise

Despite the brief intermezzo in China, Astor focused on the business within America as long as the embargo was in effect. Trading in furs and real estate produced his income during these years. He was able to invest his profits from the pre-embargo China trade in New York real estate. The city had grown significantly over the years. Astor shared his thoughts about the future of New York with his close friend, DeWitt Clinton. Both of the men assumed more immigrants would come from Europe.

They were right: between 1790 and 1800 the number of inhabitants nearly doubled, from 33,000 to 60,000.[41] Even if Astor was not certain if the city would ever encompass all of Manhattan, he saw the business opportunity. To him the logical step was to buy up real estate that was still outside the city limits. The China trade had provided Astor with the financial means to go ahead with this idea. He wanted to use the growth of the city to make a profit. Up to 1819 he invested $715,000 in Manhattan real estate.[42] At the time this was most of his cash and all of the profits from the China trade. Today this would be almost $12 million. The risk paid off. While he continued his fur trading, the city grew to more than 312,000 inhabitants in 1840. Real estate soon was heavily sought after by the newcomers.

Astor continued investing in real estate and housing. The second heyday of his real estate investments stretched from 1819 to 1834, when he retreated from the fur trade. During these years Astor invested another $445,000 in real estate and buildings.[43] The third phase of acquiring real estate followed when he stepped back from the presidency of his American Fur Company in 1834. He continued his efforts in real estate up to his death in 1848. He was then convinced that the real estate business was a perfect business. Each year thousands of immigrants tried their luck in the city. He invested again. This time he spent about $832,000 between 1834 and 1848 on real estate.[44] In total he bought Manhattan real estate for the current equivalent of $2 million.

Real estate in New York was the most important of all of Astor's enterprises. In the end the profits made here were the reason why Astor's fortune surpassed those of all his contemporaries. His business instinct and foresight about the future development, the growth and expansion of the city of New York and his courage to invest in unsettled farmland made him the richest man in America. Trading with furs and instruments only accounted for $2 million of his fortune. Most of his remaining fortune was made in the real estate business.

Gustavus Myers used those land purchases as an argument against the multimillionaire. He accused Astor of speculating in the acquisition of cheap grazing land and its sale, at the expense of poor immigrants. Myers wanted to interpret Astor's land purchases as a greedy and inhumane act without regard for the fate of the million immigrants coming from Europe who could not afford Astor's land and real estate.[45] This biased view of events hides the fact that Astor was a businessman with a lot of foresight. Indeed, his real estate business in New York and in some other regions brought him immense wealth. His idea that New York would spread one day all over Manhattan encouraged him to purchase wide swaths of seemingly worthless land outside the city. The coming of the immigrants and the actual growth of New York pushed up the value of his land. It was not his recklessness but his vision, and his courage to invest in undeveloped farmland and soil north of the city's borders, that made him by far the richest man in the United States. As a result of his vision, John Jacob Astor owned one-twelfth of all real estate of the city of New York in 1844.[46]

Acquiring real estate was not Astor's only favorite occupation. He was known among his friends as a theater lover. Reportedly, "He seldom missed a good performance in the palmy days of the 'Old Park.'"[47] Right from the time of his arrival he was interested in finding out what were the favorite pastimes of New York's upper class among whom he found his customers. He and his wife often attended public events and used them to mingle with potential new customers. In those days New Yorkers, the established Dutch and Anglo-Saxon families in particular, but also the "new" New Yorkers, met at the Park Theatre, the most popular among New York's theaters.[48] It opened with Shakespeare's *As You Like It* on January 29, 1798. The rich and famous were drawn to this three-story theater. Even those who were not interested in the plays came to enjoy the atmosphere and mingle with their business partners.[49]

Maybe it was Astor's joy in the performing arts like theater, literature, and music that led him to buy the Park Theatre on April 21, 1806, together with John K. Beekman.[50] Maybe it was just another clever investment. The joint ownership of the theater meant that Astor was in control of the most important social meeting space in the city. However, he neither tried to take over the directorate nor got involved in artistic decisions. Certainly he was more interested in owning the theater because it would make him even more integrated in New York's upper class than before. To underline its sophistication, the theater's interior was renovated over three months in 1807 by an English architect named J.J. Holland. Gas lighting was installed and coffee rooms added.

Astor and Beekman leased the Park Theatre to Thomas A. Cooper as manager. Cooper brought in Stephen Price as his sponsor, who rented the theater for $8,400 per year. When the building burned down in 1820, Astor fully restored it and leased it to Edmund Simpson, who would be the new manager from 1828 onward.[51]

In the early 1820s, the Park Theatre was New York's only theater, and the lack of competition allowed it to enjoy its most profitable period.[52] In her landmark book, *Domestic Manners of the Americans*, Frances Trollope, an English writer, stated: "It was the only house in town licensed by fashion."[53] She continued: "The piece was extremely well got up, and on this occasion we saw the Park Theatre to advantage, for it was filled with well-dressed company."[54] Again Astor's investment paid off. Due to the steady improvements and renovations, the value of the building soon rose to $150,000.[55] Simpson led the theater to fame, and artistically it was soon one of the leading theaters in America, with actors from England and opera singers from Italy supporting

Founding the American Fur Company

The international trade along official channels was severely hurt by the Embargo Act. Pirates and smugglers were on the rise. In the end Astor had been forced to give up his imports and focused on real estate and the fur trade within the United States instead. However, he faced his international competitors on the home front, too: two large British-Canadian companies dominated the fur trade in North America. There was the Northwest Company which was the largest one, and the Hudson's Bay Company, which was the oldest one then and the only one that still exists.[56] The fur traders Benjamin and Joseph Frobisher and their partner Simon McTavish founded the Northwest Company.[57] Right from the beginning there was a rivalry with the significantly older Hudson's Bay Company. King Charles II had chartered the Hudson's Bay Company in 1670. Its trading posts were located around the Hudson Bay. This allowed the company to use the bay and the rivers that led up to it as infrastructure. These were the ways on which the furs were first transported from the hunting grounds in the Canadian hinterlands to the trading posts, and from there to London.[58]

The Northwest Company established its trade a little further down south. It controlled fur trade right from the Great Lakes via Montreal and the St. Lawrence to the northern parts of New York State. Both companies fought over the fur trade monopoly from the end of the 18th century onward. At times this even led to guerrilla attacks between the rivals. Trading ships and trading posts of the respective opponents were regularly attacked and destroyed.[59] At the beginning of the 19th century the battle over new hunting grounds had begun. When new hunting grounds were located the companies tried hard

Portrait of John Jacob Astor (Vereinigung Walldörfer Heimatfreunde).

to make it impossible for each other to actually hunt in the same locations. In order to expand their businesses and discover formerly unknown regions for the fur trade, both sent trappers into the Mississippi River and Rocky Mountain territories that were added to the United States in the Louisiana Purchase of 1803. The trappers moved so far west that soon three-quarters of the furs traded by the companies came from the American territories. Neither American politicians nor businessmen like Astor were happy about his. Furthermore, American fur traders were fully dependent on the prices set in Montreal, the center of the North American fur trade. This situation hindered the further development of the American fur trade and presented a sharp contrast to the political and economic aims of President Thomas Jefferson.[60]

When he was a young merchant, Astor had to give in to the conditions set by the two mighty organizations. The more experienced he was and the wealthier he got, the more interested Astor was in the fur trade. He understood early that success in this business was closely linked to the establishment of an American company that was strong enough to face the British-Canadian competitors. In his view this was the only way to actually break the monopoly of the Northwest Company and the Hudson's Bay Company. Furthermore, it was the only plausible way to secure the American hunting grounds for American fur traders. Meanwhile, 45 years old and with the Embargo Act still in place, Astor thought it was time to realize his plans to make a move against the British monopoly in the fur trade. Over the years he had carefully listened to Jefferson's words about the vast Louisiana Territory in the west. After buying Louisiana, the United States had almost doubled in size. President Jefferson sent Meriwether Lewis and William Clark to explore the unsettled regions that stretched to the Pacific. Jefferson hoped they would find a waterway to the west, collect research on the west, and make contact with some tribes of the Native Americans in the region. In respect to the native population, Lewis and Clark were to pave the way for trade relations between them and the Americans. Though the return of the explorers was celebrated as a big success, the trade relations the president had hoped for had not been established.[61] The president told Meriwether Lewis his goals in a letter: "The object of your mission is to explore the Missouri river, and such principal stream of it, as by its course and communication with the water of the Pacific Ocean may offer the most direct and practicable water communication across the continent, for the purpose of commerce."[62]

This is where Astor saw his niche. He developed the idea to connect the West with a series of trading posts to the Pacific. The trading posts were to be used to trade with the Native Americans, but also to fight back attacks by the British. This enterprise was to be managed by a American merchant. His objective was to push the British fur traders out of the region. The trading posts should form a chain that reached the Pacific in order to stress American claims to the Oregon territory.[63] All this was meant to weaken the British competition considerably. At that point in history, not only the British were challenging American interests. The Spanish still were in the possession of California, and the Russians still controlled a good portion of Alaska in their quest to secure their stakes in the Northern Pacific region.

Astor did not want to shoulder the risk of such an endeavor all alone. He would have to build his own small army if he wanted to make sure that the British would not overrun one of his trading posts. However, not even Astor could afford to hire and equip an army of his own. He needed presidential support, not only in words but also in military strength.[64] Astor was very convinced that his plans were just what Jefferson had in mind too. He wanted to both serve his country and make a profit. There seemed no contradiction in that.

Just a month after Jefferson had issued the Embargo Act, Astor turned to his friend DeWitt Clinton in this matter in a letter from January 25, 1808.[65] DeWitt Clinton's uncle served as vice-president under President Thomas Jefferson. Therefore, Astor hoped that he could establish a connection to the president with the help of the Clinton connection. This is why he explained his plans to his friend and hoped that Clinton would not only readily support him, but also that he would introduce his plans to the vice-president or even to President Jefferson himself. Astor predicted: "Such an undertaking would be pleasing to our government."[66] Once he had convinced his friend DeWitt Clinton, he provided him with more detailed information for the vice-president. Clinton brought to plan to the ears of his uncle, with the result that George Clinton liked Astor's ideas, too. The vice-president was literally overwhelmed by what his nephew had told him. So it is safe to assume that contact was easily made with the president.

Initially Astor had intended to travel to Washington by himself to present his plans directly to the president. But then he changed his plans and wrote a letter. In this letter to the president, dated February 27, 1808, Astor asked for Jefferson's permission to trade west of the Mississippi with the tribes of the Native Americans. Astor also inquired about the possibility of receiving governmental help in the form of military support in the case of emergencies like attacks by hostile Native Americans and the British.[67] His correspondence with Clinton had been full of financial details, but his approach to Jefferson was different. Astor wrote about a big idea and explained that his vision was "to carry on the fur trade so extensively that it may in time embrace the greater part of the fur trade on this continent."[68] Furthermore, he argued that he needed governmental support for this enterprise, which he carefully said supported the "countenance and good wishes of the executives of the United States."[69]

Jefferson was delighted when he read Astor's letter. The merchant from New York had made an impression on the president. Astor's plans met Jefferson's own vision of how to develop the west. One letter followed the other and soon Astor had painted his picture of the trading posts, the patriotic cause and the expansion to the Pacific. Also, Astor hoped to get military support from the government in case of any threat or danger.[70]

The New York merchant wanted to know which role the federal government would play in the westward expansion. Therefore, he settled a meeting with President Jefferson in Washington. Astor had often talked about a trip to Washington, but now it felt necessary. As historian James P. Ronda shows there is no record of that meeting. The only sources that survived are Astor's notes from 1813 describing that he had met Jefferson as well as Secretary of the Treasury Albert Gallatin, Secretary of War Dearborn, and Secretary of State Madison. That gathering must have taken place between April 6 and April 13, 1808. Astor presented a full and detailed plan how to establish the fur trade in the west and how to take over the trade with the Native Americans. President Jefferson's answer must have pleased the German-American merchant.[71]

Jefferson and Astor agreed on many of the points. Both were disgusted by the British-Canadian monopoly on the fur trade. Furthermore Jefferson intended to increase trade with Native Americans in the territories that had become part of the United States in the Louisiana Purchase. In 1812 Astor wrote to President Jefferson: "I believe that it will afford you some satisfaction to be informed that with the progress which has been made in carrying on a trade with the Indians, which at it's commencement was favoured with your approbation."[72]

Astor's ambition was to gain control over the new fur trade in the relatively unexplored territories by establishing his own fur trade company.[73] New York was to be the enterprise's headquarters. He intended to coordinate all his fur trade efforts from there and therefore streamline his business operations all the way from St. Louis to the Pacific along the route of Lewis and Clark's expedition. Astor did not only want to make use of the experiences the expedition had brought home. He also wanted to take advantage of what the region offered enterprises in terms of infrastructure. After the Louisiana Purchase the Mississippi River was now fully controlled by the United States. Astor planned to use the river as the main route to the border territories. The natural network of rivers in the region promised a direct access to the hunting grounds and trading posts west of the Mississippi. The furs were to be brought to St. Louis first, then shipped down the Mississippi to the Gulf of Mexico. Lastly the furs would be taken by sea to New York. The headquarters of Astor's American Fur Company were perfectly located to ship the furs to Asia and Europe.[74]

4. Visionary, 1800–1815

With his letters Astor had made a good first impression on President Jefferson. Now the president was interested in getting a second opinion. So he consulted with General Henry Dearborn, who served as Secretary of War in his administration. Dearborn assured the president of Astor's excellent reputation: "[He is] a man of large property and fair Character, and well acquainted with the fur and peltry business."[75] Jefferson was glad that his first impression held. He thanked his secretary for his evaluation and further encouraged Astor in his enterprises. Astor received several positive letters from the president. The first one stated: "I learn with great satisfaction the disposition of our merchants to form into companies for undertaking the Indian trade within our own territories."[76] On April 13, 1808, Jefferson explicitly expressed his support of the merchants in the west: "All beyond the Mississippi is ours exclusively, and it will be in our power to give our own traders great advantages over their foreign competitors."[77]

In order to finally start his western business, Astor impatiently waited for the approval from New York authorities. With a little help from his friend DeWitt Clinton, he received it on April 6, 1808. Clinton had just entered his second term as mayor of New York and viewed the opportunities in the west equally lucratively as Astor did. Astor called his new business the American Fur Company to stress his patriotic spirit. The trading company was incorporated for 25 years and owned $2 million in assets to start the business off. He did not see any point in obtaining more assets by taking in investors. Astor preferred to keep the financial control in his own hands. The increased finances if investors bought stock in the company did not make up for the loss of control in Astor's eyes. In return he was ready to bear all the financial risk himself. So he tailored the organizational structure of the American Fur Company to his needs. He was the leader and did not share any decision making with the nine managing directors who were responsible to him.[78] Washington Irving, who wrote about that enterprise on the behalf of Astor, described the organization of the American Fur Company as follows: "[Astor], in fact, constituted the company; for, though he had a board of directors, they were really nominal; the whole business was conducted on his plans, and with his resources, but he preferred to do so under the imposing and formidable aspect of a corporation, rather than in his individual name, and his policy was sagacious and effective."[79] Astor had secured presidential support for his endeavor by stressing the patriotic cause and the usefulness of trade in west for the further development of the United States of America.

Jefferson felt it necessary to spread the news about the founding of the American Fur Company. On July 17, 1808, he wrote to his old friend Meriwether Lewis, who meanwhile served as governor of the Missouri Territory and reported about Astor's achievements. Jefferson was convinced that the

American Fur Company would finally set structures for the development of western trade. Jefferson was full of praise: "Under the direction of a most excellent man, a Mr. Astor merchant of New York, long engaged in the business and perfectly master of it."[80] To Jefferson the founding and organization of the American Fur Company was an expression of national interest. A good deal of the further development of the economic situation of the United States depended on self-sufficiency, and Jefferson intended to act on this. Only a very small portion of the territory that was added to the United States in the Louisiana Purchase had been explored. Almost none of it was ready for settlers or even trappers. A new fur trade company that would drive the British companies from the U.S. territory was the ideal means support Jefferson's own plans for the west. Astor used Jefferson's conviction for his own business interests. The historian James P. Ronda described the double motivation of the American Fur Company as follows: "Fur and the flag marched in company."[81]

Astoria, Oregon

On March 1, 1809, President Jefferson ended the embargo. During the last four days of his presidency, Congress passed the Non-Intercourse Act, which was nearly unenforceable. It lifted all embargoes on American shipping except for ports in Britain and France.[82] Though it was designed to hurt the French and English economies, it actually backfired and added to the rising tension between the U.S. and Britain, which would erupt in the War of 1812. For the time being American merchants could finally trade legally again with other countries.

A few days later James Madison became the next president of the United States. This was a big disappointment for Astor. His friend DeWitt Clinton had run for the presidency, and Astor had hoped to receive even more support had Clinton become president. Astor was still unhappy with the legal framework surrounding international trade.[83] His ships could sail to Canton again, but he still was not able to resume trading in instruments from London. After carefully evaluating, he accepted that he had to discontinue trading with his brother. He had to stop what had originally triggered his success story.

Astor's trading business with his brother George in London had been the backbone of his business for almost 30 years. But not just John Jacob, but also George profited from their trade business. In that way, George was able to expand his instrument business tremendously after 1783 when John Jacob had left for America. After their transatlantic business became profitable, George rented a bigger shop in Cornhill Street 79. Later he merged his business and continued trading under the company name Astor & Harwood. They expanded their portfolio and produced notes from then on, along with all kinds of instruments. However, the turbulent Atlantic took a hard toll on George. He lost many shipping loads on the seas, and from 1800 onward he ran into financial troubles. In December 1813 he died without having regained his previous wealth.[84] His wife continued the business until 1831.[85] She eventually died in 1842.

Astor's hands were tied when it came to trading with Britain. So he had to concentrate his efforts on trading with China.[86] In order to make the most of his remaining businesses he started to combine the fur trade and his China business. That would expand and optimize his enterprises considerably. He had a business triangle in mind: Canton, New York, and a trading post of the American Fur Company on the American west coast. That outpost would serve as central collection point for the furs of the northwest. This would facilitate trading with China and speed up shipping because the ships could be loaded right where they would leave for China.

The flag of Astoria, Oregon (Vereinigung Walldorfer Heimatfreunde).

Even if Astor and Jefferson never explicitly discussed the establishment of a trading post on the Pacific coast, he had been thinking about it for quite some time. He had waited for the embargo to be lifted before finally getting these plans working. Where did this vision come from? How could a German immigrant play such an important role in the westward expansion of his new American mother country?

Astor was always a good observer. It was easy for him to separate important from unimportant information. When he had traveled to Montreal many years before, he heard fellow merchants talk about an outpost like this. Many fur traders, including the British ones, dreamed of a trading post on the Columbia River at the Pacific. So did Alexander Henry, a fur trader. He wrote in 1786 to William Edgar in New York that he planned to establish an outpost on the Columbia River.[87] But he never realized his plan.

No one considered himself capable turning this dream into reality — not until Astor decided to take on the challenge. He viewed the issue as a rare chance to achieve something great — maybe even to go down in history. His vision had even larger dimensions, however: an American settlement on the Pacific Coast could provide the means for the entire region to be claimed and settled by the United States, possibly even one day be granted statehood within the Union.[88] And Astor, a once penniless German immigrant, would be the founder of the first American city on the Pacific Coast!

Only a few Spanish missionary posts existed on the Pacific Coast at the time; the rest of the land remained for the most part unsettled. Furthermore, the land tenures in the west beyond the territory of the Louisiana Purchase were still open; some districts were located under the authority of more than one power at the same time.[89] Aside from the two rival British fur trading companies that were asserting their influence in the northwestern corner of the continent, the Russian empire of the Tsar also laid claim to areas of land north of the Oregon territory up to Alaska. Moreover, Oregon shared its southern border with California, which belonged to the Spanish crown at the time and continued to expand northwards. The claim to the Oregon Territory, which was not part of the Louisiana Purchase, presented the only possibility for the United States to extend its national territory to the Pacific Coast in the early 19th century. However, only a handful of politicians were as far-sighted as Astor and Jefferson. Most continued to believe the prospect to be impossible well into the 1840s.

In order to provide protection for a future trading post, Astor began to look around for potential partners and alliances against the British. The Russians appeared to Astor to be the ideal alliance partners. Fortunately for Astor, the Russian General Consulate Andrew Daschkoff came to the United States in June of 1809 on a diplomatic visit.[90] He also desired a peaceful coexistence on the Pacific, which led him to complain to the government in Washington of a group of American traders who had sold weapons and munitions to the Native Americans settled close to the Russian region of influence. In doing this, the independent American traders were endangering the lives of the Russian settlers, should the supply of weapons enable a Native American uprising.

Newly elected President James Madison, however, did not see himself in a position to prevent the weapon deliveries, and bid farewell to the disappointed General Consulate. The shortsighted Madison did not view the area beyond the Rocky Mountains as being of interest to the country. He did not consider the expansion of the United States to be an issue of great importance. Nor did he believe that cooperation with the Russian Tsar was necessary.[91]

Astor had traveled from New York to Washington, D.C., especially to meet the Russian diplomat personally. When he heard that the talks had failed, he reacted swiftly and took up negotiations with Daschkoff independently. Astor's concerns found resonance with Daschkoff, and both parties were quickly in agreement that cooperation would be advantageous for both sides. They named their joint goal as being the pushing back of the British trade companies from the Pacific Coast.[92]

Both trade partners agreed that the business collaboration should be approved by the American government. James Madison, who felt that his authority had been passed over by Astor's direct negotiations, now faced the question of whether to handle the agreement between the fur trader and Daschkoff as a public or private matter. He interpreted the agreement as clearly having a private nature, and he, as president of the United States, was not obliged to approve it. He wanted to have nothing more to do with the matter. He had his friend Albert Gallatin, who was Secretary of the Treasury under Jefferson and stayed on for Madison's administration, relay the message to Astor that President Madison would neither approve of the agreement with Daschkoff nor support the American Fur Company in any way.[93] In contrast to his predecessor Jefferson, Madison did not view Astor's intentions as a patriotic act, but rather as the dishonest attempt to create a monopoly. The New York tradesman quickly became a sore point to him. Madison confided in a letter to Gallatin on September 12, 1810, that support for Astor would, in his opinion, be going against the principles of the Constitution of the United States of America.[94] Furthermore, Madison perceived the unconfined economic liberalism of the age as unpatriotic. In his opinion, tradesmen such as Astor should be made to pay higher taxes.

The president's response was a hard blow to Astor. He did not understand the president's antipathy and accused him of being too rigid and lacking enough imagination to comprehend Astor's vision.[95] Should the United States fail to establish outposts in the Oregon Territory, its claim to the region would be weakened. How could these intentions be unconstitutional in principle? Moreover, how could the president accuse him of wanting to create a monopoly when his goal was precisely the opposite, by countering the British monopolists? Disappointed by President Madison, the fur trader reminisced over the more gratifying correspondence with Thomas Jefferson, who had understood the importance of the endeavor. In the end, Astor had no other choice but to realize his plans without the president's approval. Because he could no longer count on the government for support, Astor knew it was that much more important for him to continue negotiations with the Russian general consulate personally and to ensure their successful finalization. In order to avoid further conflict with Madison, Astor, acting on behalf of the American Fur Company, made an agreement with Andrew Daschkoff, acting on behalf of the Russian-American Company, to mutually assist one another. They also agreed not to trade with the Native American tribes living in the region of influence of the other company.

Astor found his desired partner in the Russian-American Company and could rest assured that his outposts would have the necessary security. In a letter written on November 7, 1809, Daschkoff reassured Astor of their joint intention to push the Northwest Company out the region.[96] The next planned step was for Astor to send one of his ships with provisions and goods to the Russian base at New Archangel — today Sitka, Alaska, at Norfolk Sound. Astor's captain and the governor of the Russian territory, Alexander Baranoff, were to sign the accord apart from the American government.[97]

Astor endowed Captain John Ebbets,[98] a man Astor trusted well, with the power of authority to sign the accord. The captain was already acquainted with the Russian governor from earlier travels and was further qualified for the mission due to his longtime experience with the natives. On November 15, 1809, Ebbets set sail from New York Harbor[99] with Astor's new vessel, the *Enterprise*. Astor bought this ship on September 1, 1809. She was constructed in 1807 in Philadelphia.[100]

However, John Jacob Astor's plan was that the *Enterprise* had to sail by direct route to the Columbia River for two reasons: Astor wanted to found a trading post at the estuary mouth of the Columbia, and Astor had charged Ebbets with establishing the first friendly ties to the Native Americans there.[101] After 204 days at sea, Ebbets and his crew reached the Indian village on the northwestern Pacific Coast. Fulfilling Astor's wish, Ebbets formed an initial friendly contact with the village's inhabitants. After a stay of a few weeks, he again set sail on June 23, 1810, toward New Archangel, which he finally reached sometime at the end of June or early July.

The second part of the mission would prove to be more difficult. As Ebbets was prepared to sign the accord with the Russian-American Company, Baranoff began to make new demands and called for more supply deliveries from Astor. Ebbets was not prepared for such demands, nor did he have the authority to negotiate with the Russians on Astor's behalf. Ebbets insisted that Baranoff sign the version of the accord that had been agreed upon by Astor and Daschkoff in previous negotiations. The talks escalated, and since neither of the two main actors were discerning diplomats, the negotiations came to an abrupt end. Enraged, Ebbets departed with the *Enterprise* from the harbor of Russian military base. Although the accord with the Russian-American Company had failed, the two fur-trading companies were able to maintain the status quo so that violent conflicts never erupted between the two fronts.[102]

In the meantime, Astor had entered into a very risky alliance while on his annual trip to Montreal in 1808. The American government had abandoned him and his list of allies was short. While contemplating the possibilities for a new alliance, his thoughts turned to the idea of binding those whom he feared most to a mutual contract, namely the British-Canadian fur traders. If he could successfully get them on board and win their cooperation with the trading post, then his plans would be fulfilled and the outpost would be safe from British attacks. In September 1808, Astor made his first move. He offered the Montreal merchants $550.000 for the troublesome Michikimachinac Company and said he would add another $50,000 for a free hand in the still undeveloped Columbia country. But the British-Canadian fur traders refused Astor's offer and asked instead for $700,000. This move stopped the negotiations.[103]

When Astor returned to Montreal in the following year, 1809, the Canadians blew alternately hot and cold toward Astor's attempts to settle an agreement. To make the alliance more attractive, Astor would yield a percentage of the profits to his British partners. Because the American president indicated that he had no interest in an outer post, Astor figured that he could dispense with the patriotic character of his plan. If Madison did not share his vision, then Astor was now determined to concentrate on his own commercial operations. With this attitude, it was not long until Astor encountered a great deal of interest among the traders in Montreal, and he managed to awaken the curiosity of a few members of the British trading companies.[104]

Half a year later, Astor invited Alexander McKay, Donald McKenzie, and Duncan McDougall, all members of the Northwest Company, to come to New York, where they signed a preliminary agreement on March 10, 1810, regarding a possible collaboration.[105] Until the signing of the final contract, Astor continued to negotiate with further potential partners. His aim was to unite the members and create a Pacific Fur Company, which would be subordinate to the American Fur Company.[106] The name of the new enterprise not only pushed the national motif further into the background, it also provided the partners with a commercial name with which they could identify. Meanwhile, Astor successfully recruited further members for the endeavor: Wilson Price Hunt, a businessman from St. Louis; Robert McClelan and Joseph Miller, who were active in the Missouri fur trade; David Stuart and his nephew Robert Stuart from Canada; and Ramsay Crooks. On June 23, 1810, these fur traders, tradesmen, and trappers joined forces under Astor's leadership and celebrated the founding of the Pacific Fur Company. With the creation of the new company, the way was clear for Astor, and he could begin with the establishment of a fur trading post on the Columbia River.

The company started with two expeditions. According to Astor's plan, one expedition would sail around Cape Horn and up the northwest coast to the mouth of the Columbia on Astor's ship *Tonquin* with the materials and provisions needed to begin setting up the trading post.[107]

The second expedition, the so-called Astor Expedition, had the assignment of crossing the continent, beginning in St. Louis and continuing along the path of the established trading posts of the American Fur Company. The expedition resembled that of Lewis and Clark just a few years earlier. Under the leadership of Wilson Price Hunt and Donald McKenzie, the expedition team was instructed to build friendly relations with the various Native American tribes they met along the way. Most importantly, they should win the trust of the natives and establish preliminary trading contacts.[108]

In October of 1810, Astor traveled to Montreal one last time to conduct negotiations for a peaceful coexistence with the Northwest Company. Prior to these negotiations, it was Astor who actively made every effort to reach an agreement accommodating the cooperation with the Northwest Company. However, after news of the founding of the outpost reached those in charge at the Northwest Company, Astor found himself in a position of power. Now the British-Canadian side went to great lengths to encourage conciliation for a peaceful coexistence. Both sides signed an agreement on January 28, 1811, making the American Fur Company a partner of the Northwest Company in the Great Lakes region. However, the agreement did not apply to the regions beyond the Rocky Mountains and on the Pacific Coast. Astor hoped that his company would dominate these regions alone.[109]

In the meantime, the venturous land expedition gathered in St. Louis, the edge of civilization at the time. None of the participants really knew what lay ahead. Hunt, McKenzie, and Crooks had arrived in St. Louis on September 3, 1810, and awaited the arrival of the other "Astorians."[110] The expedition finally set off along the Columbia River on October 21, 1810. They followed the waterways as far as they could, traveling up the Mississippi River and then continuing along the Missouri River. On November 16, they made camp for winter on the bank of the Missouri. It was here that the frontier man Robert McClelan joined the group.[111] Hunt returned to St. Louis for the winter in order to report back to Astor, who at this time charged Hunt with the sole leadership of the expedition.[112]

With the land expedition well underway, Astor equipped the group for the second expedition, which was to sail to Oregon via Cape Horn. He chose to deploy his new ship *Tonquin* and to give the command to Captain Jonathan Thorn, whose rank in the Navy was first lieutenant. Thorn was a disciplined, tenacious, and occasionally inconsiderate person, whose sole interest was the navigation of his ship. He was not an explorer, a visionary, or even a tradesman. Astor chose Thorn because Captain Ebbets had not yet returned from New Archangel with the *Enterprise*. Astor also preferred Thorn because of his military background and his combat experience at sea, since Astor feared military conflicts with the British or with the Native Americans.[113] Astor placed four members of the Pacific Fur Company at Thorn's disposal: Alexander McKay, Duncan McDougall, and David and Robert Stuart.

Years of perpetual political tensions between the United States and the British crown, and the resulting attacks at sea that brought on the Embargo Act just a few years earlier, left the British members of the Pacific Fur Company feeling very uneasy prior to the departure of the second expedition. Had they become part of an American company? Or could Astor be trusted that it was all a matter of business? These uncertainties led Alexander McKay, prior to his departure from New York, to call on the British emissary to the United States, Francis James Jackson, without Astor's knowledge. McKay made inquires regarding what would happen to him and his property should war break out between the United States and the British Empire. The emissary assured him that, in the case of war, the British military would treat him as a British citizen and not as an associate of an American trading company and that there was no need for concern. McKay was relieved to know that he could partake in the endeavor.[114] At the same time, however, Jackson planted the idea in the minds of the British members of the Pacific Fur Company that, in times of doubt, they could remain loyal to the British crown and betray Astor. What course would the endeavor then take? Would the alliance of tradesmen be able to withstand the importunities?

On September 8, 1810, the *Tonquin* set sail in the direction of the Columbia River. The American frigate *Constellation* escorted them out of the New York Harbor.[115] The plan was to sail around Cape Horn during the winter and then set course for Hawaii. After a short stay, they would then turn again toward the Columbia River. However, the hard and ruthless command of Captain Thorn caused a number of conflicts during the expedition between him, the crew, and the passengers of the Pacific Fur Company. In the end, open disputes erupted between the hardened captain and McDougall, McKay, and David Stuart. McDougall finally put an end to the standoff by drawing his pistol and forcing the captain to give in. Thorn was not used to such rebellious behavior from one of his passengers. He feared further escalation of the situation or even mutiny by the "Astorians," who disassociated themselves from the choleric captain over the course of the trip, partly due to defiance and partly due to fear.[116]

Aside from this incident, the remainder of the trip went as planned without encountering a British warship. The *Tonquin* eventually reached Hawaii, and a short time later, on March 1, 1811, set sail again for the Columbia River.[117] After a relatively calm phase on board, the quarreling began again between Captain Thorn and the members of the Pacific Fur Company, causing the situation on board to remain tense. On March 22, the long-awaited coast of Oregon became visible, and Captain Thorn dropped the anchor. Now that the *Tonquin* lay at anchor, the men of the Pacific Fur Company began the search for an ideal place to set up camp. They also followed Astor's orders and established contact and began trading with the natives living in the area — the same tribe that Captain Ebbets, traveling with the *Enterprise*, had formed friendly relations with a year earlier. The natives proved to be peaceful trading partners, showing no hostility. After the fur traders had successfully accomplished Astor's first task, they moved on to their historical mission: the construction of the outpost on the Pacific. Under the command of Duncan McDougall, they left the area of influence under the protection of the *Tonquin* and moved out to explore the region around the mouth of the Columbia River for one month. After their return, the small group that had been chosen for the settlement began to clear the land that had been selected.[118]

After a number of weeks of hard work, the pioneers officially christened the settlement with the name "Astoria" on May 18, 1811. The name was a clear allusion to the initiator of the bold endeavor, who represented the mission like no other.[119] Astoria was now both the field headquarters of the Pacific Fur Company and the most distant outpost of an "American empire west of the Rockies," as historian James P. Ronda claimed.[120]

Astor secretly looked forward to the moment when President Madison would receive word of the successful founding of the post, which he had denounced only a few months earlier. However, it would take a while before news of the settlement would reach the East Coast. Nearly one year to the day later, on May 24, 1812, the former president, Thomas Jefferson, congratulated Astor on his patriotic establishment of the fur trading post on the Pacific Coast. It was clear that they both continued to share the same vision:

> I remember well having invited your proposition on that subject, and encouraged it with the assurance of every facility and protection which the government could properly afford. I considered as a great public acquisition the commencement of a settlement on that point of the Western coast of America, and looked forward with gratification to the time when its descendants should have spread themselves through the whole length of that coast, covering it

with free and independent Americans, unconnected with us but by the ties of blood and interest, and employing like us the rights of self-government."[121]

While the construction of the trading post progressed, Captain Thorn and Alexander McKay of the Pacific Fur Company set sail again on June 1, 1811, on the *Tonquin* in order to further explore areas along the Pacific Coast.[122] The rest of the fur traders remained in Astoria. For weeks on end, they had no news of the whereabouts of the ship, nor of their business partners. The pioneers persisted impatiently in the small outpost of civilization they had created. In mid–August, Native American traders traveling to Astoria brought with them initial rumors of the possible sinking of the *Tonquin*. Another native, arriving in October, attested to the rumor and claimed to have witnessed the sinking of the ship. This news terrified the small troop of Astorians. They feared that Thorn had insulted and provoked the native tribe to such an extent that the native warriors would turn against Astoria as well.[123]

What really happened to the *Tonquin*? During the exploration, the *Tonquin* came into contact with other Native American tribes around the Clayoqout Sound. Captain Thorn showed no diplomatic tactfulness and treated the strangers with contempt, making no attempt to respect their traditions and customs. Thorn appeared to have lost his mind one evening in a meeting with the tribe's chief when he pushed a bundle of fur into the chief's face, incurring the chief's hatred. Peaceful negotiations, as Astor had ordered, were no longer a possibility. Contrary to Astor's insistent warning, the next day, Thorn allowed the Native Americans to come aboard the ship. They came, but not to negotiate, as he had assumed. They came to take revenge on Thorn and the crew. During the attack, the *Tonquin* caught fire, which led to the explosion of the gunpowder. The pieces of the ship sank to the bottom of the ocean. No one, including Thorn and McKay, survived the attack.[124]

Astor did not learn of the terrible news until nearly half a year later. According to Washington Irving's work, which was influenced by Astor: "The loss of the *Tonquin* was a grievous blow to the infant establishment of Astoria, and one that threatened to bring after it a train of disasters. The intelligence of it did not reach Mr. Astor until many months afterwards. He felt it in all its force, and was aware that it must cripple, if not entirely defeat, the great scheme of his ambition."[125] Washington Irving quoted a letter of Astor, which the millionaire had written at that time.

However, after the terrible news reached Astor, he went to the theater in the evening to see a play. There he was approached by a friend, who also knew the disastrous intelligence. This person expressed his astonishment that Astor could have a calm spirit for amusement considering the horrible loss of the *Tonquin*. Astor shrugged his shoulders and responded indignantly:

"What would you have me do? [...] Would you have me stay at home and weep for what I cannot help?"[126]

Nevertheless, the loss of the ship weighed heavily. Without the protection of the ship, the Astorians were trapped on the Columbia River and they had lost both manpower and supplies. Moreover, they feared further acts of revenge by the natives. Their only hope now was the next supply ship that, according to plan, would be arriving in Astoria the following year. Until then, they would be forced to remain in the newly constructed trading post — without being able to explore the rest of the coast. They were trapped in Astoria, far away from any other Canadian or American outpost or settlement.

Astor originally planned that the second ship to Astoria would arrive there around the same time the overland expedition would reach their final destination. He equipped the *Beaver* for this mission. She left New York on October 11, 1811. This time there was a member of the Astor family on board. Astor's nephew George Ehninger, the son of Astor's sister Catherina, who had left Walldorf as last of the siblings, accompanied the men on the *Beaver*.[127] Catherina married his father Georg Ehninger in 1782. In 1783 her son George was born and named after his father. Her family first settled in New Jersey. Later she settled in New York. Catherina's husband died early when his distillery exploded. She asked her brother to employ her son as one of his fur agents to secure some income for him. However, Astor and his nephew did not work well together. While Astor was ambitious and hard-working, George could not meet Astor's expectations. George was neither business-minded nor successful in the trade. Years after that expedition, when George started to make a show of his uncle's immense wealth and indulged in a lavish lifestyle, Astor broke off all contact with his nephew.

More than nine months had passed since the *Tonquin* was lost when the *Beaver* reached Astoria on May 10, 1812.[128] Despite their concerns the "Astorians" had survived in safety. The *Beaver* brought provisions and munitions, but more than anything else, hope and progress to Astoria. As planned by Astor, some men of the overland expedition had reached Astoria a little before the *Beaver*. In order to increase the chances to finally reach Astoria and move around the wilderness faster, the expedition party had split in four groups. Three of the groups reached Astoria as early as spring 1812. The fourth and last of the groups arrived at the fur trading station only one day after the *Beaver* on May 11, 1812.

The precarious period after the *Tonquin* was lost had finally come to an end. With the arrival of the new business partners and the food they brought with them, Astoria finally started to prosper. On September 26, 1812, the new trading offices were opened, and the newly built schooner *Dolly* sailed down the Columbia River for the first time. Astor's — and Jefferson's — vision finally became reality. With the establishment of Astoria, Astor had secured his spot on the Pacific coastline long before the westward expansion of the United States of America, following Manifest Destiny, had even begun.[129]

Thus, he demonstrated to American businessmen, politicians and dreamers the way the nation would go during the 19th century. Furthermore, he showed what economic and political advantages the control of the Pacific Coast embodied. Thomas Hart Benton, the senator from Missouri, who always urged the expansion of the United States westward assessed Astor's prospects about a decade later in a speech in March of 1825, which he held in the U.S. Senate, as follows:

> The Region of the Rocky Mountains would be the chief seat of the American Fur Trade, the empires of China and Japan would be the chief markets for their sale and disposition. In the region of the Rocky Mountains the furred animals are found in the greatest abundance, and the fur itself attains its highest degree of shining and glossy richness. In China and Japan is the greatest demand for these furs, and the highest prices paid for them.[130]

The War of 1812 and the Loss of Astoria

The War of 1812 between the United States and Great Britain is also known as the "Second War of Independence" or even as "Mr. Madison's War." Over the past years there had been a conflict between Britain and France on sea, and the commercial shipping of the American merchants suffered. This was an issue that President Madison and his predecessor Jefferson agreed upon. During Madison's first term a considerable number of members of Congress demanded he take military action. A war seemed the only option to cope with the tensions.

Astor was highly concerned. War would not only mean another period of embargos but also a high risk for the merchant-shipping sector as such.[131] For him war would jeopardize both his trade with China and Astoria. Helplessly he had to watch the warmongers stir up the atmosphere. Most of them came from the South and the West in the United States, and they had no connection whatsoever neither with the merchant shipping nor with the trade sector in general. Anti-British sentiments were rising all over the United States. Speech after speech in the Senate as well as within public debates, article after article in the newspapers, the warmongers fueled the atmosphere of hysteria.

Finally, the concerns of the settlers in the west triggered the American declaration of war on Britain. They feared an uprising by a reunited confederacy of Native Americans under the lead of Shawnee chief Tecumseh, who was supported by the British, and his brother Tenskwatawa. The British tried to call up a "pan–Indian confederation" in order to resist against the further westward expansion of the Americans. This conflict started like many others of its kind. William Henry Harrison, governor of the Indiana Territory, used some minor quarrels between Native Americans and American settlers to justify attacks against the Indians. These incidents were used by the War Hawks in the Senate to support the idea of a threat from a pan–Indian attack further on.[132]

In fact, from 1805 onward Tecumseh and his brother Tenskwatawa formed a tribal confederacy that fought the westward movement of the American settlers. Tecumseh tried to unite the tribes in the east in a military alliance that was supported by the British. Astor feared a rebellion led by Tecumseh. In March 1812 he wrote his concerns to Thomas Jefferson: "It is probable that unless our Government does something by which the Indians may get their usual supplies there will be a great uneasiness on their part, if not actual hostility."[133]

However, the House of Representatives voted 79 to 49 in favor of a war against Britain on June 4, 1812. The majority of votes against this decision came from those states who engaged in trade and shipping in New England, in the northeastern part of the United States. They would have much preferred a peaceful resolution of the conflict.[134] Two weeks afterwards, President Madison officially declared war on Britain on June 18, 1812.[135] This war would last two years till a peace treaty was signed at Christmas 1814 in Ghent and took effect on February 18, 1815. The war ended without major changes and the status quo was reestablished. However, the American government popularized the peace as a victory for the United States. Though there was no territorial gain, the United States of America had definitely gained respect from the British politicians who started to see them as an individual, independent country rather than the former colonies from then on.[136]

In the past decade John Jacob Astor had managed to establish close personal contacts with the leading politicians of his time. Thomas Jefferson, Albert Gallatin, Henry Clay, DeWitt and George Clinton, as well as James Monroe, corresponded regularly with him and sought his advice and vice versa. President James Madison was a different story. Madison delegated all communication with Astor to third persons.[137] Another Madison did not share this desire to keep a distance from Astor. Dolley Madison, the president's wife, was an ardent admirer of Astor, which was probably just the thing that fueled Madison's dislike of Astor.[138] Dolley Madison was the first wife of an American president who understood herself as the "First Lady." Even though she was not interested in obtaining a political office or leading a foundation like many First Ladies later did, she was influential in Washington society as well as among politicians.

Already, before the outbreak of the war, Astor had bestowed Mrs. Madison several times with a muff and other valuable products from his best furs, as well as with exotic teas from all over the world. With his presents he wanted to make sure that Dolley Madison was on his side and would — in case of an emergency — argue in his flavor.[139] Astor hoped to benefit from the possible goodwill of Dolley Madison and tried to take advantage of the influence of the First Lady on the president for his concerns. After the loss of Astoria, John Jacob Astor never grew tired of emphasizing what a good friend of the couple he was.[140]

On the other hand, Astor gave up all hope of coming to terms with Madison when he declared war on Britain. The immigrant did not want to see his new home slide into a war. So he decided to act. In letters he turned to President Madison in order to let him know he thought that the war was a bad idea. Madison still did not hide his dislike for Astor[141] and strongly opposed forwarding these letters to the Department of State, which would have been the natural addressee for Astor's warnings about the consequences of the potential war for the American international trade. Madison not only refused to listen to Astor; he even publicly dressed him down by letting Gallatin remind Astor that the president had not forgotten Astor's unilateral negotiations with Daschkoff, the Russian diplomat.

Instead of the guerrilla and militia warfare of 1776, now the Atlantic was the big battlefield and the eastern coastline was the new trench. However, the war also spread north to Upper Canada, where the United States attempted to gain some territory. This not only blocked Astor's Atlantic trading routes but also the overland routes north to where his trading posts on the Great Lakes were located. The fur trade in the eastern United States was on hold. Astor's biggest concern, however, was that the war could spread west and Astoria would be drawn into the battles. His small group of settlers and fur traders had not yet received any news of the declaration of war.

On July 4, 1812, the celebration held in Astoria had nothing to do with the war; it was rather customary. On that day, the assembled partners, clerks, and employees of Astor's Pacific Fur Company raised the American flag and fired guns in salute. They represented a bewildering mixture of ethnicity. Most of the party were men from Scottish, French, Hawaiian, Native American, and American origin. This might have been a mirror of how the population of the Wild West might look within the next decades, but the biggest part of the group were not citizens of the United States.[142] Precisely this proved to be Astoria's fate.

Historian James P. Ronda argues that what the July 4 gathering saluted was not the past and future of the American nation. These fur traders followed another vision: they imagined an empire in the west beyond the Great Divide, as well as personal wealth and fame, because they were part of its beginning.[143] The men can arguably be considered greedy, egoistic, and without a sense of common purpose, either for the American nation or for Astor's enterprise.

A first taste of what Astoria had to expect brought David Thompsons, a member of the Northwest Company, to Astoria. On July 15, 1812, Thompsons arrived at the trading post. He informed the "Astorians" about the outbreak of the war and demanded the British members of the Pacific Fur Company should remain loyal to the British crown. According to Thompsons, Britain had already claimed the Columbia River region.[144] The "Astorians" were uncertain as to whether they should believe Thompsons or not. In any case, they were alarmed and feared a potential British attack. Whereas the atmosphere at the post had been much relieved when the *Beaver* arrived with new provisions in 1811, now it reached a boiling point, Robert McClelan, Joseph Miller and Ramsay Crooks left the Pacific Fur Company.[145] The remaining "Astorians" discussed their next steps on June 27, 1812. They were still convinced that the post had a bright future ahead. They decided that Wilson Price Hunt should take the *Beaver* and sail to Canton to trade there.[146] In his absence Duncan McDougall was to lead Astoria. Astor himself had lured the Canadian away from the Northwest Company. David and Robert Stuart were sent overland to report to Astor.

This famous Stuart expedition across the continent reached St. Louis on April 30, 1813,[147] and New York on June 23 in the same year.[148] They were the first Europeans to cross the continent west to east. The papers were full of this "American Enterprize."[149] The *New York Herald* praised Astor and his partners' patriotic vision. Astoria made headlines for the first time. Suddenly the west was not just something far, far away. There was an American settlement there, and people went back and forth. The chances of settlements on the Pacific Coast suddenly appeared attractive and many people started to dream of the west. It was proven: It was possible to make a living there! The *New York Herald* reported: "By information received from these gentlemen it appears that a journey across the continent of North America might be performed with a wagon."[150]

The Stuarts had their own share in the euphoria. They had discovered the South Pass of the Oregon Trail on their way back. This passage allowed carriages to cross with more luggage. Suddenly traveling west not only seemed possible, but moving what was needed to establish oneself in the west by carriage was possible too. So it was discussed for the first time to equip an overland trek to Oregon.

Naturally Astor spent his days in New York highly alert. He had no idea where the *Beaver* was and how far Astoria had progressed. The war with Britain added to his worries. A little before the Stuarts reached New York, he had received word from one of his friends in London. Apparently the Northwest Company had allied with the British navy and sent out a ship to the Columbia River to take over Astoria![151] His fears had come true. A few years earlier he had readily received the support of President Jefferson and his administration. Now Jefferson's successor was at war with the British and Astor saw his trading post in danger. The Northwest Company, however, had the advantage of governmental support. There had to be a way to convince President Madison to send a vessel to Oregon to protect the first American settlement on the Pacific Coast. Maybe the press coverage and the vivid discussions among the public had convinced Madison of the national importance of Astoria. Since Madison did not communicate directly with him, Astor directed a letter to Secretary of State James Monroe, stressing the patriotic motivation of the enterprise and asking for help:

> I mean in time of peace, I think I could have made a stand against that company [the Northwest Company]; in the present, it becomes doubtful and hazardous, and, in case of an interference on the part of the British Government, impossible for an individual to hold possession of a country which may become a source of wealth and comfort to many.... I am sure the Government will readily see the importance of having possession and the command of a river so important and extensive as the Columbia, the fountain of which cannot be far distant from that of the river Missouri.[152]

He also begged Monroe to send military help[153] and asked him to inform President Madison about the British war plans.[154] Many times he tried to influence several politicians and senior officers and convince them to defend Astoria with American warships.[155] In order to accomplish his purpose, John Jacob Astor also expressed his concerns in a detailed letter to the Ministry of Foreign Affairs: "As soon as war was declared I considered Columbia in danger if not lost."[156] In this letter, Astor did not use the name of "Astoria" for his foundation settlement; instead he wrote about "Columbia" to suggest to the government that this was a matter of national interest and not a personal concern of his alone.

However, the government in Washington, D.C., hesitated. They had underestimated the war efforts. Those advocating for the war were only interested in Upper Canada, but the American attack was repulsed. In total numbers 12,000 American soldiers faced about 6,000 British soldiers who had been deployed to Canada. There were no men to spare for a trip to the Pacific. While the public dreamed of the west, the politicians felt haunted by it, and reducing the number of American troops in favor of sending them on an uncertain path to the west did not seem rewarding at all. The Oregon territory did not belong to the United States and there was no inkling that it would any time soon. So why should the American government get involved there?

Frustrated by the resistance Astor met in Washington, D.C., he turned to Thomas Jefferson. As in their very first exchange of letters, Astor stressed how much it was in the national interest to protect Astoria. In his letter to the former president he invoked Astoria as: "Our establishment ... our plan ... and our property."[157] Astor explained his concerns: "I am fearfull that our pepol [sic] will be Driven off and perhaps dispers and it may not be easey to get tham together again.... I have great fears."[158] But this time it was not in Jefferson's power to help Astor.

Before it was too late for Astoria, Astor decided to act on his own. Although he was disappointed with the American government, there was no way he would just stand by and watch the British destroy his vision. In a rush he equipped the *Enterprise*, which was about to leave as third support ship to Astoria, with cannons and weapons, so that she would be able to defend herself and Astoria in case of a British attack. Maybe the *Enterprise* could save the trading post. Astor's rescue mission was doomed to fail. The *Enterprise* could not even leave New York's harbor. The British blockaded the harbor so that it was impossible for any ship to leave New York. With no hope left, Astor was forced to stay in New York and wait for potential bad news. His vision could be destroyed without his having even the slightest chance to intervene.[159]

The news of the war reached Astoria on January 15, 1813, with the arrival of the members of the Northwest Company, J.G. McTavish, Angus Bethune, Jon Stuart, and James McMillan. These British fur traders had come overland to the Columbia River and were surprised that they did not find a British frigate at the northwest coast as announced to them in a letter.[160] Among the remaining "Astorians" the spirit sunk. They were in the middle of nowhere and suddenly this wilderness was turned into a battleground. All they wanted was to trade. Without the provisions the third support ship would bring, the post had to be given up. Should the *Enterprise* be destroyed or sunk, the end of Astoria was close. Soon some members of the Northwest Company reached Astoria on the continental route. They were truly surprised when they did not find a British frigate on the Columbia River. After Astor had had the upper hand during the last years, the members of the Northwest Company saw a perfect opportunity to exploit Astoria's hopeless situation.

The Astorians were still waiting for the *Enterprise* and fear got the better of Duncan McDougall. He was the acting leader of the post and his loyalty to the Pacific Fur Company melted at the sight of the representatives of the Northwest Company. As former member of the Northwest Company, McDougall was more than happy to assure the British of his loyalty and sold all goods in stock to the Northwest Company at a bargain price.[161] Later Astor expressed his doubts about him and described McDougall as follows: "This man it is believed has been bought over by the Northwest Company."[162] The

Northwest Company received goods at a face value of $200,000[163] and only paid $42,000 to the Astorians.[164] Astoria's fate was irreversible now. On November 30, 1813, the British frigate *Raccoon* finally arrived on the northwest coast as everybody expected.[165] Astor's sources in London were right. A British war vessel had indeed been sent out to take Astoria. When the American government lacked interest, the British surely and forcefully demonstrated theirs. On December 12, 1813, Astoria, the first American settlement on the Pacific Ocean, turned British.[166]

An American Freemason magazine, the *National Freemason*, reported in 1866 that Astor was enjoying a theater play when he received the news of the unfortunate loss of his ship *Tonquin*.[167] Furthermore, the article mentioned that Washington Irving asked Old Astor, while researching for his book *Astoria*, why he did not stopped watching the play and went home directly. Astor was indignant and answered Irving: "What would you have me do? Would you have me stay at home and weep for what I cannot help?"[168] This reaction has been used repeatedly to show Astor's pragmatism as emotional coldness. By contrast, when he in turn learned of the arrival of his successful overland expedition to the mouth of the Columbia River, had he reacted emotionally and extroverted. The *National Freemason* quoted him as follows: "I felt ready to fall upon my knees in a transport of gratitude."[169]

For Astor this meant more than just losing a post. He lost the chance to establish his envisioned series of trading posts across the continent. Astoria even lost its name. Its new owners, wanting to avoid any association with the founder, renamed it St. George after the patron saint of England and protector of the British crown. On a personal view, Astor had overestimated his influence on the American politicians for the first time. He did not give up, though. In a meeting with James Monroe he wanted to discuss the possible peace treaty between the United States of America and Britain. This led to a correspondence between the two men, in the course of which Astor begged Monroe to ask President Madison to end the war and claim Oregon as American territory. Astor's game plan was to make sure Astoria would be returned to the United States in the final version of the peace treaty. On Christmas 1814, Britain and the United States finally signed a peace treaty. Until the news of the treaty was spread, fighting continued, and the war officially ended in February 1815.

Astor and the Peace Treaty of Ghent

The subsequent demands for the return of Astoria from British possession to its founder were based on the following lines from the peace treaty of

Ghent in 1814: "All territory, places, and possessions whatsoever taken by either party from the other during the war, or which may be taken after the signing of this Treaty, excepting only the islands hereinafter mentioned, shall be restored without causing any destruction or carrying away any of the Artillery or other public property originally captured in the said forts or places."[170]

The trading post had not been explicitly mentioned in the treaty text, but the comments of James Monroe, who negotiated as foreign minister together with Albert Gallatin in Ghent, showed that the United States government saw Astor's fur trading outpost on the Columbia River as part of the wording of the agreement. James Monroe wrote to John Quincy Adams and Albert Gallatin: "Should a treaty be concluded with Great Britain, and a reciprocal restitution of territory be agreed on, you will have it in recollection that the United States had in their possession, at the commencement of the war, a post at the mouth of the river Columbia, which commanded the river, which ought to be comprised in the stipulation, should the possession have been wrested from us during the war."[171] Looking back in history, this was the first official document of the United States talking about the Oregon question.

As already mentioned, Astor hoped that he would get Astoria back after the signing of the treaty. Full of confidence, he wrote his nephew George Ehninger: "By the peace we shall have a right to the Columbia River and I rather think that I shall again engage in that business."[172]

But the demise of Astoria had not meant the end of the activities of the American Fur Company, because John Jacob Astor was a "bounceback" and he trusted his friendship with James Monroe and Albert Gallatin. Both politicians were close friends of his in the Madison administration. Moreover, Gallatin, who was a long-term friend of Astor, joined Monroe in the negotiation of the peace treaty after the War of 1812 in Europe.[173] Astor had already met with him in 1814 in Washington. There, the two had discussed a possible peace treaty between the United States and the United Kingdom and its consequences.[174] The result of their meeting was a correspondence in which Astor pushed Monroe forcefully to influence President Madison in that matter. The millionaire just wanted to make sure that Astoria had to be returned to him, and that this should be part of the upcoming peace negotiations with the British.[175]

Also, a letter of September 22, 1814, showed Astor's acculturation. He advised Monroe to recruit both German and French military experts for the United States, their home country.[176] This demonstrated once more that Astor felt American, and it expressed his loyalty to his new home country.

All this time John Jacob Astor impatiently waited for news about the settlement. When he still did not have any news in October 1815, he approached

Gallatin about it.[177] His friend had left for Ghent, which was part of the Netherlands then and belongs to Belgium now. Almost daily Astor wrote letters to him begging for the return of Astoria to his company. Despite his efforts, the peace treaty of Ghent remained silent on Astoria.[178] During the negotiations the Northwest Company even claimed that the trading post was rightly acquired and therefore could not be claimed by the United States.[179] In order to settle the treaty, the American negotiators had to give up Astoria. In admitting the rightfulness of the position of the Northwest Company the United States significantly lost on any potential claims to the Pacific Coast. While American traders were still in the region, their status in relation to the Canadian-British fur traders was uncertain.[180]

Both former enemies avoided mentioning the outpost explicitly during the rest of the contract negotiations. The historian Frederick Wish speculated that the United States secretly planned to eventually claim the entire Oregon country, including Astoria. But during the negotiations of the peace treaty, they avoided mentioning Astoria in order not to sound too aggressive. Furthermore, Astoria was not to be discussed explicitly in order not to open additional demands by the British side. By those means, the restoration of the *status quo ante* made by the Treaty of Ghent did not consider the situation in Oregon at all. In the following years, this led to a legally unclear situation on the Columbia River for the United States.[181] And for Astor it meant that Astoria was lost.

Unfortunately, the loss of his fur trading post meant for John Jacob Astor also the loss of his original business concept, which was based on a chain of trading posts across the entire North American continent. The loss of the outpost on the Columbia River as an important point of intersection of his commercial empire determined a change in his strategy and vision. In addition, Astoria was now owned by the Canadian-British competition, which renamed the outpost St. George in order to obscure any association with its origin.[182]

Furthermore, the outpost opened for his direct competitors new strength and possibilities. It was a bitter moment for Astor. He had been bold enough to follow the vision of an outpost at the Columbia River when no other fur trader had dared to undertake that kind of enterprise. Now, Astoria belonged ironically to those who did not initially have the courage to establish an outpost on their own.

Moreover, in terms of business, the loss of Astoria was a disaster for the New York merchant. A lot of his money had been invested there and was now lost, and Astor was very aware of the implication of that loss. Parton quoted the millionaire in his 1864 publication and reported that Astor commented to some friends: "But for that war, I would have been the richest man that ever lived."[183]

Astor was disappointed. His friends had let him down and his vision was lost; all his plans for the west had failed. However, there was no way he would let himself down, and he took a stand on the proceedings. On the one hand, he took up negotiations with the Northwest Company about dividing the territory on the Pacific and a peaceful coexistence of both trading companies. On the other hand, he tried again to use all the influence he had in Washington, D.C., and demanded that a war vessel be sent to Astoria to claim the return of the settlement.[184] His reaction to the assertions of the Northwest Company to have legally bought the trading post was to point out that this all happened when the "Astorians" were held at gunpoint and with a British frigate about to arrive. Furthermore, Astor explained how his former business partner, Duncan McDugall, betrayed the Pacific Fur Company and supported the British. The only reason that Astoria could fall into the hands of the British was betrayal and military action. There was hardly anything legal about it. Also, the owner of the settlement, Astor himself, had never agreed to the sale and he never would have.[185]

This time not only Secretary of State Monroe but also President Madison assured Astor of the importance attached to the restoration of Astoria to the United States. Of course much lip service was involved here to calm down the important businessman. Both politicians feared claiming Astoria for the United States would start yet another war with Britain, and having just ended one that had caused the death of over 2,200 American soldiers, they did not see war as an option.[186] A military action on the Columbia River would necessarily breach the peace. In the end there was nothing left for Astor but to accept the inevitable. In the following years he focused on the fur trade on the Great Lakes, where Mackinac Island became the center of his operations.[187]

Astor's willingness to engage in competition with the Canadians changed significantly after the loss of Astoria. From then on, he no longer sought a monopoly in the North American fur trade for himself and his trading company, but rather tried to come to terms with his competitors in a peaceful coexistence. In a letter dated December 30, 1816, he wrote to James Monroe: "Soon after the late War I found that the Canada Traders had pretty well established themselves ... within the boundary of the United States.... A heavy loss would probably be the result of such opposition [against Canadians]."[188] This moderate tone differed significantly from his confident letters to Thomas Jefferson, which he had written to the former president just a few years before.

Without any political solution that would settle American interests in the Pacific region, Astoria was lost to its founder, and therefore the first American settlement on the Pacific coast was not longer American soil.[189] Astor's enterprise, though, had given a glimpse of what would to be expected in the years to come. The Americans became more interested in the west. During

4. Visionary, 1800–1815

the Astoria incident both the public and politicians realized the opportunities that kind of settlement provided for the United States. The unorganized territories in the west were no longer mere unknown wildernesses. They were potential new states. The disputes about these territories along with the British-Canadian border regions continued, and it only took till 1818 for another negotiation to take place.

In the meantime, Albert Gallatin had become American ambassador to France. In Paris he settled the British and American interests in the Oregon region in the Anglo-American Convention of 1818, which granted joint control of the Oregon Territory to the former enemies. In reality, it was the Hudson's Bay Company, North America's oldest and still active trading company, that controlled the region in the 1820s and 1830s and acted as a government-like institution. The company had left Astoria to establish a new post further north: Fort Vancouver, which served as central trading post for the region. In the 1840s American interests reached a new high and the efforts to claim Oregon increased. From 1842 onward American settlers crossed the continent in organized wagon treks to settle Oregon. Therefore Washington demanded that the British to cease all claims in the territory south of 54 degrees and 40 minutes northern latitude. Because the British were trying to avoid war this time, they offered to divide Oregon along the 49th degree of latitude, with the exception of Vancouver Island, which would remain British. It was Secretary of State James Buchanan who finally secured the American share of the Pacific Coast for the United States of America. On June 15, 1846, James Buchanan signed the Oregon Treaty and brought an end to the competing claims of the United States and Britain and a formal start to the further political westward expansion.

In the wake of the negotiation, Congress debated the Oregon issue ardently. Astor was repeatedly quoted as a shining example of the possibilities a westward expansion offered. Thomas Hart Benton, the Missouri senator, praised his achievements and emphasized the importance of Astoria in the congressional debates. Furthermore, he saw how much Astoria was in the national interest of the United States:

> The valley of the Columbia is ours: ours by discovery, by settlement, and by the treaty of Utrecht. And has too often been so admitted by Great Britain, to admit of her disputing it by now.... [Astoria] was the foundation of a colony, and the occupation of the whole valley of the Columbia, and the establishment of a commercial emporium, of which the mouth of the river was the seat, and the Rocky Mountains on one hand Eastern Asia on the other were the outpost. Great Britain saw it without objection — the US with approbation; and every circumstance which proclaimed and legitimated its commencement, existence and overthrow.[190]

These words rang in Astor's ears. He had his son William contact Benton to repeatedly give him his best regards and joy about the recognition of his vision for the northwestern coast. Astor was pleased that the American public finally saw everything in the right light. However, Benton's praise for Astor might not have come unexpectedly at all. One supporter financed his political career to a great extent: John Jacob Astor.[191]

Nevertheless, in 1848 Oregon officially became a U.S. territory, and parts of this region, along with parts of Idaho, Montana and Wyoming, later formed the state of Oregon. Without the founding of Astoria and the importance of the fur trade it is hard to imagine that this development would have been possible as fast as it happened. Astoria was a trigger. Trappers came home back east with stories about the unexplored wildernesses, the beauty and fertility of the land in the west. After Astor's employees, the Stuarts, had found the passage that wagons could take, the door was wide open for American settlements in Oregon.

5

Global Player, 1815–1834

Recent historians have called the phase of American history from 1815 to 1834 the *market revolution*.[1] It is set between the political and the industrial revolution and was triggered by the fast increase in population, the continuing expansion of infrastructure, the improvements in agriculture and beginning industrialization. The interplay of these factors created economic growth in the Northeastern United States in particular. Hundreds of thousands of *common men* worked, traded, bought and sold. The *Niles' Weekly Register* of 1815 formulated what was a generally accepted rule for success: "[Buying and selling was] the almost universal ambition to get forward."[2] The new competitive age did not care much about the republican ideas of the Founding Fathers. A strong community with an equal share of all citizens was no longer a desirable thought. Now everybody sought his own luck. The common good was no longer in the center of the public's interests.[3]

The United States in the 1810s fundamentally differed from the North American colonies of the 1760s, as well as the revolutionary eras in the 1770s and 1780s. Also, French traveler, political thinker and historian Aléxis de Tocqueville, who traveled extensively within the United States by the beginning of the 1830s, recognized the business fever on every corner. He wrote: "[There is a] feverish ardor the Americans pursue their own welfare."[4] They drifted away from the moral ideals of "virtuous republic" which Thomas Jefferson envisioned. After the War of 1812, American society was individualistic and business-minded.[5] The old aristocratic hierarchies dissolved and the *common man* took action in the public. The ideals of the protective republic were sacrificed during this transformation, as well as the idea of a small republic with selfless citizens. The era of the *market revolution* did not leave any room for this. American society compensated this by offering each white male citizen incomparable chances to succeed. Careers like the one of John Jacob Astor suggested to the public that the United States offered everyone the same chance to rise in his social and economic status—irrespectively of the traditions and social conventions of the Old Europe.

The Formation of the Second Bank of the United States

However, the War of 1812 was not just destroying Astor's business. All the time, the millionaire had another iron in the fire. To finance the War of 1812, the United States government sold war bonds to various wealthy investors. One of the purchasers of war bonds was John Jacob Astor, who earned after the end of the war a considerable sum.[6] Therefore, he was extremely interested in establishing a balanced financial market within the United States.

The establishment of financial institutions that are necessary by modern standards were not taken for granted in the early republic.[7] It needed the political and economic vision of Secretary of the Treasury Alexander Hamilton to establish the political framework along with the financial institutions for the first American financial system. As one of the central institutions of Hamilton's plans, Congress chartered the First Central Bank of the United States in 1791 despite much opposition among the public. The Jeffersonians were particularly concerned because to them it was a scary thought to move away from agriculture towards commerce, which would lead to financial manipulation and corruption.[8] Chartered for 20 years, the bank issued bank notes till the critics prevented a renewal of the charter in 1811.[9] However, the financial problems surrounding the War of 1812 made even those who previously had strongly opposed the idea of a central bank reconsider. War bonds that the government had issued and would have to pay back eventually financed most of the war.[10]

John Jacob Astor was one of the public supporters of a new central bank. Often he shared his views with individual congressional politicians and members of the administration. As early as in 1811, right after the charter of the first bank expired, he discussed with Gallatin how the charter could be renewed or a successor bank could be founded.[11] Two years afterward, when the United States was still at war with Britain, Astor met with potential investors such as Steven Girard, David Parish, and Jacob Barker, as well as representatives of the American government, among them John C. Calhoun, Alexander Dallas, and Albert Gallatin, on April 6, 1813.[12] Astor wanted to discuss the possibilities of another central bank and the financial framework necessary for such a venture. The group agreed on a vague plan as to what another bank might look like,[13] though nobody thought this would be realized anytime soon under President Madison. Astor, who was suffering from the slow speed of communications with Astoria, yet again had to wait impatiently till the end of the war seemed near before it looked more promising for another central bank. Finally Astor and his fellow investors approached the president in 1814 again to support the founding of a second central bank.[14] In retrospect, Astor and his fellow investors were the most significant force in the establishment of the bank. Astor, Girard, and Paris formed a triumvirate that set everything in motion.[15]

The government took their initiatives serious. Therefore Madison and his close friend Monroe, who succeeded him as president, discussed the possibilities of such a project repeatedly.[16] In Congress, however, a heated debate started. Those opposing the central bank feared Astor and his partner could use the situation to their own advantage and public reserves of the second bank would be a mere guarantee for their own fortunes.[17] The three of them had bought most of the war bonds during the War of 1812, and therefore the American government was greatly indebted to them. Despite the debts there was no formal plan as to how to pay back what the United States owed Astor, Girard, and Paris.[18]

During 1815 the atmosphere in Congress cooled down again and the establishment of the Second Bank of the United States was seriously considered.[19] In the end it was agreed that Gallatin's successor as secretary of the treasury, Alexander Dallas, should prepare a draft together with Congressman John C. Calhoun. Both of them now got in touch with Astor and his partners in order to discuss this issue in a smaller group. In one of his letters to Stephen Girard, the second richest man in the United States, Astor inquired whether he was still ready to participate in the Second Bank of the United States. Astor did not want to risk giving the public the wrong impression if he moved forward with the plans and one of his investors was no longer on board. A clear communication was needed — one that Astor controlled.[20]

In the discussions with Calhoun, Astor demanded that a central bank be established again, fast. This was the only way the administration would be able to beat some of the private banks that aimed in a similar direction.[21] In the meantime Gallatin was able to report to the president that Astor, Parish and Girard were prepared to jointly invest $2 million in such a venture in order to get things started and allow the bank to operate.[22] This was the decisive moment. The opposition in Congress gave in. The way was free for the establishment of the second central bank in the United States. On April 16, 1816, the Second Bank of the United States was officially founded in Philadelphia. William Jones was its first president, and the American government called five directors to serve in the board and 20 more to be installed by the investors. Jones had served as secretary of the navy between 1813 and 1814 in the Madison administration.[23]

Each of the 25 directors was responsible for a local branch of the bank. Due to the repeated initiatives that had led to its establishment, John Smith and Albert Gallatin agreed to suggest that Astor should become one of the directors to be nominated by the government.[24] Even though Madison and Astor were not really on speaking terms, over the past year the president agreed and accepted Gallatin's proposal. Considering the debts the government still had, it was surely wise to unite Astor and Girard behind the national cause and integrate them into the bank on the government side. Therefore not only was Astor among the five governmental appointees, but also Stephen Girard.[25] Of course, it was Astor who was to preside over the New York branch.[26] So only a year after one of his biggest failures, the loss of Astoria, Astor was finally chosen for a public office. Whether Madison and Gallatin thought it was an adequate compensation for the loss of the trading point or a clever move to align one of Madison's greatest critics and foremost businessmen in the United States is not reported.

In the establishment of the Second Bank of the United States, Astor showed one of his characteristic character traits. Again he associated his personal plans with the national interest.[27] He looked for advantages for the United States and integrated them into his line of argumentation. The decisive motivation may have been the opportunity to finally cash his war bonds. His personal financial interests, however, were completely in line with the national interest. Only three years after Astor was elected director of the New York branch of the Second Bank of the United States, he resigned.

Business Genius

The era of the *market revolution* did not only see the re-establishment of the American Fur Company after the war of 1812, but also the final expansion of Astor's trade. Now, at the age of 52, Astor was about to expand his activities into a global trade empire. His success was connected to the general boom that came in the wake of the market revolution. Having always had the right gut instincts, Astor had already invested in the industries that were booming. So it was enough for him to expand his already successful companies. He did not engage in any new activities, but harvested what he had seeded from the time of his arrival, by passing attractive investment opportunities like the Erie Canal, which would connect New York with a direct route to Chicago. Astor was still smarting from the loss of Astoria, and taking new risks was neither necessary nor attractive enough compared to what he already possessed.[28]

So Astor first focused on trading with China again. He had to cease trade with Asia during the War of 1812, which led to a strong increase in demand for American furs in China while the United States was missing out on Chinese spices, silk and tea. So Astor seized the opportunity and expanded his

The seal of John Jacob Astor (Alexander Emmerich).

fleet in order to compensate for his losses in the war. By 1815 he owned eight trading ships: the *Enterprise*, the *Beaver*, the *Fingal* (which was replaced by the *William and John* in 1816), the *Boxer*, the *Pedler*, the *Forester*, the *Hannibal*, and the *Seneca*.[29]

The fleet soon paid off, and the China trade was the first step towards Astor's global trade empire. He started to send ships to South America and Europe. The heart of his commercial activities remained New York, where he controlled all operations. In New York he received his North American furs, the products from China, South America and Europe, and it was from here he sent these good to their final destinations, depending in which part of the world they gained the highest profits. His ships delivered Chinese, European and American goods to ports like Valparaiso, Canton, St. Petersburg, Bordeaux, Le Havre, Hamburg, Izmir, London and Amsterdam. It was not long before the new ships paid off.[30]

Unfortunately, trade relations with South America soon ceased abruptly. After some uprisings in Chile, where locals fought the Spanish under the lead of General Bernardo O'Higgins, the New York merchants hoped to open new markets after the Spanish had disappeared from the now independent South American countries. Of course, Astor was one of the forerunners of this movement. Chile was rich in natural resources and Astor hoped to trade Chinese tea and velvet as well as American fur and tin for Chilean copper and silver. Back in New York, the businessman equipped the *Beaver* and sent it to Valparaiso, the Chilean port. This time Astor was too impatient. South America was still in the middle of fights for independence. When the *Beaver* reached her destination she was immediately caught in the troubles between the fronts. In the end she was attacked and boarded by the Spanish. Astor had lost his second ship. The Spanish released the crew but kept the goods and the ship.[31]

Astor was probably less disappointed about the loss of the ship than the loss of trading opportunities with South America. This time it was not up to him to be the forerunner. The situation in South America was still too dangerous. So after this experiment he focused on trading with China, North America and Europe again. Europe in particular seemed to be looking forward a much more peaceful time after the conflicts between the European states were settled in the Congress of Vienna that ended the Napoleonic Wars.

Astor did not only expand his overseas trade but also his trade within North America. In the following years he set his mind on expanding the American Fur Company in order to control the territory west of the Appalachians to the Rocky Mountains. The first steamers were used on the Hudson and reduced the travel time considerably. Now it took only two days instead of a week to travel from New York to Albany. In 1819 the Erie Canal was opened in parts. The canal was a favorite project of Astor's friend, DeWitt Clinton, who oversaw the work as governor of the state of New York. In 1825 the canal was officially opened. It connected New York to Buffalo, the Great Lakes, and Chicago. Traveling on the canal meant saving 95 per cent on the costs of transport. Now a regular trade route between Chicago and New York could be established. The Midwest was finally connected to the ports on the east coast, and both Chicago and New York entered a new stage of trade. Chicago grew tremendously after new settlers could take an easy route west. This was a sharp contrast to Astor's early journeys, when he solemnly walked through these wildernesses in the north of the state of New York with furs strapped on his back. Settlers not only pushed into Chicago, but also poured into Buffalo and Rochester.

Now John Jacob Astor concentrated on expanding the fur trade again. His business partner for this endeavor was Charles Gratiot from St. Louis, an officer who had successfully completed his education at West Point. Gratiot fought in the War of 1812 and was responsible for rebuilding the forts of St. Joseph and Meigs that were located on the frontier. Right from the founding of the American Fur Company he had served Astor as a consultant and provided him with valuable information from the Mississippi region and the

Great Lakes. Over the years Gratiot had become one of Astor's most important sources of crucial information about the West. In 1816 the two of them met in New York in order to discuss the state of the fur trade after the war and evaluate ways to expand the fur trade to the west. During this meeting Gratiot suggested Astor should stop claiming Astoria and the Columbia River region and instead concentrate on the expansion of St. Louis as the center of the fur trade in the west. At that time, St. Louis was already the center of those trading routes following the big rivers of the West. Here the Missouri, the Arkansas and the Ohio merged with the Mississippi. The new steamers made it possible that furs could be transported from the Rocky Mountains, the Great Lakes and the Appalachians down the Mississippi to St. Louis within a short time. Therefore Astor's consultant advocated for St. Louis as an ideal location for the American Fur Company. Despite Gratiot's reasonable arguments, it took Astor a long time to make up his mind. It was obvious that the steamers might help St. Louis to become a true commercial center in the west. Furs could be transported fast and securely via the river to New York. They could easily be delivered to Canton and Europe from there. Finally he decided to follow Gratiot's advice and began to plan relocating the American Fur Company to St. Louis.

Before fully engaging in the endeavor, he first wanted to see whether it was possible to get the support of the American government in this matter.[32] After being let down on a couple of previous occasions it was important to Astor to minimize his risk. For years he had hoped to finally gain the monopoly in the fur trade in American territory. Despite Astor's repeated efforts to gain official support, there was no significant success in pushing the Canadian fur trade companies and traders out of the American territory.

Only after the law was passed in Congress did Astor start to build his new trading center in St. Louis. He separated the region in which the American Fur Company was active into two spheres of interest. Robert Stuart was instructed to control the fur trade in the region of the Great Lakes and along the Missouri from his location in Michilimackinac. A second office was established for the American Fur Company in St. Louis. Astor chose his long-term business partner Ramsay Crooks to run the St. Louis branch.[33]

It was the right decision for Astor. Only a year after he had moved his main trading operations to St. Louis, the first paddle-steamer reached the port of St. Louis on July 27, 1817. The invention of this new Mississippi ship speeded and facilitated the trade via the Mississippi. The first true east-west connection was established. After years of setbacks, Astor now was back on track on his mission to develop the west. Once more he had waited for the right moment and earned the reward his courage. This was finally the time to make the American Fur Company the leading fur company in the United States.

Meanwhile Astor's operations had grown to the extent that he was ready to delegate some more responsibilities. Therefore he was looking for new staff among his old friends. His first choice was his friend Albert Gallatin, who was no longer the secretary of the treasury and seemed available. So Astor hoped he would accept the position of a business partner of the American Fur Company, which would be paid handsomely. However, much to Astor's regret, Gallatin chose to become the American ambassador to France instead.[34] Astor further thought about whom to hire. Who would be a trustworthy and efficient partner? He had not planned for this moment to happen so soon and started to look closer to home. Would his son be ready to take over a part of the business? There was only one way to find out. He did not hesitate any further and chose his second son, William Backhouse Astor, as partner and assistant director. The board of directors of the American Fur Company now consisted of father and son, Ramsey Crooks, and Robert Stuart. Crooks was in charge of the business in the west and the trade with Native Americans. William managed the rest of the business and all trade overseas. His father still was the head of the company but he relied on his son to make the right decisions.[35]

William Backhouse Astor had been to Germany from 1808 to 1815, where he studied Social Sciences at Göttingen from August 25, 1810, onward.[36] However, William never studied at the University of Heidelberg like some authors suggested. A year after William returned from Europe he married the American Margaret Rebecca Armstrong. Her father, General John Armstrong, was American secretary of war in the Madison administration during the War of 1812. Armstrong was a close friend of the president. He had been the American ambassador in Paris from 1804 to 1810. On her mother's side, William's wife was related to the Livingstons and Beekmans, leading families in New York's society.[37]

After William's return his father's affection for him steadily increased. The little boy had grown a lot in Europe and returned as an accomplished and educated man. Astor was incredibly proud of his son. However, he was happy for his other children too. None of them had to experience the poverty Astor himself had to when he was their age. His wealth allowed him to offer them what he only dreamed about: education, choosing the professions they wanted, and marrying the partners of their choice. When he looked at William he did not see the child of a poor German immigrant; he saw a refined member of the American elite. In 1815 the proud father wrote to Dolley Madison. He described William to the wife of the president as loyal to the American nation and hoped for her support upon William's arrival to Washington, D.C., where he intended to meet the president. Astor praised his son in the following words: "He is young and ambitious to become usefull to his native country

[...] He is desirous first to make his Respects to you and to Mr. Madison for which purpose he will make a journey to Washington."[38] Astor wanted to make sure William did not inherit only his fortune, but also his contacts to the highest political circles and networks. With William at his side, Astor reached the heyday of his trading career, making it possible for him to slowly delegate more and more of his business activities to his son and heir without giving away too much control.

Returning to Europe

Over the previous years John Jacob Astor had become tired of all the troubles that came with his huge enterprise. Now he felt his age. On July 17, 1818, he turned 55 and was among the older citizens of the United States. The stresses and dashed hopes that resulted from the loss of his favorite project, Astoria, took a heavy toll on Astor. Sometimes he would feel burned out and empty. So he decided to leave New York together with his youngest daughter Eliza and his grandson, John Jacob Bentzon, who was seven at the time. His grandson was the son of his daughter Magdalen and her husband Adrian Benjamin Bentzon, a former governor of the island of Santa Cruz.[39] The three of them set out for Philadelphia and Washington, D.C.

Astor enjoyed the time away from the business and obligations in New York as well as the luxury to spend his days talking with his favorite daughter and his grandson. The three spent some time in Washington, D.C., in winter until they were suddenly torn from these idyllic moments. One day, John Jacob Bentzon met with another child without asking permission from his aunt or grandfather. The two boys ran away to skate on the Tiber Creek, which was iced over enough so that it seemed safe to do so. However, the ice was too weak to carry the weight of the two children. They sank into the icy waters and could not be recovered in time. Both boys died. Astor was shocked and sad.[40]

Disaster had struck, and even multimillionaire Astor did not have the means to stop it. All his success, all his fortune — nothing could make up for the loss of the child who had been in his care when it all happened. Nothing was the same afterwards. He was not the same afterwards. It was his negligence that had caused the accident. The child should have never had the chance to steal away on his own. Thoughts like this haunted Astor. He was in deep sorrow. This also affected the marriage of his daughter Magdalen, who never really recovered from the loss and divorced her husband in 1819. Month after month Astor felt guilty.[41] This was the first time since his arrival in the United States that he actually allowed himself to take a break. Both his psyche and his health had suffered and he no longer regularly attended to his business. In his grief he turned to his friend Gallatin in Paris: "[My grandson] was not five minutes absent before I missed him, but before we could hear where he had gone, both he and the boy had drowned."[42] Gallatin tried to cheer him up and suggested a trip to Europe might bring some distraction. Maybe away from all his duties and constant reminders of his grandchild, Astor might find some peace and recovery. This might just do the trick — after 35 years of hard work, a break might be just what he needed.[43] Astor himself also hoped that Europe might be a place where he could refresh his mental and physical strength. His son had talked about the fascination of Old Europe, and now Gallatin praised Paris as the pearl of Europe. Astor had set his mind not only on visiting Paris but on seeing the heart of Old Europe too: Rome. He had first had the idea to travel to Europe in 1803, though it just seemed unrealistic to leave home for that long then. It was business first. Now, 16 years later, he had found a worthy successor in his son William Backhouse Astor and was able to leave without regret.

Astor had established a strong board of directors for his company: William was the acting director, and he left his business partners Ramsay Crooks in St. Louis and Robert Stuart in Michilimackinac explicit orders on how to proceed.[44] The American Fur Company was well organized and the responsibilities were clearly defined. This was the foundation of the further expansion of the fur trade in the territory close to the Great Lakes.[45] A vivid example of Astor's precise and detailed working process is a memorandum he left for his son, William Backhouse Astor, upon his departure from New York. His father did not trust in coincidences and instructed him step by step how to trade, how to approach which business partner, and how to move into new directions. He also provided a full last will in case he did not return from Europe.[46]

After Napoléon Bonaparte had lost his great war, Europe's aristocracy had met under the lead of Klemens Wenzel Graf von Metternich, the Austrian foreign secretary, for the Congress in Vienna (1814–1815) to realign and redefine the borders after the war. Their goal was the restoration of the old political order that existed prior to the French Revolution of 1789. Nobles and delegates from over 200 kingdoms, dukedoms, grand dukedoms and other territories had assembled in Vienna to legitimize their rule and strengthen solidarity among their houses. The democratic and republican revolutions had to be suppressed. The voices that demanded the sovereignty of the people had to stop. Indeed, the Congress of Vienna resulted in a longer period of peace in Europe. Though the people still longed for the ideals first presented in the American and later in the French Revolution, the aristocracy had once more saved their rule and the public demands for political participation, establishment of democratic rule, and legal equality ceased — but not for long.

The once poor German immigrant and now successful American citizen John Jacob Astor left New York on June 2, 1819, with his daughter Eliza.[47] He took the *Stephania* and sailed back to the Old World. He left his wife, most of his family, and all his day-to-day business behind and arrived at Le Havre, France, at the end of the month. After 36 years he had returned to Europe. Astor and his daughter took a carriage to Paris, where he stayed some weeks with his friend, Gallatin. After the Congress of Aachen in 1818, where the decision was made to pull back the troops that occupied Paris, the city regained all her charm and esprit. Astor enjoyed the easy life of a successful businessman in Paris. Later he wrote to Ramsay Crooks in a random outburst of joy to praise the atmosphere in Paris.[48]

After his arrival, Gallatin had introduced him to the Paris higher circles. Gallatin's son James wrote in his diary that Astor was particularly fond of Elizabeth Patterson Bonaparte, the first wife of Napoleon's youngest brother Jérôme.[49] She was the daughter of an Irish immigrant to the United States and lived in Baltimore, where she originally met Jérôme. Two months later they married. But Napoleon annulled the marriage. Now in Paris, the Bonapartes and the Astors got to know each other, because they lived in the same building in Paris.[50] Due to their good relationship, Astor would have liked to see their children be engaged, but the children might have seen that differently.[51] And even Gallatin's son James suggested the same.[52] Some years later, Elizabeth Patterson Bonaparte met the Astors again. Then she found clear words to write in a letter to her father back in Baltimore: "I fancy, for his daughter, to whom nature has been as penurious as fortune has been the reverse. She may marry by the weight of her person, but any idea of disposing of her except to some pains-taking man of business, or ruined French or Italian nobleman, would be absurd. She is not handsome, and sense cannot be bought; therefore they will wander from place to place a long time before their object is accomplished."[53]

In any case, Astor and his daughter moved on to the Lac Leman.[54] Astor had a great time in Geneva, which seemed to him a perfect place to spend more time. After seeing Rome in November he continued his journey to Naples, where he spent the winter and returned to Rome in March. The remains of Roman antiquity inspired him and he decided to stay there till June.[55] Then he finally decided to return to Germany — his old home. Together with his daughter he crossed the Alps and traveled through the Black Forest. There is no source that would give us a hint as to whether Astor visited Walldorf on his way to Frankfurt am Main. All we know is that the next letter he wrote after crossing the Alps was one to James Monroe, which was sent from Frankfurt on September 5, 1820.[56] Astor might even have visited Walldorf without anyone recognizing him. He might have returned to his home, but hardly anyone would have remembered the son of the local butcher. His father had died on April 18, 1816.[57] His stepmother Christina Barbara had died on November 15, 1809—years before Astor went back to Europe. His half-sisters Maria Magdalena and Maria Barbara had already passed away at the time of the third European tour, and his other half-sisters Elizabeth and Anna lived already in New York.

Unfortunately, there are no sources today describing the successful merchant's visit, if any, to his hometown Walldorf. He would have most likely been seen around the town as an exotic appearance, with his luxurious travel luggage and clothes. So it remains a mystery whether he saw former classmates or relatives in southern Germany. Only a very disputed source makes a note of Astor visiting Walldorf. William Oertel von Horn, who wrote a biography of Astor, claims he met with locals in Walldorf: "Has his love [...] for his home town completely died? Didn't he ever consider to see his home again? Surely, Astor had visited his home town and enjoyed the pleasure to see his family and friends of his youth again."[58]

However, Horn's claim seems highly speculative. He had never met Astor in person and did not even intend to write a historical account of Astor's life. His biography was meant as an educational guide for young men, for which Astor's life provided merely a framework. Returning home to Walldorf made the Astor of his story just a much more likeable and family-oriented man because he appeared not corrupted by his wealth and followed conservative values.

Eliza Astor gave her own account of her journey with her father. Instead of mentioning a stop in Walldorf, she talks of meeting her uncle Melchior when they traveled straight from the Black Forest to Neuwied. She met her uncle, his wife Verona, and their daughters Maria Magdalena and Maria Sophia.[59] Melchior had worked as a butcher in Oftersheim, a village close to Walldorf, for six years when his brother George had invited him to London in 1783. Melchior had left Walldorf in April 1783 but only made it to Neuwied where he had met members of a Moravian community.[60]

The Moravians were the first large-scale Protestant missionary movement, which emphasized a lifestyle of prayer and worship and a form of communal living in which personal property was still held but simplicity of lifestyle and generosity with one's wealth were considered important spiritual attributes. As a result, divisions between social groups and extremes of wealth and poverty were largely eliminated. Melchior arrived in the Neuwied congregation on April 18, 1783, and never left. Fascinated by their interpretation of Calvinism and Pietism, he was torn between the wish to see his brothers in London and help them in their business, and his wish to stay in Neuwied to learn more about the Moravian mission. In the end he had to explain to his brothers in a long letter that he had been convinced to stay in Neuwied. He would not move on to London but join the Moravians. He worked as a cook in Neuwied till he had to quit for health reasons in 1805. In 1796 he had married Verona Weber, who was originally from Beinwil in the Swiss canton of Bern. She had left her home to join the Moravians in Neuwied in 1781. The couple had six children, but only two survived their toddler age.[61]

Now, 40 years after John Jacob had left Walldorf, the two brothers met again. Both of them had grown old, had their own families, and had led very different lives. One was the richest man in North America; the other was a member of a congregation that helped the poor. The brothers had much to catch up upon and to discuss. Eliza also found friends in her cousins, Sophia and Maria Magdalena. Despite her excellent education, Eliza was not fluent in German, but still grew very fond of her cousins. The visitors stayed in Neuwied for the entire month of October and left for Paris at the beginning of November.[62]

Life in Paris was so fascinating for Astor that he stayed there for over a year. There he met the renowned American author Washington Irving, who was living in Europe for a couple of years in order to collect Dutch and German fairy tales and folk stories he planned to use as inspiration. In the 19th century Irving was among the most-read American authors. He still is famous as a master of the short story. Over his life he created many characters and locations which found their place in American popular culture. He was the first to label New York with the nickname "Gotham" and to call her inhabitants Knickerbockers. Astor remembered that he had already had contact with Irving via his employee Henry Brevoort in 1803. Now they met again and became close friends.

While Astor was still in Europe, James Monroe followed James Madison in office in 1817. Despite the slow postal service via the Atlantic, Astor had kept close contact with his friends in the United States, his friends in politics in particular. Most of his letters were directed to James Monroe, who had become a close friend of Astor in the previous years. Once the politicians had asked Astor for a loan in order to support his political career. Astor lent him $5,000, but had to wait 15 years before Monroe actually had paid all of the money back. One of his other correspondents was Henry Clay, another leading politician of his time. Clay had held all kind of political offices, including speaker in the House of Representatives, secretary of state and opposition leader of the new Whig party. He had also unsuccessfully run for the presidency before. Astor was quite fond of the Whig politician, who also was a member of the Freemasons. Clay and Astor had met in 1814 when Astor was meeting David Parish, on of the investors of the Second Bank of the United States. From then on, Astor frequently funded Clay's political activities, and both exchanged frequent letters while Astor was in Europe. William Backhouse Astor continued the payments and support for the Whig politician. His father had great hopes for him. When he wrote to Clay's son, Henry Clay Jr., he stressed that his father had been a good friend to him and was always a reliable advisor in all matters.

The friendship between the two men was notorious, and the New Yorkers soon picked up on it. It was rumored, when Clay was once again begging for money, that he sent a committee to New York to talk to Astor. However, all Astor had as an answer was: "I am not now interested in these things. I haven't anything to do with commerce, and it makes no difference to me what the Government does. I don't make money any more, and haven't any concern in that matter." One of Clay's men reacted by insisting: "You are like Alexander [the Great] when he wept because there were no more worlds to conquer. You have made all the money, and now there is no money to make." Instead of commenting on the man's cockiness, Astor actually felt flattered by the comparison and was ready to reward the committee with $1,500 for Clay.[63] This story was spread widely in many newspapers after Astor's death in 1848.

Nevertheless, before Astor's departure, Clay and Monroe asked him to keep him up to date with the political situation in Europe. After the restoration wrought by the Congress of Vienna, the failure of the French Revolution and the Napoleonic Wars, they were particularly interested to learn about the democratic movements that still might be active in Europe. Astor liked this new role. Being an informant for the political elite seemed to make him even more an American citizen as before. He truly evaluated the political situation in Old Europe as an American, not in the capacity of a German immigrant. After Astor had resigned his office in the board of the New York branch of the Second Bank of the United States, he was now ready again to take over a political task while he was in Europe. He wrote to Monroe: "If I can be of use to you I would be most happy."[64] But for the president the unofficial observer was of more use than another official ambassador. One of the strongest impressions Astor documented for the president was the impact the United States had on European intellectuals. He was proud to report to Monroe: "All men of sense and information have a hope and look to our dear country for a place of safety."[65] It was hard to ignore that the presumed peace in Europe was nothing but an image upheld by the nobility. The unrest could be felt everywhere, and so Astor informed the president accordingly: "Those in Power are trimbling [sic] [...] A Revolution of extend is soon to bee lookd for."[66]

Surely Astor was a biased observer who had experienced the benefits of the American political and social system firsthand and made the most of the opportunities it offered, but leaving the bias aside, his observations were still realistic. Also his evaluations of the result of a further uprising in Europe were based on his previous experiences. It seemed most likely for him that any war in Europe would have severe consequences for the transatlantic trade that had just recovered from the War of 1812. Europe seemed so occupied with itself that Astor expected the hundreds of little kingdoms, dukedoms, and principalities to engage in fighting each other in the near future. A war in Europe seemed imminent, but it would be a war the United States would not wish to have a part in. So Astor fueled Monroe's isolationist approach to American foreign policy. Two years later, on December 2, 1823, the fifth president of the United States of America declared what was later known as the Monroe Doctrine. He feared a decolonization of the western hemisphere, and therefore the United States stated that further efforts by European countries to colonize land or interfere with states in the Americas would be viewed by the United States of America as acts of aggression requiring U.S. intervention. At the same time, it was assured that the United States would not interfere with existing European colonies nor in the internal concerns of European countries.

Henry Clay, who was interested in the South American movements demanding independence, was keen on information about the political situation in Spain, so Astor provided him with news when he was in Florence: "I Supose the new State of things in Spain will not Change our Relation with that country for the wors[e]."[67] In the same letter he voiced similar concerns as in his letters to Monroe, stressing the revolutionary tendencies in Europe: "In Europe the Revolution is addord and admird. By all who are not in government pay in Naples it has exciteed much feare. So much So that Several persons have been privetly excuted and I rather think that in less than 12 months the Spirit of Liberty will again Show itself on this Continent."[68]

Of course, Astor did not only take care of his political contacts. After all, he was still president of the American Fur Company. Therefore many of his letters also touched his business relations. Even if William Backhouse Astor was the acting director of the family business, Astor could not fully let go. He had introduced William as his replacement as long as he was in Europe, but Astor had kept the right to make the final business decisions himself. There was no way he would lose control over his company even if he felt tired and was looking forward to a break. So he had Ramsey Crooks come to Paris to discuss the further expansion of the American Fur Company in spring of 1821. They renewed their partnership agreement on March 27, 1821, for five more years.[69]

In April 1822 Astor and his daughter returned to the United States.[70]

The reasons for his return were purely commercial at this point. He felt he needed to coordinate the expansion of the American Fur Company in the western territories. However, Astor only stayed about a year in New York before he returned to Europe.[71] He had soon realized his health could not keep up with the speedy life in New York anymore. He admitted so in a letter to his dear friend Albert Gallatin on October 18, 1822: "Here I cannot pass my time but by being constantly engaged in business, which is a trouble to me and causes anxietes which I wish to avoid. [...] I can do better in Europe or more pleasantly."[72] It was easy to let go this time. Astor had seen how well his son had kept the business together, William's performance had exceeded his expectations. Also his business partners brought their part to the table so that Astor allowed himself to indulge into another trip to Europe. On June 1, 1823, he departed again together with his daughter Eliza. Somewhere in the middle of the Atlantic Ocean, John Jacob celebrated his 60th birthday.

Right after their safe arrival in Le Havre, they traveled to Antwerp, and from there straight to Lac Leman. Both of them had fallen in love with the beauty of this lake and the scenery surrounding it on their first trip. They had met Marc Turrettini when they first visited Geneva. Turrettini, who was a descendant of an old noble family, had become a good friend of theirs and vouched for them so that they could receive a residence permit and buy a villa at the lake. Astor spent $50,000 on the estate Saugy in Genthod, formerly owned by the Russian duchess Catherine de Bruce. Soon this villa became the unofficial headquarters of the American Fur Company for the following two years, but also Astor's relaxing residence where he could see himself growing old—far away from his busy house on Broadway. Now he controlled his empire from the shore of Lac Leman and corresponded with his business partners in New York, Michilimackinac and St. Louis.[73]

Originally Astor had only planned to stay in Europe till fall of 1825 and return to New York for the winter. His bad health made it impossible to return to North America as planned.[74] However, on August 20, 1825, he informed Ramsey Crooks that would stay in Geneva because there was a celebration coming up. Eliza had met a representative of the Hanseatic merchants in Paris, Vincent Rumpff. Astor's youngest daughter and the Swiss-born Rumpff fell in love and decided to get married after Astor had agreed to Rumpff's proposal. Astor liked Rumpff and indeed believed he was the perfect gentleman and husband for his daughter. So Astor was proud to lead his daughter down the isle when she married Rumpff on October 25, 1825.[75] The villa in Geneva was her wedding gift, which she happily accepted. She spent the summer months there and the winter and spring in Paris, where her husband worked.[76] Elizabeth Patterson Bonaparte commented on this wedding in a letter to her father: "Mr. Astor has at length succeeded in marrying his daughter very well.

[...] He has no fortune, but is well connected, and has it in his power to introduce her into the best company. Astor is delighted with the match. [...] Rumph is a handsome man of thirty-five, and we all think she has been very fortunate in getting him, as she has no beauty."[77]

In finding a husband for his youngest daughter, it seems that Astor's mission in Europe was complete. So, while John Jacob traveled back to the United States, his daughter immigrated to Europe and stayed in the villa near Geneva. Altogether, Astor had spent seven years away from New York, and now it was time to return for good. He reached New York on the *Danube* on April 9, 1826.[78]

Trade on the Frontier

The face of the American west began to change significantly during the first half of the 19th century. Looking for Native American trading partners, the big fur trade companies sent trappers and agents across the prairie and the Rocky Mountains. The majority of the natives had already made first contact with white folks and traded furs regularly. However, now the competition increased.

In the 1820s, the Hudson's Bay Company showed a clear strategy in their competition on the frontier. Against a petty competitor, there could be no quarter; the British company's objective was his ruination. To temporize with a rival of small capital was not only to risk the growth of his powers to do damage, but to encourage others to follow him. On the other hand, against a competitor too strong to be easily destroyed, an accommodation might be acceptable. The Hudson's Bay policy was to scour competitive areas, paying whatever prices were necessary to deny furs to rival traders or companies.

While John Jacob Astor was on his first voyage through Europe, the relation between the American Fur Company and the Native Americans in the west drastically changed under the pressure of the competition from the Hudson's Bay Company. With Astor away, his agents seemed to enjoy a loose leash and stopped trading with pearls, fabrics and wooden carvings. Alcohol seemed to work so much faster and promised higher profits.[79] Many Native Americans were addicted to this drug and were only encouraged to use even more alcohol by the traders. As soon as the agents and merchants of the American Fur Company adopted these practices, their reputation in the fur trade business sank tremendously. Astor's company would soon be known as the greatest scoundrels in the world.[80] It is unclear if Astor knew about the alcohol trade with the natives, or even if this happened under his order. Nevertheless, historian Hiram M. Chittenden wrote in his classical work *The American Fur*

Trade of the Far West of the "hard and cruel ways" of the American Fur Company toward the natives.[81]

Most of the critics could be found among the competing companies, not so much among the advocates of more rights and better treatment for the Native Americans in Washington's political circles. The problem was that the competitors readily used the same approach and gave away as much cheap whisky as they could in order to gain as many furs as possible. The American Fur Company was their target, and without Astor present the company seemed to be an easy target. During the previous years the American Fur Company had gained control over the fur trade, and the small American traders as well as the British-Canadian rivals could not regain any significant market share. So the independent traders first started to use alcohol in trade. They cut whisky, rye or rum with water and sweetened it with sugar to make it taste better. The tribes, which already had a hard time coping with the new challenges, suffered greatly from the new dangers that alcohol presented. The effects that long-term abuse of alcohol would have on the consumer were not known among the tribes. Slowly alcoholism became a widespread phenomenon in the west. When this became known, the traders brought even more liquor into the west, and even started to distill it right at the frontier. Some managed to make entire tribes dependent on their alcohol deliveries. The profits in the west were bigger than ever, and the monopoly of the American Fur Company was soon highly disputed.[82]

In 1810 John Jacob Astor had explicitly forbidden trading with alcohol when he sent his instructions to the expedition group that built Astoria.[83] His business partner Crooks had turned to John C. Calhoun in 1819, who was secretary of war then, to suggest passage of a law against trading alcohol in the territories of the Native Americans in the Mississippi region and around the Great Lakes, where the American Fur Company and the Hudson's Bay Company competed. How much Crooks was concerned with the health of the Native Americans is not clear. The law would have surely helped the American Fur Company to reduce the competition, but Astor's steady reminder that trade should not be conducted with the help of alcohol might have also resulted from his own experiences with his drinking father. So he had seen the negative effects alcohol could have on people firsthand.[84]

During the two years following Crooks's advice, the American Fur Company lost so much territory without legal help from Washington, and the pressure by the competitors was so high, that the American Fur Company had to change their business practices. Astor's dry company turned to alcohol in order to win back market shares lost to the other traders. Foreshadowing Cold War terminology, Astor defended this move in a letter to William H. Ashley by blaming his competitors from the Hudson's Bay Company for leaving him no other option than to use alcohol himself to even out the chances for both: "If the Hudson's Bay Company did not employ ardent spirits against us, we would not [...] But without it, competition is hopeless; for the attraction is irresistible; and if the British traders alone posses the temptation, they will unquestionably not only maintain, but rivet their influence over all the Indians within their reach, to the detriment of the United States, in alienating their affections from us."[85] Astor did not sound too happy, but he also saw no other option. Taking into account that he had repeatedly refused to go into this direction, it appears believable that he saw trading with alcohol as a last resort in order to retain the *status quo* and keep his company competitive in the fur trade.

Astor feared his long-term Native American business partners would turn against him if he refused to deliver alcohol to them. Thomas L. McKenney, the superintendent of the Indian Bureau, had to acknowledge the fact that the traders who used alcohol just made a better profit in a letter to James Babour, secretary of war, on February 14, 1826: "The Trader with the whiskey, it must be admitted, is certain of getting most furs."[86] After the independent traders introduced alcohol, the point of no return was passed. There was no way the trade with alcohol would just cease on its own. One after the other, the companies followed and offered alcohol to the Native Americans. Obviously the independent traders were not too happy with the fact that the big companies with vast financial resources started to imitate their trading practices.[87]

The politicians in Washington observed these developments with much growing concern. They feared alcohol would soon lead to uprisings, tribal revolts, and fights among the tribes. There was no denying the serious consequences the alcohol caused among the tribal communities. The stability within and among the tribes suffered, and soon a general destabilization of the situation in North America seemed hard to fight. When Washington finally reacted and tried to regulate the distribution of alcohol to the Native Americans by law, the efforts were pointless. The laws signed in Washington were hardly of any significance for the life on the frontier. So political actions were fruitless. There was not even a clear majority in favor of these laws in Congress. Many politicians had sympathy for the cause of the Native Americans, but they also had to keep the best business interests of the United States in mind. So forbidding trading with alcohol seemed also to punish American merchants. Congress had first passed a law allowing the president to forbid trading alcohol with the tribes in 1802. The law explicitly reserved the right to issue a law in this matter to the president himself. Though the presidents held this right, neither Jefferson nor his successors Madison and Monroe made use of it. Only after the first major tribal wars in the wake of the War of 1812 did the politicians start to take this option more seriously. In 1815 the administration forbade building distilling sites in the west. This was, of course, doing more lip service than actual good. The alcohol continued to pour into the West. In 1822 the next law in this matter followed. Now it was no longer allowed to transport alcohol into the Native American territories in order to trade it for goods. It was a major problem for the administration that their legislative authority did not reach into the Native American territories. So it was hard to execute in the west what was ruled in Washington. Also, traders could always claim they were transporting alcohol for medical or personal use. Therefore it was often very easy to argue that the law did not apply.[88]

When Astor started to allow his agents to trade with alcohol, he knowingly ignored an American law. He had often freely interpreted the legal framework to his benefit, but this time it seemed less of an innocent gamble than a measure to secure the survival of his American Fur Company. He felt it was his right to protect his property when the government neither stepped in on his behalf, nor executed laws forbidding trading with alcohol in Native American territory. In a letter to Ashley he explained his point of view: "Wherever the trade is exclusivly in the hands of our own citizens, there can be no doubt, that the uniform and complete enforcement of such a law will be beneficial both to the Indians and the traders, but at those points where we come in contact with the Hudson's Bay Company we must either abandon the trade or permitted to use it. [...] Our rivals can introduce any quantity they please."[89]

However there were rough times ahead for the American Fur Company. Major John Tipton, a governmental Indian Agent, caught one of Astor's employees, William H. Wallace, selling alcohol to Native Americans. Tipton made it his personal mission to fight the business practices of the American Fur Company. Therefore he confiscated several shipments of trading goods in the name of the government.[90] William Backhouse Astor tried in vain to regain the goods. Tipton had tasted blood and continued his vendetta. Time and again he seized trading goods from the American Fur Company till William had enough and turned to John C. Calhoun for help. On November 13, 1824, he wrote to Calhoun, who was about to leave his office within the next few weeks, and voiced his concerns about Tipton's motives. It seemed to him that the civil servant had a bigger interest in destroying the American Fur Company than serving the public interest. However, the government did not comply. All alcohol transported by the American Fur Company was destroyed without any compensation for the Astors.[91]

John Jacob Astor's business partners did not have any idea how to counter what was happening in the west. There was no united outreach to politicians or any serious effort to stop the measures taken against the American Fur Company. Only after John Jacob Astor returned from Europe in 1826 did they find their voice again. In his view there was only one solution to the problem. He needed to speak to Albert Gallatin to counter the claims made against his company. Being the good friend he was, Gallatin immediately turned to James Barbour, who had followed Calhoun in office. In a letter Gallatin expressed what a dear, long-term friend Astor was to him, but also to the American nation. He pointed out that Astor had always acted out of national interest even if it was against his business interests. In order to expand on this idea, Gallatin named Astoria as an example of Astor's perfectly patriotic attitude and explained how the businessman had risked his own fortune in order to gain the United States a spot on the Pacific Coast. Gallatin could not help but stress the fact that Astor had never been compensated for the loss of Astoria, which was estimated to be worth $100,000. Also Astor's long-established anti-alcohol politics were brought forward to demonstrate that it was not John Jacob Astor who was to blame for the sale of alcohol. On the contrary, Gallatin claimed it had only been the individual action of some low-level employees who got too ambitious. The management of the American Fur Company could therefore not be blamed for the misconduct of a small number of their staff members. It should rather be the duty of all persons concerned to stop these individuals. Gallatin ended his letter by begging the entire administration to respect Astor's company: "[This Company] should be rather countenanced than discouraged by the government [...] I think therefore that he is at least entitled to a liberal treatment."[92]

The government was not impressed. After years of taking the problem lightly, the administration had adopted a hard line on the alcohol trade. After Astor had left for Europe, his son had tried to turn from Saul to Paul by suggesting an even harder anti-alcohol law on December 15, 1829, in order to get the American Fur Company out of the spotlight. When he did not receive any response from the government, he had to do it himself. William Backhouse Astor therefore wrote to his biggest competitor, James Keith from the Hudson's Bay Company. He suggested an agreement between the two companies: "[That] not in the future, either directly or indirectly, carry in, or in any way give ardent spirits to the Indians of that region, or vicinity; provided the [...] Hudson's Bay Company pledge themselves to the same effect."[93] William emphasized his noble motives and wanted to gain the trust of the rival company by appealing to the humanity of the management to stop trading with alcohol, as would the American Fur Company.[94] Of course this letter also proves that Astor's company traded with alcohol on a large scale and not just through some individuals in low-level management.

This attempt was bound to fail. At first, the Hudson's Bay governor and committee were receptive to an agreement to stop the competition, or at least to end the use of liquor. But those arrangements were dependent not only on the good faith and trust of both sides, but on their ability to carry out their obligations. The Hudson's Bay Company monopolized the trade on the British side of the border. They controlled the fur trade completely on their territory, while the American Fur Company on the American side had not demonstrated that it could maintain the same dominance.[95] Therefore, William Backhouse Astor suspected that the Hudson's Bay Company had not the slightest intention to enter the proposed agreement and voluntarily stop using alcohol in the trade with the Native Americans. William did not see any other option than to further trade with alcohol too, if he did not want to risk leading his father's company into bankruptcy.[96]

There was only one other way to deal with competition that did not involve alcohol at the time. In 1821 the Hudson's Bay Company peacefully annihilated a competitor. It simply bought the Northwest Company and added it to its portfolio.[97] To the north of Astor's territories of interest, a new competitor suddenly appeared after the forces of the Hudson's Bay Company and Northwest Company had merged. The notion that more competition can make better business conditions was also adopted by many of the independent fur traders. Many of them formed companies of their own in order to protect their business interests. With the competition on the move, it was more than necessary to look into new directions to expand again.[98]

John Jacob Astor started to look for new alliances in order to fulfill his old dream to be the undisputed leader in the American fur trade. However, he had learned a lesson or two. He neither looked for new employees nor for new trading posts. His perspective had changed, and suddenly these newly founded little companies attracted his interest. By integrating existing companies into his mega-company he saved development costs in establishing new contacts, educating new personnel, and building new outposts. Therefore Astor instructed Ramsey Crooks to get in touch with the Missouri Fur Company and Berthold and Chouteau, two minor players in the fur trade, as well as two other even smaller companies.[99] This strategy failed when none of the smaller companies was interested in an agreement with the American Fur Company. So Astor changed his approach and turned to larger companies. Stone, Bostwick and Company seemed a potential candidate for an alliance and came with the benefit that many of the smaller companies were already their subsidiaries. Before leaving for Europe for the second time, Astor was able to negotiate an agreement that led to a temporary fusion of the two companies from April 1, 1823, onward.[100] The way the agreement worked was that all business was conducted in the name of the American Fur Company. Stone and Bostwick kept their sphere of interest around the Missouri River, with

Astor guaranteeing that none of his representatives would interfere with their interests there. Astor had made a significant step ahead. No longer did he have to fear the competition on the Missouri. Neither did he have to hire new agents nor build new trading posts. A former competitor had become a close ally — on time.

Only two other companies besides the already mentioned ones were strong enough to permanently establish themselves as competitors on the market: the Rocky Mountain Fur Company and the Columbia Fur Company. So Astor now skipped long-term negotiations and went straight to the bank: on July 6, 1827, he bought the Columbia Fur Company without further ado, and agreed with the director Joseph Renville and his business partners to a one-off payment, after which all of them left their company. Astor no longer tried to compromise with his competitors, he simply bought them. With this new strategy he eliminated all his competitors around the Great Lakes and on the Upper Mississippi. Finally the American Fur Company had got rid of its rivals and Astor had gained the long-sought monopoly. During this phase of expansion Astor had gained seven more trading posts and a sheer uncountable number of trappers, administration staff and agents who now worked for the American Fur Company. In order to make his new presence in the new territories known he changed the name of the Columbia Fur Company in The Upper Missouri Outfit of the American Fur Company.[101]

Retreat from Business

When John Jacob Astor turned 64 in 1827, he felt tired and worn out. He had not been long returned from Europe before he decided to finally retreat from some of his ventures. This meant not only that he as a person retreated, but also that he gave up entire ranges of his business in general. The first branch he shut down was the China trade. North American furs began to lose in popularity in China from the 1820s onward.[102] Astor lost his interest in the China trade when the profit began to sink. Soon it completely ceased. When there was no longer a demand for furs in China, importing silk and spices from there was no longer attractive either. It was not very lucrative to only import from China without selling anything to her because it meant the costs remained the same but the profits were cut in half. Many other companies had begun to import from China so that Astor was only one in many, whereas he had been one of the first ten years before. Other merchants and companies had caught up with him and started to imitate his business strategies.[103]

Once more Astor had analyzed the situation correctly. It was time to stop trading overseas before there were higher losses. In 1824 he still sent four ships to Canton. The following year he reduced it to one. Two years later, in 1826, Astor sent two last ships to China and sold all his ships the following year.[104]

Obviously, it was easy for Astor to end his trading business. It could be considered a strength of the millionaire that he was able to stop whenever it was necessary and not hold onto old connections and friends. This behavior seems to be typical for John Jacob and can be observed all through his life: he could leave his home town and immigrate to another country; he could leave London for America; it was easy for him to spend years overseas in Europe, leaving his wife, children and friends behind him; he could stop his trading business; and he could step back from the fur trade. All these steps seem to be possible because Astor was resting neither upon old connections and business relations nor on friendship or even love. Due to the fact that he had suffered many losses in his early childhood, he may not have been able to establish strong connections to other people — in private life as well as in business.

Continental transport significantly changed during these years. While ships were easily lost in heavy weather or hostile encounters, the railways promised a more peaceful infrastructure. In the 1820s the first railways started to operate in New England and Pennsylvania. On private initiatives, New York experienced its first steps into the railway business.[105] Astor had mostly been interested in developing New York real estate and therefore his focus was the city of New York rather than the state as such.[106] Shortly after his return from Europe, Astor read in the papers about G.W. Featherstonehaugh's decision to found the Mohawk & Hudson Railroad Company.[107] On April 17, 1826, Featherstone-

Portrait of John Jacob Astor (Vereinigung Walldorfer Heimatfreunde).

haugh's company was chartered and now he tried to attract new investors for his railway. The first line was supposed to run from Schenectady and Albany along the Hudson to New York City. He was planning to carry both goods and people. Reading about these plans, Astor immediately realized the opportunities that came with this endeavor. Connecting New York to other parts of the state with a reliable means of transportation would guarantee safe travel for persons as well as for goods. He could safely send his goods by rail, and his real estate in Manhattan would not depend on sea travel anymore. Therefore the value of the real estate was expected to rise. So he took initiative and bought 300 of the 500 available shares of the Mohawk & Hudson Railroad Company. This made him the second largest shareholder of the company.[108]

He was not the only New Yorker to spot this opportunity. The management of the Mohawk & Hudson Railroad Company combined some of the most distinguished businessmen of New York. All of them understood what kind of new opportunities lay in the improved infrastructure offered by the railways.[109] Astor was elected one of the nine directors of the Mohawk & Hudson Railroad Company.[110] Initially, John Jacob Astor was fascinated by the new technology and the possibilities opened by the railroad. He must have sensed that it was a new business in which he could invest. Moreover, he wanted to attract more investors and wrote his business partner, Gerrit Smith of Albany, the son of Peter Smith, about the railroad company: "You will become interested."[111]

John Jacob Astor was director of his own businesses most of his life, but now he had to compromise with his fellows. His new partners confirmed him in his office over the next three years. During these years Astor used all his business experience to manage the Mohawk & Hudson Railroad Company, planning the routes the tracks should follow through the state of New York and what goods and passengers should be transported. In total, 51 meetings of the directorate were held — most of the time in Astor's house on Broadway. As previously in the case of the fur trade and the imported instruments, Astor observed closely the ways others did business. So he carefully evaluated the other railway companies, their business strategies and their personnel while optimizing his own construction efforts. He made it his new mission to bring railway transport and travel to the state of New York and supported his new endeavor with $35,000 to secure the financial future.[112] After five years the railway was ready for its first journey. On September 24, 1831, he could celebrate the official opening of the first line. Maybe this new achievement led Astor also to look back on the times when he traveled the woods in the northern regions on his own, which now could be reached comfortably in a railway cabin with hardly any limits as to the amount of goods transported. However, at nearly 70, he did not have the ambition to actually manage the operations of the Hudson & Mohawk.[113]

John Jacob was happy to have started and set up the new business, but now that the tracks were laid he had reached his primary goal, to improve the infrastructure in order to increase the value of his Manhattan real estate. So he was not interested in the further development of this company. Therefore he gave up his office as director and was free to travel to Europe for a last time.[114] His family overseas had grown. Eliza was looking forward to seeing him, and her sister Dorothea followed her to Europe. Dorothea had married Walter Langdon and the couple had eight children together. So Astor wanted to see his children and grandchildren. Another reason for his travel might have been to see a French physician whom he had previously met and who had suggested some treatments for his age-related health issues as some authors suggested.

On June 20, 1832, Astor left for Le Havre. After 19 days at sea he reached Europe once more.[115] This was so much faster than the months he had to spend on the rough seas when he traveled to the United States for the first time in the winter of 1783-84. Not only the infrastructure on shore had seen significant improvements. The ships had gained in technical inventions and comfort over the last 50 years, but sea travel was still a burden for Astor. He was very tired when he took the carriage to Paris, where he spent much of the remaining months of the year recovering under the eyes of physicians.[116] Only in the springtime of 1833 did he finally go south to see his daughter Eliza and her husband in Geneva. Astor was overjoyed to see his beloved family in the familiar setting of the Lac Leman. But the happiness was soon spoiled, when news reached them that back in New York, Astor's brother Henry had died in April 1833.[117]

Henry Astor and his wife were not blessed with children, but they too had gained a considerable fortune in New York. Despite being overshadowed by his brother in the view of the public, Henry enjoyed a high reputation among New York's politicians and his trading partners. Philip Hone, the former mayor of New York and long-term friend of John Jacob Astor, made note of Henry's funeral in his diary on April 25, 1833. Hone pointed out that he had lost a friend and New York had lost a fine longtime citizen and highly cherished businessman. Although Henry always lived in the shadow of the success of his brother, he had made also good profits with his butchery and took the money to invest in banking and real estate. When he died he left a fortune of $800,000, which Henry left in total to his nephew, William Backhouse Astor.[118]

Astor had planned to be back in New York in the fall of 1833. However, his health did not allow him to travel. All his physicians urged him to stay

5. Global Player, 1815–1834

in Geneva, and he was ready to oblige. Astor used the time to prepare himself for the trip and finally left in the spring of 1834. On April 4, 1834, he reached New York on the *Utica*,[119] but unlike when he returned from his previous travels, he did not return to the American Fur Company. He officially resigned from his office as director of his company. The captain had left the ship. Astor had decided to do so when he was still in Europe and wrote to his son, William, to inform him about leaving the company for good. In the same letter, he asked William to spread the news among their business partners and prepare everything for his return in 1834.[120]

It was time for him to retreat again. Times had changed, and while Astor had been a forerunner during most of his life, now a new generation pushed forward and Astor was business-minded enough to see it. He had the courage to actually take the consequences and leave on a high note. He knew it was time to go in the same way he knew when he had to stop trading overseas and reduced the fur trade. The continental expansion was no longer a wish; it was happening. The routes to the west had been explored and developed. Fur trade was no longer an adventure of a few courageous individuals. It had grown into a solid business. The infrastructure had improved to a point that initial advantages by good contacts and intimate knowledge about the best routes did not matter anymore. More and more competitors had stepped in. But the public had lost interest in fur coats and hats out of beaver skin. The demand dropped with more and more companies pushing on the market at the same time. New York's fashion turned to silk and away from fur in the 1830s. Formerly profitable fields of business, like the fur trade, weren't considered current anymore.

6

New Yorker, 1834–1848

Astor rose during a time when New York's bourgeoisie was developing and the first New Yorkers earned their great fortunes. A clearly visible sign of this financial elite were the first multimillionaires of the city. In 1845, John Jacob Astor and Peter G. Stuyvesant were the only two millionaires in New York; a decade later there were already dozens of them.[1] The second richest man of that time was Steven Girard, who was a citizen of Philadelphia. Despite the success stories of the few, many underprivileged families could not even dream of the luxury enjoyed by the financial elite. They lived in the same city but in a totally different world.

Four percent of the population owned half of the property in the city of New York. More and more newcomers poured into the city. In the 1830s the population had reached the number of 200,000. Immigration was the most key factor causing the increase in trade in traffic, banking, shipbuilding, insurance and many more industries. Not only trade grew; the city itself also expanded. In the previous years all houses were concentrated on lower Manhattan, but now the settlements slowly crawled up north. The first new settlement was the part known as Greenwich Village today. Broadway remained the center of the city and the rich continued to build their big mansions there, showcasing New York's glamour to the international visitors and immigrants.

For many years John Jacob Astor was the only millionaire in New York. In the 1840s he got company. Other businessmen made their fortunes in the new economy and accumulated millions. The following decade counted a dozen millionaires in New York.[2] This new financial elite presented a new class of people both for the established, aristocratic families as well as the underprivileged classes. Suddenly the question was publicly discussed what was to be expected from these new self-made millionaires. It was argued that since their money was mostly earned in trade and most of the profits came from the New Yorkers, they also had a moral obligation to return something to the community. So the New York papers saw article after article that discussed what was to be expected from the behavior of the financial elite in politics, economy and culture. The main issue was what they should give back to the city of New York in particular and the United States in general.

Being the richest man in all of the United States from the 1820s on, Astor was in the hot spot here. His fortune made him a public person. There had not been a millionaire before him in North America. Therefore it was rarely discussed what a big fortune required the owner to do within a republic. In 1828, only one percent of the New Yorkers owned more than $34,000 in total, while Astor spent $50,000 a year on railways alone. Even those considered rich in New York could not compete with Astor's finances. Therefore some of his contemporaries thought it was only fair that Astor should return his fortune to the community. Being the first millionaire, of course Astor was also the first to be confronted with these demands. After Astor's death in 1848 these demands were headline news in New York for many weeks. Even today the rich Astor who kept his wealth to himself is the dominating image in the public. Journalists in the mid-1850s agreed that every individual had the duty to serve the republic. Being a millionaire seemed to make it true for him a million times more.

Of course, to establish personal liberties within a republic of individuals was a cornerstone of the American Revolution, but with the liberties came the moral obligations to participate in the republic of equals and support the community. Only this would guarantee the stability and the prosperity of the community. Borrowing the political ideals of Greek and Roman antiquity for their republic, the Americans also integrated the concept of a benefactor as a model citizen in their republican ideals. Roman aristocrats built baths, held games and gave donations to the public, so Americans had high expectations of those who made the most of the unlimited opportunities in the United States of America.

From the time he immigrated, Astor had tried to become a part of New York's elite. Over 50 years after his arrival in New York he finally was not only part, but also at the center of this circle. He had established a reliable economic, social and political network around him, and now his primary concern was to make sure that his family would remain in this position permanently. None of his children, grandchildren and relatives should ever experience anything close to the poverty he had seen in his childhood. However, Astor had realized that securing his fortune was not enough to establish his family's position in the long run. He also needed to become the ideal republican citizen. Therefore he started looking for the right projects to support as a benefactor and better opportunities to engage in projects in the city of New York to improve his standing with the locals again after he had quit the theater business a couple of years before.

The Astor House

One of Astor's first major projects in New York was the Astor House. As early as April 3, 1828, John Jacob Astor invested $101,000 in the City Hotel.[3] Once more Astor's business-mindedness led him on the right track. The City Hotel was one of the finest hotels in New York and was widely know among New Yorkers and visitors. It attracted many rich and famous visitors from within the United States as well as from abroad who were ready to do business in New York.[4] He merely varied his overall business strategy in nuances: again he turned to the rich and offered them luxury. This had proven the most efficient strategy in the cases of the fur trade and the instrument trade already.

Astor hired Chester Jenings, an experienced hotel manager who had worked in high-level management positions, and employed him from 1817 onward. As in other instances Astor did not intent to engage too much in the operations. At the beginning of his career he and his wife controlled all operations; meanwhile, Astor was wealthy enough to hire the best people to do the job so that he could retreat to a position as supervisor and director.[5] The City Hotel was a successful venture for Astor and brought him good profits right up to April 25, 1833, when it burned down. The news reached Astor in

The Astor House (Vereinigung Walldorfer Heimatfreunde).

Europe and he was devastated. In the previous years he had quit the sea trade to minimize the risk of losing entire ships, and now he had lost an entire hotel in the middle of New York. There was a significant difference from the sea trade. While he bore all risk himself on the sea, he was conveniently insured on shore. So he decided to rebuild the hotel with the money issued by his insurance.[6]

When Astor returned on April 4, 1834, from his last trip to Europe,[7] more bad news reached the traveler. He had already heard that his brother Henry[8] and his daughter Magdalen had died[9] while he was on the other side of the Atlantic, but now he was informed that his beloved wife had passed away only a couple of days prior to his return. Sarah had died at 72, and Astor remained heartbroken.[10] His friend Philip Hone met him after his arrival and gave a vivid picture of Astor's state in his diary: "He looks poorly and is much thinner than he was when he went to Europe. The hand of death has laid heavy upon his family during his absence, and his spirits are much depressed in witnessing the blanks which have been created."[11]

Back from Europe, where he had been among two of his daughters and many, many grandchildren, he now felt alone in the big city. Without his wife, the house on Broadway was not the same. He felt lonely. Often he had spent time away, but this was the first time he had returned without his wife waiting for him. The next decision was easy to make: Astor left the old house behind. It was no longer his primary goal to connect to the other businessmen on Broadway. He was at a different stage of his life. Now he tore down his old house at 229 Broadway.[12] (It is unclear when he had moved from 149 Broadway to this location.)

When Astor left for Europe, he already had plans to swap the home on Broadway for a cozy new one for his wife and himself that would better serve their needs as senior citizens. Therefore he started a new project: a new hotel, which was to be the best in New York.[13] In his novel *Astoria*, Washington Irving weaves a story that is based on Astor's personal memories. When the businessman walked down Broadway very early in his career, he took a good look at all the new houses and thought to himself: "I'll build, one day or other, a greater house than any of these, in this very street."[14] Maybe this was the time when Astor remembered this. He built a house, but not one of the large villas that already lined Broadway. On the spot of his former home he built the newest, most modern hotel in the entire United States.

The hotel business is a good example for Astor's business strategy in his later years. He more and more remained in the background and let others run his businesses. It was enough for him to set the businesses up and lead them into the right direction by taking on management responsibilities in the beginning and hiring someone to do the job as soon as the processes were established. He was not the most innovative businessman; he was rather a perfect observer and evaluator. Identifying strengths and weaknesses in other businesses helped him to develop his successful strategies.

In case of his new hotel, the Astor House, the Tremont Hotel in Boston had served as an inspiration for Astor, but he intended to make a better version for New York.[15] Jefferson Williamson, the author of *The American Hotel*, described Astor's mission and his love for New York as follows: "John Jacob Astor ... felt that if Boston could support a house like the Tremont, surely the metropolis could support one even finer."[16]

In 1832 Astor started to set his plans in motion. His son William was chosen to work together with Isaiah Rogers, the architect, who had already constructed the *Tremont* in Boston, in order to come up with the blueprints of the new hotel.[17] With his genuine sense for public relations and patriotic gestures, Astor laid the cornerstone to his new hotel in a big public celebration on July 4, 1834.[18]

Over the next two years New Yorkers were curious to see what was happening on the construction site and took peeks on their Sunday promenades. In May 1836 the waiting time was over, and the Astor House finally opened its doors. In his diaries, former New York mayor Philip Hone called it the "New York Palais Royal."[19] Jefferson Williamson quoted American poet Fitz-Greene Halleck, who had been Astor's secretary over the last 16 years, with: "Astor copied all the features of the Tremont.... However, the Astor was a more impressive building than its Boston prototype. It was two stories higher, it had nearly twice as many rooms, and the architect had had afterthoughts which elaborated the exterior and interior."[20]

The hotel was built in the style of Greek antiquity. It had six floors, 300 rooms and 17 bathrooms, which were extraordinary numbers in a time when baths were still considered a luxury.[21] The Astor House resembled the Tremont only on a first glance. Astor made sure his hotel surpassed the Boston benchmark by far. So not only in construction and comfort, but also in its technical equipment, the Astor House was state of the art. Once more Astor had taken an idea and added his business-mindedness in order to bring about an improved version. The *New York Constellation* raved about the luxurious equipment and technological innovations used in the hotel: "The House was lighted by this gas everybody is discussing. But the Quantity consumed being greater than common."[22] A novelty was running water on the upper floors. A brand new steam engine pumped the water up. No other hotel in the United States had a similar system working.[23] The furniture was exquisitely carved from black walnut wood. All interior design was of a standard that was unseen before in a public building. Astor had not saved a dime on the mundane fittings.[24]

Astor hired the two brothers Simeon and Frederick Boyden, who previously ran the Tremont Hotel in Boston, to manage his hotel, severely damaging his competitor's business.[25] From the day of its opening onward, the richest, most important individuals resided in the new number-one hotel on Broadway. Soon the Astor House was also the prime venue for political, cultural und economic dinners in New York.[26]

Astor had not named his hotel Astor House from the beginning. After it proved to be a financial success, he officially referred to it as the Astor House. Of course, after all his years in business, his long-term address on Broadway would also be known among the locals as Astor's house. So it is not surprising that a new name like Park Hotel was soon dropped because many people would simply have the Astor House in their heads when talking of Astor's Broadway hotel.

The hotel's return on investment was not noteworthy for Astor in terms of money, but was high when it came to prestige and setting his own landmark in New York. With marketing and advertising still undeveloped, branding and naming of products, like the Astor House, was Astor's way to make his name known to the public. He had come a long way since the beginning of his career when he bought one-line ads in the *New York Packet*. Now he had his name on New York's best hotel, widely visible on Broadway. To many people, Astor and luxury became more and more synonymous. He established his name as a brand and loaded it with meanings: glamour, wealth and success. Due to the raving critique of the papers, the Astor House was soon known for its splendor among the New Yorkers, but this did not stop in New York. Visitors and papers spread the news about the Astor House around the North American continent and to Europe. Soon Astor's improved copy of the Boston Tremont was copied itself. The name Astor was used to imply the high standards and luxury ambient even when Astor had nothing to do with a certain business, like the Astor House, San Francisco, which opened during the 1848-49 gold rush.[27]

It might not have been Astor's initial impulse upon entering the hotel business, but it was this branch of his business that actually started a family tradition. Hotels were owned by Astors for generations. Moreover, nowadays his name is connected with the famous Waldorf-Astoria in New York, although he was long dead when the hotel was founded by two of his great-grandsons: in 1897 the two cousins John Jacob Astor IV and William Waldorf Astor finally united their family hotels, the *Waldorf* and the *Astoria*, to create the legendary first Waldorf-Astoria. This New York landmark also used naming and branding techniques to keep the family name a public topic. In order to stress the equal shares of the two hotels in the newly merged hotel, the two parts of the name were connected into Waldorf-Astoria. It closed for good in

THE WALDORF-ASTORIA, NEW YORK

May 1929. After a luxurious ball, much of the original equipment was auctioned off for a total of $350,000. It was by far the most famous, most modern and biggest hotel of its time and the first one that provided more than 1000 rooms. The original buildings were torn down, and on their site the Empire State Building was built in 1931. In the fall of 1931 the new Waldorf-Astoria opened on Park Avenue. The costs of the construction were in the region of $40 million. It was again a state-of-the-art building that also was the highest hotel building of its time. In front of the building there was a special driveway for automobiles, and in its basement a station of the New York Central Railroad was integrated. With 2253 rooms it surpassed its predecessor by far, and its interior design set standards for all 1930s buildings.[28]

Washington Irving's *Astoria*

After Astor had torn down his former residence on Broadway in order to build the Astor House, he moved to his country house, Hell Gate, outside of New York City in 1834,[29] which would be nowadays located around East 87th Street close to York Avenue. Today nothing is left of this residence. From his new residence, Astor could look over the East River to a small village, which is nowadays called Astoria, Queens. This part of New York was named after John Jacob Astor in 1839 to persuade him to donate money to the village's young ladies' seminary, a college for young girls. Although he only invested $500, one quarter of the sum they hoped Astor would give, his name remained.[30]

At Hell Gate, Astor lived together with his secretary Fitz-

Portrait of John Jacob Astor (Vereinigung Walldorfer Heimatfreunde).

Opposite: Postcard of the Waldorf-Astoria (Alexander Emmerich).

Greene Halleck, who was actually a poet.[31] But to Astor, Halleck was more than just a secretary. Years later, the *New York Times* described Halleck's importance to Astor, his business and his family: "Mr. Astor was very fond of giving liberal entertainments, and at all of these Halleck was the life and the soul of the company. Although Halleck was employed by Astor as chief agent and representative in his business, he was always regarded more in the light of a confidential friend, and as such Mr. Astor's house was practically Hallecks's home. [...] Mr. Astor never gave a public dinner or entertainment without the presence of Halleck."[32]

After his last return from Europe, Astor had realized that public opinion was no longer favorable for him. New Yorkers called him avaricious. To them it seemed obvious that Astor was not ready to share his wealth with the community. When Astor talked to his friend Philip Hone, he was very concerned about the public image of him. Hone noted in his diary: "I have great pleasure in recording this munificent act of Mr. Astor's, because public opinion does not give him as much credit for liberality as I have thought him entitled to."[33] Hone had always thought highly of Astors as benefactor because: "He [...] has come to the wise conclusion that as he cannot take his money away with him the latter days of his life are not likely to pass less pleasantly for the reflection of his having sprinkled a little sweet into the bitter cup of the widow and fatherless."[34] On November 5, 1835, the former mayor of New York made an entry in his diary about Astor's donation of $5,000 for the Society for the Relief of Aged Indigent Females.[35] Nowadays this would be about $122,000. Two years later he donated the same sum again to the same association.[36] Another $20,000 was added to this sum posthumously. Astor had provided that the money should be used as an endowment and the interest should be used to fund the Society annually.[37]

Astor also showed a particular interest in his employees and their families. However, he had high expectations. Only those who proved to him that they were hard-working, diligent and canny could count on his support. Without much public mention of it, according to his letters he supported families of his employees if the bread-earner died in the course of his staff duties with an Astor company. When his employee Jacob B. Taylor died, he supported his son Moses till the boy was old enough to earn his own living.[38] Astor also jumped in when Captain John Ebbets died. The captain had been a loyal friend and led the first expedition to build Astoria. With the help of Astor the young John Jacob Ebbets studied at Yale, and after he graduated, Astor employed him in the American Fur Company in 1832.[39]

There are many more little donations mentioned in Astor's letters. In June 1835 he donated $100 to the survivors of a tornado in New Brunswick to help those in distress, "in aid of the needy who have suffered."[40] Another

$200 and $500 were donated to the Fire Department Fund.[41] There is no full record of all of Astor's donations, but his last will gives a more detailed account of his charity work. Posthumously he left $5,000 each to the Institution for the Blind and the Society for the Relief of Half-Orphans and Destitute Children, as well as another $2,000 to the New York Lying-In Asylum.[42]

Starting his new life in Hell Gate Astor hired Washington Irving, the famous American author, to write a story about the founding of Astoria on the Columbia River based on the papers and accounts of the American Fur Company, as well as on Astor's personal notes.[43]

Washington Irving had spent the last 17 years in Europe and only returned to the United States in 1832. The two men had met in Europe before, and Irving was welcomed back to New York with a big reception at Astor's City Hotel. Without any imminent jobs planned, Irving was flattered and agreed under the condition that his nephew Pierre Irving could accompany him. After he had traveled the west twice after his return from Europe in order to work on his piece *A Tour of the Prairies*, the story of Astoria seemed like a perfect extension of this story. Astor wanted the story to be based on his business papers and his own accounts. Not only had Astor and Irving knew each other for some time, their families too knew and liked each other. Peter Antelyes, a literary critic, argued that there are references to Irving's admiration for the millionaire at many places in Irving's work. Irving himself describes his intentions to write *Astoria* and Astor's wishes in the introduction: "[Astor] expressed a regret that the true nature and extent of his enterprise and its national character and importance had never been understood, and a wish that I would undertake to give an account of it."[44]

There could not be any doubts that Astor worked hard to rectify his image in public in order to be known again as the honorable, patriotic businessman he was. He feared nobody would remember his achievements in the westward expansion. Over the last couple of years, several accounts of the Astoria adventure had been published, but none of the authors had even bothered to ask Astor for any information or statement. Among the publications were the volumes of Gabriel Franchère[45] and *The Columbia River* by Ross Cox.[46] Both had experienced the founding of Astoria firsthand and both blamed Astor himself for the failure. In 1849, *Adventures of the First Settlers on the Columbia River* was published by Alexander Ross.[47] The news about Astoria also spread east, over the Atlantic. In 1858 Dr. W.F.A. Zimmermann published *Astoria oder Reisen und Abenteuer der Astorexpeditionen* (*Astoria or Journeys and Adventures of the Astoria Expeditions*).[48] But this novel, written in German, found recognition only in Astor's birth country.

After Astor had offered Irving the job, the writer informed his nephew Pierre in a letter on September 15, 1834, that John Jacob had invited both of them to Hell Gate as long as they worked on the story, to sift through the business papers. Irving was happy to also announce that Astor had offered both of them $3,000 per year in order to finish the story.[49] His nephew was as happy about this as Irving himself, and they both moved into Hell Gate in August. They enjoyed Astor's hospitality and luscious lifestyle.

Astor had opened his private archive so that Irving could use all papers and memorandums that were relevant to the story. Pierre was chosen to look through all of this material and preselect important documents for his uncle.[50] As early as October 8, 1835, Irving managed to present a first draft to Astor. With much joy he invited Irving to stay on at Hell Gate to continue his story. Therefore Irving could spend the winter with Astor[51] and his favorite grandchild Charles Astor Bristed, who was the son of his daughter Magdalen and her second husband John Bristed. Charles studied at Yale and only rarely visited his grandfather.[52]

During his time at Hell Gate, Irving met many fur traders and adventurers but also politicians on the estate. One of the guests was Captain Benjamin Louis Eulalie de Bonneville, a former officer on the American army who had received financial help from Astor to fund a three-year expedition to the west. Bonneville had left in 1832 and now returned to New York to report to his investor. Irving listened and loved Bonneville's stories and the hand-painted maps. So he decided to write another book on the west, *The Adventures of Captain Bonneville*, which would be his last book on this matter.

Irving finished his *Astoria* in February 1836. The book followed the rise and fall of the first American settlement on the Pacific Coast. John Jacob Astor is portrayed as the benevolent patriarch and inspired creator of the venture. Irving presumably let a bit of bias shine through in his portrait of Captain Thorn. He had known the captain since they were young and did not appreciate his undiplomatic, nervous temper. In any case, he needed to juxtapose the good Astor and an antagonist. So Thorn seemed the appropriate choice. He had caused many tensions in the exploration party, and in the end it was a fact that he was responsible for the sinking of the *Tonquin*. Astoria fell to the British because, due to Thorn's failure, the post was defenseless.

At the end of October, Irving's book was finally published and Astor was happy to see New York's bookstores advertise the book in the local papers. Had he known Rupert Murdoch's example, he just might have bought a paper to guarantee adequate press coverage. But even without his further engagement, the *New York Daily Express* published on November 1, 1836: "Washington Irvings New Work this day is published. Astoria—or anecdotes of an enterprise beyond the rocky mountains, by Washington Irving, in 2 vols [...] just received and for sale."[53]

Even if Irving was critical when it came to the literary quality of Astoria, he was happy that the book received positive reviews. Financially the book was a big success. Irving's American publisher paid him $4,000, and his British publisher paid him another £500. The joint venture of Washington Irving and John Jacob Astor caught the public's attention. Only months after the Astor House was officially opened, Astor not only had a building that carried his name, but also a book by a respected author that spread it in big letters. Philip Hone commented the release in his diary: "The result of Irving's rustification at Mr. Astor's [...] last summer has just come out, in the shape of a new book called "Astoria." I have not read it, [...] but it is said to be a beautiful little work, one of those true stories [...] in which sober history is so gracefully decked by the pure ornaments of his style and so garlanded by the flowers of his poetical imagination."[54]

Of course, there were also critical voices about the publication of *Astoria*. Gabriel Franchère, for example, saw himself forced to have his account of the Astoria story translated into English. Originally he had published it in French, but reading Irving's *Astoria* really stirred his mistrust. He did not feel like any of the facts were represented correctly.[55]

Irving was happy that Astor was fully satisfied with his *Astoria*: "Old Mr. Astor appears to be greatly gratified, which is very satisfactory to me," he wrote to his nephew; "William Astor also expresses himself in the most gratifying terms, and seems surprised that the subject have been made so interesting and entertaining. In fact, I have heard more talk about this work, considering the short time it has been launched, than about any other that I have published for some time past."[56] Astor liked the way he was represented in the novel, and Irving did not spare with his praise for his benefactor. The newspaper *The Examiner* quoted the famous writer in its issue on October 23, 1836:

> [Astor] was already wealthy beyond the ordinary desires of man, but he now aspired to that honourable fame which is awarded to men of similar scope of mind, who, by their great commercial enterprises, have enriched nations, peopled wildernesses, and extended the bounds of empire. He considered his project establishment at the mouth of the Columbia as the emporium to an immense commerce; as a colony that would form the germ of a wide civilization; that would, in fact, carry the American population across the Rocky mountains and spread it along the shores of the Pacific, as it already animated the shores of the Atlantic.[57]

With those warm words about Astor, Irving not only restored a positive image of the millionaire in the public mind, he also produced a piece that would end up on the canon of world literature still read in English departments today. Not only did Astor's name gain eternal fame, but the dream of the first

American outpost and the westward expansion was preserved for future generations. After the opening of Astor's hotel, this publication brought him for a second time into the center of public interest. With both these projects, John Jacob Astor managed to associate his name with a positive image, success, boldness and — with the success of the Astor House — with luxury.[58]

Since Irving and Astor had already established friendly relations in previous years, the time they spent together on Hell Gate must have intensified their friendship. In December 1836 Irving reported about one of Astor's many visits to Irving's new residence of Sunnyside on Hudson River: "Old Mr. Astor most unexpectedly paid me a visit [...] He spent two days here, and promised to repeat his visit as soon as there shall be good sleighing."[59] Astor enjoyed his intellectual discourses with Washington Irving. He developed a strong affection for the author. Early in 1837 Irving introduced his friend to Joseph G. Cogswell. Born in 1786, Cogswell had studied at Harvard and Göttingen. In 1820 he became the head librarian of the library at Harvard University. Astor and Cogswell soon became good friends. Cogswell was particularly impressed with the multimillionaire. The man he met at Irving's house did not seem to correspond to his public image at all, and Cogswell stated: "He is not the mere accumulator of dollars, as I had supposed him; he talks well on many subjects and shows great interest in the arts and literature."[60]

Astor and Cogswell met again in October of the same year. This time Astor had invited Cogswell to Hell Gate. He found Astor in a good mood but physically his age could not be denied. He seemed fragile, and a little worn out. Cogswell saw the letters piling up on Astor's desk. Many, many people were asking for donations. Cogswell wrote home that he was surprised by the number, though it was known everywhere in the city that Astor was a charitable man. Astor had felt his age for many years now. After his wife had died and his siblings had passed away too, he thought about what would happen after his death. With all his children married and financially secure, he could think about his last will in more general terms. What should he leave to New York?

New York had become a rich and busy city with many buildings where stocks were exchanged, merchants traded, and harbors built. But it was lacking a public library. The rich already kept huge book collections in their homes, but publicly the classical literature was not available. Astor had not had access to books himself when he was young. A newspaper article describing his daily life in 1842 also underlined his interest in books and literature in general: "Mr. Astor has been reputed ignorant, but this is a libel, for he is in part, and always has been, a great reader, especially of light literature. Likewise he is a very liberal patron of literary men, as is partially evidenced by the fact of his warm attachment to Washington Irving, and his choice of Fitz Greene Halleck, for his right hand man."[61]

It seems that the idea behind the library was that Astor wanted for other people to be able to educate themselves even if they could not afford private tutoring. So he decided to leave enough money for the city of New York to establish a public library. In honor of the donor, it was agreed that this should be the Astor Library. It is not documented whether Cogswell had suggested this plan, but Astor surely was consulting with Cogswell how to proceed. Astor planned to leave $400,000 for a nonprofit public library and hired Cogswell to acquire the books. In 1839, he finalized an inventory list and Astor allowed him a budget to travel to Europe, where Cogswell bought more books in a total value of $60,000.[62]

Economic Crisis and Immigration Waves

In 1837 several European countries as well as the United States were haunted by an economic crisis that caused the most serious distress in the global economy of the 19th century. Several factors contributed to the collapse of the highly interconnected markets in North America and Europe. The crisis was triggered by President Andrew Jackson's economic policies and the bankruptcy of several American banks that had invested into some risky projects. More than 850 banks had to close. The boom slowed down so much that the United States had more jobless people than ever before. The economic depression lasted for the next five years. Jacksons's successor in the office of president, Martin Van Buren, did not manage to solve the economic problems either. In an effort to secure the governmental finances, he refused to grant any federal loans or other financial support for businesses.

The economic crisis hit New York hard. As center of the American commerce, the city had many operations that fully depended on a strong economy. Real estate prices fell to an all-time low. Astor was fortunate enough that he did not have to fear any major losses because he had cleverly diversified his wealth in cash, stocks and real estate. So he did not panic. He tried to find ways to make the best out of the crisis. However, his first measure was to help his long-term business partner Gerrit Smith, who was the son of his agent Peter Smith from Albany, with a loan in the amount of $100,000.[63]

Astor got the idea that he should invest not only despite all the panic around but also because of it. He had always trusted New York's ability to rebound and grow, as it had after the War of 1812. So when everyone around him tried to get rid of seemingly unprofitable goods in order to raise at least some cash, Astor saw cheap real estate everywhere on the market. When the economy bounced back in the 1840s, the value of these low-cost investments multiplied.

The crisis also pushed many immigrants away from Europe to North America, where they were looking for a better life. Since the crisis also existed on the other side of the Atlantic Ocean, many new immigrants from Europe still lived in poverty when they reached their land of dreams. A great many of those immigrants came from the German southwest. To them Astor was the shining example of how they could leave their own poverty behind. They all came from areas where famines struck and their economic situation and social status were simply unbearable. The lives of many of these German immigrants did not take the turn they hoped for. They did not find the Eden they had pictured in New York, but a city that was two-faced: a glamorous rich one and a indescribably poor one. The only thing that seemed certain was that the city suffered greatly from the economic crisis.

On the one hand, the city was full of the brick houses and villas of the rich; on the other hand, the primitive, wooden, and mostly improvised huts of the poor lined many streets. With the fast influx of immigrants, even more of these huts appeared, and people remodeled tents and stables so that immigrants could live there. The situation resembled modern-day slums. People shared their quarters with animals, and dirt and garbage piled up everywhere. Hundreds of thousands of Irish and German immigrants poured into the harbor of New York and settled in Manhattan. The city rapidly grew in size and numbers. In the 1840s Manhattan reached as far north as to today's 40th Street.

Astor had watched these developments closely. It was much harder for the new immigrants to successfully integrate than it had been in his case in 1784. The city was different now and it was much harder for it to absorb all of them. However, Astor soon realized what kind of role he played for the German immigrants. Many of the papers that informed those who had decided to leave Germany used Astor and his career as an example. Emigration agents, who earned their living by recruiting poor Germans ready to leave home, used Astor to promote their services. As much as Astor had always wanted to be a true American, he had not fully lost touch with his German origins. So he decided to engage in a new endeavor for a last time. This time it was a true nonprofit, though. He pledged to help the German newcomers. Astor had been a member of the German Society of the City of New York from 1787 onward.[64] However, he had joined more to please his brother Henry, who was an active member there, than to participate. He had never been to any of the society's annual assemblies before. Now the German Society seemed a perfect platform for his plans to help the German immigrants and to send accurate information back to Germany. Now he ran for the office of the president of the German Society of the City of New York. As long as Astor was president of the Society, he donated annually $5,000 from 1837 to 1841. In addition, Astor also left $20,000 to the Society posthumously.[65] The money was to be used to establish a permanent office that would be a one-stop office for the new arrivals. In the 1850s this office became a part of the official immigration office, at Castle Garden, the former Fort Clinton at the very south end of Manhattan. In 1892 the office was moved to Ellis Island.

The Lower East Side was one of the hot spots for German immigrants. Many of them settled there and opened typically German businesses like bakeries, butcheries, restaurants, and beerhouses. Breweries were established on Bowery. This so-called Little Germany became the cultural and economic center for the German immigrants, with German schools, club houses and theaters. The houses differed in their architecture from the American houses in other districts and the signs in the windows were only in German, so that English-speaking New Yorkers had a hard time finding their way around. The way of life the Germans established in New York seemed strange to the locals: balls, fests, singing competitions and sports tournaments did not appeal to the English-speaking majority of New Yorkers.

As had been the case many times before, Astor was criticized for his actions. Over half a century later, authors like Gustavus Myers used the fact that he was president of the German Society in support of their arguments. According to Myers, Astor only wanted to use the reputation of his office to sell his overpriced real estate to poor newcomers. His actions during these years might seem irritating at a first glance. Of course Astor was looking for ways to make profits even in the years of crisis. However, only these profits allowed him to support his charities in the end. What was irritating many was that he did not simply open his purse and pour money into the market. He rather invested in the establishment of institutions that would help people to help themselves to find long-term solutions and efficient help. Today it is taken for granted that the state offers assistance for people in financial and other sorts of distress. In the 1830s self-preservation was man's first duty. However, Astor simply set up an immigration consultancy office, which undoubtedly was a model for similar institutions later established by the state and federal governments.

When it comes to his real estate business, he saw himself as developer in the true sense of the word. He provided the land on which houses, apartment buildings, shops, offices, public buildings, and streets were built. He neither acted as a greedy capitalist, as he was portrayed by his critics, nor did he emerge as a philanthropic benefactor who intended to build an ideal city based on the community principle. He did what he always did: act as a businessman. He engaged in a business he truly believed in and helped his fellow German immigrants without losing his business-mindedness.

Age and Death

After his wife died in the spring of 1834 Astor felt weaker and weaker. Hone had noticed before that Astor lost more and more weight: "He looks poorly and is much thinner than he was when he went to Europe."[66] He continued: "I am sorry to observe since Mr. Astor's return from Europe that his health is declining. He appears sickly and feeble, and I have some doubt if he will live to witness the completion of his splendid office."[67] Astor never did fully recover from his third trip to Europe, which was haunted by so much bad news like the loss of his wife Sarah, his brother Henry, and his daughter Magdalen. He would see even more loved ones pass away. In 1838 his beloved daughter Eliza died in Geneva. This news broke him in the same way the death of his favorite grandchild, John Jacob Bentzen, had done, and he retreated to his country home to mourn.

Hone was not the only one who observed the changes in Astor. William Backhouse Astor had a similar impression. He regularly wrote to his niece Sarah, another of those members of the Astor family who had returned to Europe, and informed her and her husband, Robert Boreel, of his father's weakening constitution.[68] Philip Hone also commented in a similar way in his diary: "Mr. Astor presented a painful example of the insufficiency of health to prolong the life of man. [He] with his fifteen millions of dollars would give it all to have my strength and physical ability.... He sat at the dinner table with his head down upon his breast, saying very little."[69]

Astor spent his final years on his estate in the countryside, Hell Gate. Here he had found peace after he left most of his businesses to his son William. The old millionaire had the house equipped with all that was valuable and luxurious: artwork, elegant furniture and expensive instruments. But he avoided an excessive lifestyle and remained the canny businessman he always was.[70] Sometimes he invited members of the New York elite as guests.[71] Other than that he only met with his former employee and director of the St. Louis office of the American Fur Company, Ramsey Crooks, and another former trading partner, Pierre Chouteau, to play some cards once a week. Washington Irving described Hell Gate in a letter to his brother Peter: "I have not had so quiet and delightful a nest since I have been in America. He has a spacious and well-built house, with a lawn in front of it, and a garden in rear. The lawn sweeps down to the water edge, and full in front of the house is the little strait of Hellgate [...] Halleck, the poet, lives with him, but goes to town every morning, and comes out to dinner. The only other member of his family is one of his grandchildren [Charles Astor Bristed]."[72]

Some years later, in 1842, the *New York Tattler* published what we would call nowadays a lifestyle report. They visited Astor at Hell Gate and stayed with him for a day. The writers of that article proudly presented: "We wrote this sketch, thinking it might gratify the reader to learn something of the habits, manners etc. of an old gentleman whose daily income is four thousand and odd dollars."[73]

In this report Astor is described as an old gentleman who enjoys life:

> Mr. Astor is now at the wrong side of eighty, and naturally begins to feel the hand of time press heavily on his constitution; but still he enjoys himself, cracks his joke, empties his bottle (for though no inebriate, he is far from being a teetotaler), smokes, and interests himself in the rise and decline of stocks. In fact, though old, there is nothing of the dotage, the second childhood of old age about him. His mind, on the contrary, is as sound as a bell, and his head as clear as when he used to be shoveling in Spanish dollars by the ship load.[74]

Furthermore, Astor does not seem to be dried-up old greedy person, as some later historians described him:

> The Labors of Mr. Astor's day, at the present writing, are divided somewhat as follows: He rises early, dresses without a valet, and smokes half a pipe of tobacco. He then breakfasts sometimes on milk, but mostly on the most fragrant description of Mocha coffee. Another attack on the pipe follows. The papers then are called for, when his still keen eye falls foul of the money article — but afterwards he goes through the editorials and chit chat of the day, and is mightily tickled when he finds anything better than usual. Pipe again. Then, when he's able, a saunter about and a crack with the neighbors concerning stock or the weather. Next, a two hours' siesta, and then to dinner, whereat John does great execution, for he is a wonderful hand at the trenchery for an old man. The pipe, chit chat, and a mild glass follow, and then the time is spent until 9 o'clock, when he calls for his chamber lamp, and takes up line of march for Blanket Alley.[75]

Music had been of special importance to Astor. His time in London and trading in instruments had made a big personal impression on him. Now at his senior age, he regularly held musical events in his country home and invited family and friends to enjoy some professional pianists or string quartets. He loved to introduce this kind of music to his grandchildren. The old John Jacob was particularly pleased whenever William's oldest daughter Emily Astor Ward and her sister-in-law Julia Ward sang solo or as a duo on these occasions. Astor could not be prouder.

On December 15, 1846, one of the most significant events in Astor's later years happened. On this date was the wedding of John Jacob III, Astor's grandchild and oldest son of William Backhouse Astor. John Jacob III had followed his father's example: he first studied at Columbia University, and then spent some time in Europe, where he studied in Göttingen. After he returned from Europe he completed his studies at the Harvard Business School and became the main legal and financial advisor of the Astor family business. He married Charlotte Augusta Gibbes. Charlotte came from a rich family from South Carolina. Astor had not only invited all family members but also many of his business partners and friends in the New York upper class. A day before the actual wedding, Astor invited his friends to a reception in William Backhouse Astor's house on Lafayette Square. All the rooms were filled with candles and decorations. The guests wore the most expensive and fashionable suits and dresses and the ladies were adorned with valuable jewelry. The party guests danced, string quartets played, and everyone enjoyed the elegant atmosphere. This was the way Astor liked it.

In 1847, a fire broke out in New York close to the location where the Astor House was standing. Due to the help of many firemen, the hotels were saved and remained untouched by the fire. Astor was relieved. He thanked the fire department and gave them an acknowledgment of their "great and efficient exertions in subduing the fire at the Astor House."[76]

At the beginning of November of 1847 Astor left Hell Gate for the last time to spend some time in the city in his townhouse t 585 Broadway. This three-story building had been built according to his wishes over the past few years, and he had also bought the houses in the vicinity for his family. The *New York Times* wrote about this building: "The house at 585 Broadway, which was always pointed out to visitors as one of the interesting sights of the city, being the home of the wealthiest man in this country, was a good-sized three-story brick house. [...] It was a very handsome, elegant home."[77]

Washington Irving visited his friend a last time on 585 Broadway. He had only returned a few months before from his assignment as American ambassador to Spain. Irving had been in Europe again from 1842 onward and had not seen his friend after the joint Astoria adventure. So he was shocked to see his friend very frail, bent down, and much aged.[78]

At the end of February 1848 William informed his brother-in-law Vincent Rumpff in Paris about Astor's failing health: "[My Father] has for some weeks past suffered from an attack of cold which has reduced his strength much and made him quite thin and altho' now much recovered from the cold he is so debilitated that he can leave his bed but for a few hours at a time."[79]

Only a few weeks before John Jacob Astor would have celebrated his 85th birthday, he died in his house on 585 Broadway on March 29, 1848, at about 9 o'clock in the morning. The papers claimed he died peacefully of old age without suffering.[80]

A few days afterwards Astor was buried on the afternoon of April 1, 1848. In order to prepare for the funeral, six priests, family members, friends and business partners met in William Backhouse Astor's house. However, the funeral of New York's richest citizen was an event of public interest. The streets were lined with people who wanted to see the coffin because they felt sympathy or simply because they were curious.[81] The streets leading from William's house on Lafayette Square, later renamed Astor Place, to St. Thomas Church on Broadway were bursting with people. Even European newspapers were writing about the event. For example, the *North Wales Chronicle* published a paragraph about Astor's funeral: "Crowd after crowd gathered to the spot, to witness the last tribute to the dead. The coffin was placed in the hall [of 585 Broadway], and the doors thrown open that every one might have an opportunity to see him; and thousands rushed in, until the hall was crowded almost to suffocation."[82]

The bishop of New York would celebrate the funeral service in St. Thomas and so many people tried to join the service that the only option was to keep the doors open during the service.[83] Black velvet covered Astor's coffin and a small glass window allowed a last peek at the great businessman and family patriarch. Afterwards he found his resting place in the churchyard of St. Thomas.[84] Among the coffin bearers were Astor's closest friends: Philip Hone, Ramsay Crooks and Washington Irving. Irving in particular was devastated by the death of his dear friend. The *New York Tribune* announced that a mausoleum was planned in another churchyard where Astor would find his final resting place.[85]

Sometimes it is claimed that Astor's grave was next to the Alexander Hamilton's in the Trinity Churchyard. Maybe it just seemed fitting that the two great men of the early republic would find neighboring permanent resting places on Broadway facing Wall Street. It would have been a perfect match, but Astor's mausoleum was built in the Trinity Cemetery in Washington Heights on 155th Street in Harlem, where many members of the Astor family were buried.[86]

Astor's Last Will — Founding a Dynasty

Almost two weeks after Astor's death, the *New York Herald* came to the conclusion that "the great object of the will is to create an Astor dynasty by entailing the property upon the regular successors of the individual, for ages to come."[87] The newspaper criticized Astor harshly for his last will, and it has to be questioned whether this criticism was justified or not. But in one point the *New York Herald* was right: Astor wanted to found a dynasty.

During his lifetime the millionaire was always very cautious about his public image. He discussed it often with his advisors and decided that the strategy to make sure his name was always associated with positive achieve-

The Astorhaus in Walldorf (Vereinigung Walldorfer Heimatfreunde).

ments and economic success was to name the most successful or most prestigious projects after Astor. Therefore the outpost in the Oregon territory on the Pacific coast was named Astoria; his most prestigious hotel was the Astor House; the library he donated was the Astor Library and the poorhouse he donated to his hometown of Walldorf was the Astorhaus. The public library was the project with the largest endowment. The Astor Library had its first rooms on Astor Place, formerly Lafayette Square, close to William Backhouse Astor's house. John Jacob Astor wanted to enable all New Yorkers to educate themselves without respect to class or financial means. He was grateful for the education he had enjoyed even in the poor Walldorf and cherished learning as highly valuable good. However, it was also true that Astor intended to set himself a landmark in his beloved city.

Most of his contemporaries appreciated the opening of the Astor Library. The intellectuals in particular thought it was an excellent initiative. The famous American author Herman Melville spoke highly of New York's public library on many occasions. In the preface to his *Bartleby* he explicitly praised Astor for his charity and thanked him for the establishment of the Astor Library, which he referred to as his second home: "I do not speak it in vanity, but simply record the fact, that I was not unemployed in my profession by the late John Jacob Astor; a name which, I admit, I love to repeat, for it hath a rounded and orbicular sound to it, and rings like unto bullion. I will freely add, that I was not insensible to the late John Jacob Astor's good opinion."[88] But the library did not guarantee Astor a long-term good reputation. About 50 years after Astor's death the administration of the city of New York merged the Astor Library with the Lennox Library and the Tilden Trust to the New York Public Library. Astor's library lost the connection to its founder when his name was removed. However, the front of the current building still proudly shows the visitors Astor's mission: "The Astor Library founded by John Jacob Astor for the Advancement of useful knowledge MDCCCXLVIII." Inside, the first room is still called the Astor Hall. But the moment the library was renamed and reorganized, the city took away the common memory that Astor had sponsored New York's biggest library.

The second largest donation made in his last will was the establishment of a home for the poor and needy in his hometown Walldorf in Germany. There, care would be offered for the poor, ill and impaired. The city of Walldorf was happy to receive Astor's donation and starting building the house in 1852, as the late millionaire wished. It was opened proudly in 1854.

Astor had plans for academia, too. In the first version of his last will he

The front of the New York Public Library (Alexander Emmerich).

planned to endow a chair at New York's Columbia University with $25,000. However, this donation was announced under one condition. The professor to be hired should teach German literature and be able to teach German language, too. Columbia University could not settle with Astor's attorneys, so in the final version this endowment was deleted from the will.

Of course the main purpose of Astor's will was to provide for his family. None of his children, grandchildren and relatives would experience poverty as he had in his childhood. William was the main heir. Having already inherited his uncle Henry's fortune, William was suddenly the richest man in the United States of America and followed Astor also in the role of patriarch of the Astor family. The Astors were an integral part of New York's elite and were not only accepted among the established families, they had become one of them.

John Jacob Astor had been the proud patriarch of his family, a true *pater familias*, and happily took care of his own and shared his wealth with them. However the rewards he bestowed on them came with a high price. Astor demanded success and discipline from his family. Family members could only win his trust and support with eagerness, diligence and entrepreneurial achievements of their own. He hated under-achievers and despised those who did not work to increase the family fortune. If family members did not meet his expectations he was ready to break off contact or at least break off financial support for them. His nephew Georg Ehninger, for example, led an excessive lifestyle while he was working for Astor, which ended in his uncle sacking him. Ehninger was the only one of Astor's close relatives who was not mentioned in the will. The other family members received enough money to lead an independent life.

By his last will he bequeathed to his descendants at least his fortune's social and symbolic capital, so that his children and grandchildren were able to maintain or strengthen their social status. Finally he took for himself the last step and became a philanthropist, as is usual for millionaires nowadays. In 1848, no one, neither Astor nor the public, understood the responsibility which a millionaire has for society and the public. Therefore, the cost of his sponsoring of both a poorhouse in Walldorf and a public library in New York, in relation to the size of his fortune, started a discussion about the responsibility of a millionaire as well as of the taxation of entrepreneurs. The two sides could not be more opposed: Did he had to give back all his money to the republic he lived in? Or was he free to earn all his fortune based on the ideas of a free economy and the pursuit of happiness?

John Jacob Astor surpassed his previous donations and gifts to the public, and eventually emerged as a sponsor. The primary function fulfilled by the will, however, was the ability to transmit the fortune to his family and not to give it to the American community. In fact, with his wealth, Astor anchored his descendants as an American dynasty in the New York society of plutocracy.

John Jacob Astor's eldest daughter Magdalen was born on January 11, 1788. The first child of the Astors was named after her German grandmother, John Jacob's mother. At age 19 Magdalen married Adrian Benjamin Bentzon, who had just returned from his post as governor of the island of Santa Cruz[89] on September 14, 1807.[90] Their son, John Jacob Bentzon, tragically died in 1818 while on a trip with John Jacob Astor to Washington. One year later, Magdalen was divorced from her husband. Her second marriage to the Englishman John Bristed also ended in divorce. Their son, Charles Astor Bristed, was born on October 6, 1820. He was known as Astor's favorite grandson. After Magdalen's death in 1832, the boy did not come to live with his father, who became a priest in Bristol, Rhode Island, but with his grandfather. Young Charles was smart and Astor supported his later career.[91] He paid the school's fee so that Charles could study at the famous Yale University in New Haven, Connecticut.[92] Astor's special relationship with his grandson Charles is also visible in Astor's last will, in which he gives his house on 585 Broadway, his villa Hell Gate, and an additional $115,000 to his grandson. Furthermore, Charles Astor Bristed became one of the trustees of the Astor Library.[93]

The second child of the Astors was named after his father: John Jacob Astor Jr. He was born in 1791 and should have become the head of a new dynasty. But unfortunately, the child was sickly and suffered from a mental disability. Washington Irving described the unfortunate young man in a letter written in 1821: "[John Jacob Astor Jr.] is in very bad health, and seems in a state of mental stupor. His situation causes great anxiety and distress to his father and sister; and there appears but little prospect of his recovery."[94] In his last will Astor gave his son a yearly stipend of $10,000 as well as a house on 14th Street.[95]

Eventually the third child and second son, William Backhouse Astor, born on September 19, 1792, fulfilled his father's wish to become the future head of the Astor dynasty. He enjoyed an excellent education in the United States and was also sent to Germany to study at the University of Göttingen. Therefore, William spent most of his time between 1808 and 1814 abroad in Europe before his father called him back to New York in order to make him his business partner.[96] After John Jacob Astor's final retreat in 1834, William took over the family business and he eventually became the main heir of Astor's last will.[97]

William and his American wife Margaret had seven children: Emily, John Jacob III, Laura, Mary Alida, William Backhouse Jr., Henry and Sarah, who died as a child. Emily Astor Ward, considered one of Astor's "singing birds," died shortly after her marriage to Samuel Ward Jr. Her daughter Margaret Astor Ward was raised afterwards together by her father and grandfather William Backhouse Astor.[98] Later, this child founded a world-famous cosmetics company. William Backhouse Astor's oldest son, John Jacob III, became the main heir like his father before him.[99] His son Viscount William Waldorf Astor (1848–1919) was one of the two founders of the Waldorf-Astoria Hotel. In 1893 he left New York and the United States to immigrate to England. There he became a nobleman and received the title of viscount. He became the head of the English line of Astors of Heever Castle.

William Backhouse's son William Backhouse Jr. was the father of John Jacob IV. This great-grandson was the second founder of the Waldorf-Astoria. He tragically died in 1912 aboard the *Titanic*.

The next child of Sarah and John Jacob was Dorothea. She was born on January 11, 1795, and named after John's sister-in-law, Henry's wife.[100] In 1812 she followed an invitation by Albert Gallatin and traveled to Washington. There, she got acquainted with Colonel William Langdon of New Hampshire. Soon after, the young couple married on September 24, 1812, and one year later, Sarah Astor Langond, the first of nine children, was born. According to Astor's testament, every grandchild got an immense sum. Moreover, Astor left his City Hotel behind for his granddaughter Sarah.[101]

The youngest daughter of the Astors was Eliza. She was born in 1801 in New York and was her father's favorite. In 1819 John Jacob traveled with her to Europe to find her a husband. There, she got to know the Swiss-born Hanseatic ambassador, with whom she fell in love. They got married in 1825 in Paris and moved afterwards to Geneva. There, Eliza died in 1838, ten years before her father.

However, John Jacob Astor did not leave behind money for only his children and grandchildren, he also took the children of his siblings into consideration. After his oldest brother George died in 1813,[102] John Jacob took care of his brother's family and regularly sent money to Elizabeth.[103] Also in his testament, he took care of her and left her a yearly sum of £200 for the rest of her life.[104] His brother George and his wife had four daughters and four sons. At least three of them came to the United States. George Jr. worked for his uncle as a fur trader.[105] When he died in 1832, John Jacob watched after his nephews son George Peter Astor Jr., who got the sum of $3,000 according to John Jacob's last will.[106] Two more sons of George, Benjamin and William Henry Astor, also came to New York.[107] But Benjamin did not become successful. He worked as a luggage carrier and died in 1834.[108] When Benjamin died, John Jacob Astor wrote to his niece, Benjamin's sister Mary

Reynell: "I suppose you have been informed of the death of your brother Benjamin. He left his wife penniless."[109]

The other brother, William Henry, seems to have inherited the musical skills of his father. He came to the United States and worked as a music teacher.[110] From his uncle, he got the yearly sum of $5,000 for the rest of his life.[111] Joseph Astor, the brother who stayed in England, got a one-time payment of $50,000, while the three surviving daughters, Sarah Oxenham, Mary Reynell and Catherine Epworth, each got $20,000. The fourth daughter had already died in 1845.[112] Later Astor reduced Mary's legacy to $15,000.[113]

Astor's second oldest brother Henry had no children. Therefore, Henry gave all his money after his death to William Backhouse Astor.[114] The daughter of his brother Melchior, Sophia Astor of Neuwied, got $5,000, as well as a yearly payment of $300.[115]

It seems that the members of his sister Catherina's family were the black sheep. Catherina died before John Jacob. But nevertheless an earlier version of his testament shows that she would have only gotten $1,000. Nevertheless, her son George Ehninger, who worked for Astor, never managed to gain the recognition of his uncle. He was the only surviving close relative who did not get anything from his uncle.[116]

Thus, John Jacob Astor saw himself primarily as a patriarch and the head of a dynasty. Having had the experience of poverty and hunger as a child, he wanted to assure that his family would never suffer as he had. Therefore, the primary goal of his testament was to provide for his family and to attempt to establish a dynasty. From his birth onwards, he had chosen William as his heir. He got the biggest part of the fortune and he got all social and political connections.[117] In that way, William was not the son of an immigrant, but a fixed part of the New York society. Finally, John Jacob Astor made his son head of the Astor family. Astor also made sure that almost every family member could live a good life. During his lifetime, he tried to employ many family members, while others he just supported financially.[118]

Nevertheless, he demanded from his family a certain amount of discipline and perseverance. To be able to gain his recognition, one had to show an inclination for hard work, ambition and business acumen. If they neither showed those skills nor attained success, they failed in his point of view, as for example his nephew George Ehninger. In that case, there was no understanding in Astor's eyes.[119]

But at the same time, Astor realized that he had to give money away to those who needed it. The sources tell us of some of his sponsoring actions. All the minor donations were for people in need. The two biggest donations, the Astor Library and the Astorhaus in Walldorf, showed that he wanted to help people in the difficult situations in which he had been as a child. The idea behind the library was that everyone in New York, whether rich or poor, could gain access to books—and in that way to education. With the foundation of the Astorhaus for the poor of Walldorf, he wanted to offer direct help to those who were like he once was.

Considering all this, the *New York Herald* was right in appreciating Astor as follows: "In reading over this will, with its numerous codicils, the conclusion to which the mind is led is the following—that the great purpose of the testator was to leave the bulk of his fortune to his eldest son, W.B. Astor, and to get round and evade in some way or other the American law which prohibits primogeniture, or the concentration of the whole of a mans's property upon one heir, to the exclusion of the others. This our American law, and a wise law it is."[120] But nevertheless Horace Greeley's paper did find Astor's will unrepublican and against the law.

Besides amassing money and building a dynasty which lasts until today, John Jacob Astor left the City Hotel, the Park Theatre, the Astor Library and the Astor House to his fellow New Yorkers.

Astor's Public Image and Legacy

The memory of a historical person is an important aspect of his legacy, a practice that has won in influence in analyzing a person's life in the humanities and cultural studies during recent years. Since the early 1990s, there has been wide discussion[121] about memory and the memory of a society.[122] According to the Egyptologist Jan Assmann, the past "in itself" is not self-contained or immutable. It is always a construction by the later generations, each having their own memories and creating their own past. Therefore, one must always analyze who constructs the past, in which context, and also which media promote these images.[123]

This can lead to different, sometimes very diverse interpretations. Additionally, each individual has, according to his own character and circumstances, his own memory within a community. Depending on the milieu, background and each individual, those memories come together and form a collective memory.[124] Thus, memories are not fixed recollections set in stone, but snapshots rather than exact copies of a historical fact of the past.

Whenever one is analyzing Astor's public image it becomes clear that the millionaire's name evokes both good and bad associations. Besides being hailed as one of the most industrious and successful men of his time, he has also been portrayed by historiography as being greedy, cold, and without any heart for those who were not as fortunate as he had been.

Astor's Image During His Lifetime

The first biographical sketches concerning Astor were already written during his lifetime. The works of David Jacques for the *Hunt's Merchant Magazine* in 1844,[125] and of Moses Yale Beach for his own work "Wealth and Biography of the Wealthy Citizens of the City of New York" in 1845,[126] showed a positive image of Astor's person and career, and both writings describe Astor's meteoric rise from poor immigrant to a leading person in U.S. economy. They focus on his monopoly position in the American fur trade, his important role for U.S. trade relations with China, and his farsighted investment in land on the outskirts of New York, which later became the center of the American metropolis. Basically, the two accounts led almost logically to Horatio Alger's novels from the 1860s, in which the writer established an ideal image of a poor, industrious boy who came to great wealth through honest work.

These two early works praised both Astor's service and his vision. They highlighted Astor's social awareness, his zeal for the nation's westward expansion and the construction of the Astoria outpost, the foundation of the Astor Library in New York, and the support of other German immigrants arriving on American shores. Both biographical sketches also recognized his achievements as a businessman, manager and real estate speculator. They marked his career in uncritically positive terms.

But this positive image was not the only one prevailing. During his lifetime Astor had to face criticism. The three Astorian clerks, Gabriel Franchère,[127] Ross Cox and Alexander Ross, published their view of the establishing of Astoria, in which they blamed the multimillionaire for the failure of the outpost. Franchère started the debate with his French publication in 1820. This book was later translated into English. His publication was followed by Ross Cox's book *Adventures on the Columbia River* published in 1832,[128] and Alexander Ross's book *Adventures of the First Settlers on the Oregon or Columbia River* published in 1849.[129]

These writings damaged Astor's reputation considerably. In response, the American public had not long to wait for the multimillionaire's answer. As described earlier in this chapter, Astor asked the famous and celebrated writer Washington Irving to write the narrative *Astoria or Anecdotes of an Enterprise Commissioned Beyond the Rocky Mountains* in 1834. This publication would particularly emphasize Astor's role in envisioning, financing and building the trading outpost on the Pacific Coast before the War of 1812. Washington Irving's book, which told the story of Astoria from Astor's perspective, sold successfully in the 1830s and 1840s[130] and helped the multimillionaire to get a better reputation in the United States for some years.[131]

Especially the old, aristocratic families accepted Astor as one of their own, as the reactions after his death showed. Many went to the procession on the street, to the church, or visited Astor's coffin. Especially Philip Hone, who could be regarded as the mouthpiece of the New York money aristocracy, praised Astor's life and career in his diary. Hone shed some light on Astor's public perception when he wrote on the day Astor died: "He came to this country at twenty years of age; penniless, friendless, without inheritance, without education, and having no example before him of the art of money-making, but with a determination to be rich, and ability to carry it into effect."[132] In Hone's little resume of Astor's life, only catch phrases such as "millionaire" and "from rags to riches" and "from a dishwasher to a millionaire" were missing to describe what was later known as the American Dream. Never before had anyone made so much of the opportunities offered by the land of unlimited opportunities. His story was the raw model for generations of immigrants to come. Astor had fulfilled his personal American dream that he had envisioned in the little village of Walldorf when his brother's letters first showed him a life beyond social barriers and territorial frontiers in Germany. The United States of America allowed him to live his American Dream, and he tried to give back what he could: his drive to explore the west at his own expense and add significantly to the mapping of the territories west of the Appalachians; his clear business vision that helped several branches of industries to develop by his investments; and his vision of a perfect infrastructure on Manhattan Island that still shapes modern New York.

Change After His Death

But all this changed by the time of John Jacob Astor's death in March 1848. His rather positive image was about to falter completely.

There were some soft-spoken positive voices among journalists after Astor's death, as this example shows: "The New York Star says: 'It is rumored that he has willed large sums to religious societies, hospitals, and benevolent institutions, including the German Emigrant Association. Various individuals in his employment, besides his descendants, are also supposed to have received legacies or pensions. Among others whose names have been mentioned in this connection, are Fitz Green Halleck, the poet, Washington Irving, the historian, and Mr. Bruce the latter for thirty years a clerk in the office of deceased."[133] This article is remarkable because it is the only one mentioning that Astor did indeed sponsor some projects besides his library and the Astorhaus in Walldorf.

Also Parton confirmed, years later in 1865, Astor's sponsoring: "We are told that he did, now and then, bestow small sums in charity, though we have failed to get evidence of a single trustworthy instance of his doing so."[134] And the famous American writer Herman Melville praised the multimillionaire in the preface to his novel *Bartleby, the Scrivener* for his charity and thanked him for the foundation of the Astor Library[135]: "John Jacob Astor; a name which, I admit, I love to repeat, for it hath a rounded and orbicular sound to it."[136]

But obviously no one was interested in reading newspaper articles like that. As the public had to deal for the first time with a person who rose from poverty to immense, incredible wealth, the first conclusion was that Astor must have been a bad man.

Soon after Astor's death, the debate on how to appreciate his life turned into a full-fledged vendetta. The critique was highly biased, and many of the accusations brought forward were later repeated over and over again in most of the later publications on Astor. Independent or neutral voices were rare. Most of the journalists used the controversy around Astor's person to increase their circulation. It was not their intention to give a true and unbiased account but a vivid picture, even if many stories were pure imagination. Date, names, and entire storylines were simply made up by the muckrakers of the time.

In the days following Astor's death, his life was still portrayed with numerous nuances. Whig politician and journalist Horace Greeley[137] praised Astor's hard work and economic finesse. He suggested Astor as a model for the young generation. On the negative side, Greeley did criticize Astor's behavior in the War of 1812, when he bought a great amount of the war bonds issued by the government.[138] Greeley accused Astor of using the war to become even richer. When it came to Astor's real estate, Greeley did not explicitly state any critique, but suggested the taxation of private property and general limits to real estate owned by an individual: "Man of his keen and acute intellect may no longer be permitted to engross millions of acres and [...] town lots."[139] Greeley was certainly not a social revolutionary, but he saw the need for some social reforms. With knowledge of Astor's land speculation, he proposed the taxation of personal income and a restriction of land ownership for individuals.[140]

On March 30, 1848, the *New York True Sun* revealed that the immigrant had left $20 million. Though the public had an image of Astor's being rich, the height of his fortune he left to his family seemed so unreal that it was widely considered unbecoming.

The Accusations of James Gordon Bennett
(New York Herald)

Astor's fortune of 20 million heated further critics. Among them was James Gordon Bennett, the publisher of the *New York Herald*. This newspaper had revolutionized the way news was published during the previous years and reached high publishing numbers with easy-to-read reporting. Bennett was not happy that he was not one of the first to publish the Astor news.

Bennett in particular demanded a return to the old republican ideals. It just seemed unfair that money that was essentially earned from the New Yorkers should not at least in part benefit the community. At the time Astor died nobody had ever left that kind of wealth, simply because no one had ever earned that much. Therefore the fathers of the Constitution, who strongly opposed being taxed by George III, did not even think of introducing a new taxation system in the new republic. Consequently, neither private property nor inheritance was taxed.

With the publication of the testament, the *New York True Sun* seemed to win the upper hand among the New York papers. So Bennett was looking for the better story that promised higher sales.

It was Bennett himself who accused Astor in a lead article of having lived off New York's citizens and made his fortune by speculating in real estate. For this reason the journalist demanded that it would be nothing but fair if New Yorkers actually now profited from his fortune in return, and therefore half of Astor's inheritance should be donated to the city of New York: "If we had been an associate of John Jacob Astor, the first idea that should have put into his head would have been that one-half of his immense property — ten millions at least — belonged to the people of the city of New York. [...] The farms and lots of ground [...] have all increased in value entirely by the industry of the citizens of New York."[141] The *New York Herald*'s opinion on Astor was clear: Donating a public library was not enough to compensate for what New Yorkers had lost in real estate payments to Astor.

James Gordon Bennett seems to have summed up all the negative stereotypes associated with Astor. Bennett wrote: "[Mr. Astor] was industrious in the accumulation of riches, he was likewise very penurious and niggardly in money matters. What he saved he kept and locked up to the day of his death. He would, however, never object to subscribing for charitable objects when solicited to do so; but would almost invariably insist upon having others subscribe first."[142] Furthermore, Bennett accused the multimillionaire of some rather dark characteristics when he wrote:

> He added immensely to his riches by purchases of State stocks, bonds and mortgages etc. in the financial crisis of 1836 and 1837. He was a willing purchaser of mortgages from their needy holders at less than their face; and when they became due he foreclosed them, and purchased the mortgaged property at the ruinous prices which ranged at that time. A few weeks before his death, he sent a hundred thousand dollars to each to Mrs. Landgon and Mrs. Kane, for the purpose, as is supposed, of economy, and to keep them from troubling

his executors.[143] Bennett's words influenced many later researchers and writers.

Nevertheless, one has to consider the context of the article and the fact that Bennett's opinion was extremely biased. Astor and Bennett had never been friends. Twelve years before Bennett wrote this article, they had an encounter which shaped Bennett's view of Astor. Astor sent an employee to subscribe to the *Herald* with cash for one year in advance. Bennett refused to take the money, although it would have meant an important sum for his newly founded newspaper. He disliked the fact that one person could afford to pay so much in advance. Furthermore, he published this episode in the next issue of his newspaper.[144] Taking in account Bennett's harsh way to deal with this subscription leads to the conclusion that he might not have personally liked the millionaire. Nevertheless, journalists like Bennett, animated by personal connections, sympathies and antipathies, constructed Astor's image for later generations.

Can Astor's Work Be Considered as "Labor"?

The fact that Astor's career was controversial in the eyes of his contemporaries was already discussed by the *Daily Herald* in 1848. Its journalists picked up the following lines from the *New York Globe*: "When we reflect, however, that wealth is the product of labor, and that he possessed millions of what others had produced, we need not to be surprised that a diversity of opinion exists whether the life of Mr. Astor has been a benefit or an injury to mankind."[145] Obviously, in the opinion of the *New York Globe*, Astor's business did not count as labor because he was not producing anything.

The *Daily Herald* defended the millionaire by asking if physical work is worth more than the labor of the mind: "But what does that word labor designate — the labor of the mind or the labor of the body, or both? Is it not apparent that the physical labor of the strongest of us, apart from intelligence to guide and inform it, ... is less valuable than the labor of a horse, simply because a horse has greater physical power than a man? ... To say that Mr. Astor possessed millions of what others had produced is a fallacious assertion."[146]

Judging Astor's career from today's perspective, one would certainly declare Astor's work as "labor." But in the mid- and late 19th century a strong debate about labor and the protest of the labor class created a momentum for a certain political view that would later become socialism. Authors who focused on this perspective could never justify an individual career from rags to riches without giving back all riches to the community. Therefore they criticized Astor harshly. He did not fit into their view.

Economic Liberalism vs. Republicanism

Moreover, as soon as the press jumped onto the Astor wagon, the critics of economic liberalism followed. The death of the millionaire was just too good an opportunity to miss as a platform for their own views. They claimed to be surprised and shocked after Astor's real wealth was revealed, and used his example to illustrate the negative effects too much money has on people. They showed that it leads to avarice, greed and egoism without any sense for community. It was important to them that following the pursuit of happiness without any virtue or social responsibility was spreading like a disease in the 1840s. To them it was more than obvious that the once glorious community of early republicans who fought for equal rights had given way to capitalist individuals without any regard for republican values.

Anecdotes, hearsay, vague memories and plainly fictional accounts about Astor suddenly appeared. His contemporaries did not hesitate to use him as the perfect example of anti-republican thoughts. On the occasion of the 29th anniversary of the founding of the Boston Mercantile Library Association in 1849, it was Horace Mann who elaborated on Astor for the public. In his view Astor missed the point of living in a republic because he did not use any of his money for the community or charities. Again Mann publicly criticized the lack of a tax on Astor's inheritance, which meant that not only was Astor in no way bound to return something to the community, but his heirs would inherit the same lack of social responsibility. Therefore, the Astors would continue to be enslaved by the fortune of their forefather if they did not turn to charitable work. Thus, John Jacob Astor had enslaved his subsequent generations, who would have to carry the burden of wealth for the rest of their lives without feeling guilty for that. Mann was sure: Without real work the Astor family would not be able to get real satisfaction in their life.[147]

Mann portrayed Astor as someone who had never done any good deed in his life, never used any of his money for the community, and in no way fulfilled his social and moral duties to his fellow citizens in order to demand a return to the republican values that lay at the heart of the American Revolution. In 1849 Mann published in *A Few Thoughts for a Young Man* an account of this lecture that again focused on the dangers of millionaires for the American nation: "The Millionaire is as dangerous to the welfare of the community in our day, as was the baronial lord of the Middle Ages."[148] Again he used Astor as an example of unpatriotic, unrepublican and un–American behavior that needed to be stopped before it could spread among his contemporaries.

These claims provoked a reaction among the Astor family. Astor's favorite grandson, the publicist and Yale graduate Charles Astor Bristed, countered Mann's claims in *A Letter to Horace Mann*[149] and defended his grandfather. Charles emphasized how the public benefited from the Astor Library in New York and the Astorhaus in Walldorf, Germany, and how his uncle intended both institutions to improve the lives of the citizens in the respective communities by giving them free education and free support in distress, making them independent of both governmental and individual finances. Therefore not only the citizens benefited from Astor's donations, but also the cities themselves, who were not burdened with additional charitable work. Of course Charles also referred to the patriot motives of the establishment of Astoria and the founding of the American Fur Company. It was particularly hard for Charles to see his uncle constantly compared to Stephen Girard, the second richest man of New York and Astor's former business partner in the Second Bank of the United States. Girard was praised for donating almost all of his fortune to charities in Philadelphia and New Orleans, though he obliged these charities to ban any religious influences in their institutions, like the famous Girard College he donated. To Charles this was a clear violation of everything the city of brotherly love and the nation under God stood for. Therefore it was Girard who was in fact antireligious and un–American. Charles admitted that Astor had revised his last will and charities previously selected for donations had ended up receiving nothing in the end. However, he stressed that Astor's lawyers had played a big part in these revisions, and when his uncle was frail and had lost most of his close ones he wanted to make extra sure those who were left behind would not run into any risk of having to fear for their financial security anymore. Astor had not acted against his fellow citizens but in favor of his own family. In the end it was easy for Stephen Girard to leave most of his fortune to the community, because he did not have any children or family that survived him.[150]

Astor's negative image was maybe mostly fueled by James Parton's 15-page biographical sketch in *Harper's New Monthly Magazine* in 1865. Parton cemented Astor's image as a greedy old man. He quoted anecdote after anecdote in order to emphasize how heartless, greedy, and avaricious Astor was. Being widely available and easy to read, Parton's biography was soon the master narrative of Astor's life. Many of the Astor biographers of the generations to come quoted Parton's account without ever questioning his sources or having a look at Astor's papers and letters themselves. Parton was widely known among his contemporaries as an author of historical fiction. Previously he had written about Albert Gallatin, Thomas Jefferson, Benjamin Franklin, Andrew Jackson and Aaron Burr and was a regular contributor to *Harper's*. His Astor was a troubled and conflicted man whose only qualities and achievements were his business-mindedness, the founding of the Astoria outpost and construction work in New York. Parton never claimed Astor had used illegal or unfit measures to reach his goals. However, it was highly disturbing for Parton to see that Astor had experienced so much poverty of his own during his childhood and still did not share with the community, but kept everything for himself; therefore he concluded that Astor had failed as a citizen. To him, Astor was nothing but an immoral, unrepublican and un–American capitalist who left everything to his family and nothing to the community. Parton claimed to base his account on statements he had collected in the 1860s among those who knew Astor. To some, this was hearsay; to others, the authority of these statements was not to be doubted. In any case, along with the anecdotes that were already around, these statements were the foundation of Parton's biography — mostly because they conveniently supported his line of argumentation, not so much because they gave a true picture of Astor's life.

In the wake of the Progressive Era, Astor was again in the spotlight of those criticizing capitalism. Burton Hendrick once more used Astor as negative example, in his article on "The Astor Fortune" in *McClure's Magazine*,[151] the platform for all muckrakers in the early 20th century. The magazine constantly decried the social grievances of the time. However, most of the articles gave an opinion rather than fact-based, well-researched articles, despite the magazine's claims to publish investigative, revealing articles about selected businessmen and companies. Hendrick was a regular author for the *McClure's Magazine* from 1905 to 1913. His goal was to show that Astor had made his fortune using illegal and immoral practices when he developed his New York real estate. To Hendrick there was nothing special in Astor's business skills. He argued that all of Astor's success came down to manipulation and the only reason for Astor to leave his fortune to his family was that he did not want to share it, not because he was concerned about his family's financial security. Hendrick used most of Parton's arguments to suggest all of his statements were carefully researched, but he never followed up on Parton's sources. In Hendrick's portrait Astor was nothing but an average merchant who did not deserve his fortune because he neither worked hard nor achieved anything of importance.

In 1910 Gustavus Myers picked up on the progressive critique on Astor. He published a three-volume *History of Great American Fortunes*, which included a biography of Astor among the biographies of other entrepreneurs.[152] Myers, a socialist, not only criticized Astor, he vilified him. This seemed to be a personal mission for Myers, who was the child of poor German immigrants and never advanced in society but became a member of the New York City Social Reform Club. Myers apparently could not accept that fact that someone with a similar background had had such a different life from his own, and remained an advocate of the poor all his life. He even added more fiction to the Astor story to support the image of the greedy old capitalist: "To the last breath, squeezing arrears out of tenants; his mind focused upon those sordid methods which had long since become a religion to him; contemplating the long list of his possessions with a radiant exaltation; so Astor passed away."[153] Myers never analyzed any source in order to paint a balanced picture of Astor. He claimed that Astor sold alcohol to the Natives all the time, even during his first voyages through New York State. Furthermore, he purported to show Astor's greed by claiming that he had never shared his wealth with anyone.[154]

Astor's critics seemed to be supported by the first edition of James Gallatin's diary *A Great Peacemaker: The Diary of James Gallatin* in 1915. While Albert Gallatin, James Gallatin's father, was a close friend of John Jacob Astor, his son despised Astor wholeheartedly. In James Gallatin's eyes, Astor behaved like a farmer and lacked social competence: "I am not surprised, as Astor was a butcher's son ... came as an immigrant.... He dined here and ate his ice-cream and peas with a knife."[155] James considered himself as part of the international elite who lived according to the French etiquette, and he could not forgive Astor's rustic behavior. In his view Astor did not belong to his social circle despite Astor's love of classical music and literature. Maybe he envied Astor's good relations with his father; maybe James was simply harsh on Astor because he denied him permission to marry his youngest daughter Eliza when they had met in Europe. All in all, James's negative portrait of Astor seems to be based on personal animosities rather than on a general view.[156]

But not just the press painted a negative picture of the millionaire. The old Astor got into the focus of the famous British writer Charles Dickens. Dickens had visited the United States for the first time in 1842 and stayed for some days in Astor's City Hotel. On his trip Dickens had the chance to meet many important people in New York.[157] Manhattan's old and aristocratic society prepared a reception for him. In his honor, a great ball and several evening dinners were organized.[158] At these events, Dickens also met Washington Irving, William Backhouse Astor, and Philip Hone.[159] And he met John Jacob Astor, a 79-year-old millionaire, at a dinner on February 19, 1842. This dinner was held at Astor's first hotel, the City Hotel.[160] As long as Dickens stayed in New York or traveled through the United States, he behaved very politely. But when he returned home, he did not hesitate to announce what he really thought of his trip.[161] Some months after his return to the Old World, Charles Dickens published an article about America. He showed himself strongly impressed by New York's moneyed aristocracy.

Back in England, Dickens criticized the New World with harsh words. Considering all his points, Astor's person and wealth could have inspired Dickens to create the character of Ebenezer Scrooge of his famous work "A Christmas Carol," which he wrote after his return to Europe. This Christmas story is about the old millionaire Ebenezer Scrooge, who turned greedy and cold by gathering a fortune.[162]

The German Perspective

In Germany, however, less was reported about Astor. During his lifetime, some accounts of his success circulated in German newspapers and immigration pamphlets. They used him as a positive example of a German emigrant. From time to time newspapers from Mainz and Bremen reported about Astor, naming him "a philanthropist and benefactor."[163] In general, the German press placed his life and career in a positive light. However, they never analyzed his life as intensely as the Americans did.

In addition to the German press, many contemporary writers praised the emigration of John Jacob Astor to America as an excellent example. Franz Löher presented Astor in his 1847 book as follows: "[Astor] is the greatest businessman in America. The country is grateful for the dedicated comprehensive ways and areas of trade, which he opened, not only in intelligence and stamina, but also in boldness and confidence, he surpassed all Americans."[164] Twenty years after Astor's death German writer Friedrich Kapp dedicated an entire chapter to him in his work about German immigration to the United States. There he described Astor's life and ascension. However, Kapp did not just praise Astor as Löher had before. He must have been aware of the criticism of Astor when he wrote: "You can not love him, one is often tempted to despise him, but you have to admire him anyway."[165]

Nevertheless, the most comprehensive publication of the 19th century in Germany is Horn's book *John Jacob Astor: A Portrait for the Youth*. According to Horn's writing, Astor is an ideal role model which should serve to teach the German youth. He intended to encourage a young readership, by Astor's example, to believe in God and a better future.[166]

In 1868, Franz Otto published a German book called *The Book of Famous Merchants*, in which Julius Engelmann dedicated to Astor a chapter of 20 pages. The New York merchant is listed among other famous merchants like Marco Polo, the Fugger family, and the Medici family. Engelmann praised him as one of the greatest fur traders of all time, founder of Astoria, and one of the developers of a global trade system. However, he overlooked many aspects of Astor's life. Nevertheless, this book might have some influence on those Germans who thought about immigration and a better life in North America.[167]

German historians joined in the chorus of praising Astor. Some took him as an example for great success, like Professor von Langdorff of the University of Heidelberg in 1864, who held a lecture on John Jacob Astor: "Astor

Inside the Astorhaus (Vereinigung Walldorfer Heimatfreunde).

or the right way from misery to glory and happiness."[168] The professor praised Astor's career and used it as an example as Horn had done a decade earlier. But besides these examples, Astor was never in the focus of German academia.

More than 200 years after Astor's birth, the former German chancellor Kurt-Georg Kiesinger remembered the life and success of John Jacob Astor. Together with Gavin Astor, 2nd Baron Astor of Hever, one of the multimillionaire's descendants, who had come from London on behalf of the English branch of the family, he took part in the celebrations of Astor's 200th birthday in Walldorf, Germany.[169] During the celebrations Kiesinger spoke in front of a crowd in Astor's hometown Walldorf. Later he wrote: "I spoke of poor immigrants who came to success, and remind myself that I celebrated [...] together with Lord Astor the 200th Birthday of John Jacob Astor in 1963. [...] The story of this man and his family is amazing."[170]

Kiesinger was not the only one who praised Astor and his extraordinary career. According to Arthur F. Burns, U.S. Ambassador to Germany from 1981 to 1985, John Jacob Astor stood next to Wilhelm von Steuben, Carl Schurz and Henry Kissinger, as he underlined in an address of March 14, 1983. He praised the four personalities and asked: "Where would America be today [...] without the enormous contributions of German immigrants?"[171] To him, John Jacob Astor was as important for the development of the United States as the two politicians and the general fighting in the Revolutionary War.

But as we have already seen, Astor's image in public opinion is by far not as good as these two examples might show. Though he was accepted as a successful businessman during his lifetime, his image changed after his death.

In this way, the quote by Kiesinger shows that the collective memory in Germany celebrates Astor nowadays as a brave and daring German immigrant, who made an enormous career in a foreign country. People in Germany admire John Jacob Astor, during his lifetime as well as nowadays.

Today: Two Opposing Images

The image of the greedy of millionaire is not the only way Astor has been described since the time of his death. But it was the strongest image journalists, writers and the public constructed. Therefore, it become the most widely known image of Astor.

Contrary to the United States, the Europeans remember him as being a much better person. His success as an emigrant, his visions as an entrepreneur, and his braveness to immigrate are in the center of this memory. But nevertheless, the overall opinion of Astor did not change, and those more positive articles defending the millionaire did not have any influence on public opinion.

John Jacob Astor polarized and is still polarizing public opinion. But the debate surrounding him showed how unsure all journalists were. Nobody really knew how to handle the phenomenon in a way that would give a balanced view. It was too easy to be either a fan or a foe. In the end many of the articles, books and other publications about Astor used him to discuss basic ethical questions about liberalism and republican values rather than aiming at a true account of his life. Today the public has a much more differentiated opinion about millionaires—and a great number of lawyers make sure that publications are much less one-sided than in the 1850s. Laws protect individuals and their property, and now journalists risk high fines if they misrepresent facts about modern-day "Astors" like Rupert Murdoch, Donald Trump and Bill Gates. During Astor's days neither the standards of the journalistic profession nor the legal framework banned speculative articles that were published without any proof for the claims made. In order to get a true view of Astor's life it is necessary to look behind the fiction, hearsay and anecdotes and take a close look at the author's motivation and unbiased accounts of the public's reaction to Astor's death.

Therefore, two fundamentally different images of the multimillionaire spread around the public. On the one hand, this was the image of a miserly man whose only interest was the acquisition of wealth, and who declared money to be his religion. On the other hand, an image of a curious and bold economic genius was drawn. Behind his spectacular economic skills was a man who had experienced great poverty during his youth.

The Name Astor

Nowadays the name Astor is associated with a variety of different famous and luxurious hotels all over the world. Those hotels, with the names Astoria, Astor Hotel, and Waldorf-Astoria, actually do not belong to a chain owned by the Astor family, but these names are nonetheless synonyms of luxury and comfort. Considering John Jacob Astor's Astor House and the fact that he wanted to associate his name with opulence, his plan seems to have succeeded.

Nevertheless, the general public opinion is that John Jacob Astor himself founded the Waldorf-Astoria. Nobody knows about his role model, the Astor House. In that way, John Jacob's name is also strongly connected with the New York Waldorf-Astoria. However, without the Astor House, there would not have been a family tradition of owning luxurious hotels, and John Jacob's great-grandson would have never built the Waldorf-Astoria. Thus, the beforementioned example of the Astor Hotel in San Francisco, which opened during the gold rush in 1848–49, is no exception. It was the first of many hotels all

Astor Place, New York (Alexander Emmerich).

over the world that use and bear the name of Astor today. Most of them do not know to what or whom they refer to.

Knowing that Astor wanted to associate his name with success, it is surprising that his company was named the American Fur Company. But due to the fact that Astor asked for governmental support from President Jefferson and that he wanted his enterprise to be a national cause, it seems only logical that the company was not called the Astor Fur Company. If it had had his name, it would have been not as easy for Astor to ask for military support, as he actually did.

Nevertheless, the fur-trading outpost along the Columbia River was finally named "Astoria" in memory of its founder John Jacob Astor. Nowadays, the city still bears that name.

In the 19th century, many other cities and small communities all over the United States of America were named after Astor and his family. One finds cities named Astor or Astoria in the states of Florida, Georgia, Iowa, Kansas, Illinois, Missouri, South Dakota, New York, and of course in Oregon. In New York City, there are several public places that are directly or indirectly

6. New Yorker, 1834–1848

Waldorf-Astoria cigarettes (Alexander Emmerich).

associated with John Jacob Astor and his family: the Astor Place, Astor Boulevard, Astoria in Queens—a neighborhood originally named Astoria for German immigrants.

Although there are many places named after Astor, there is almost no active culture of memory to remember his person or his career besides in Astoria, Oregon, and in Walldorf, Germany. Both cities are sister cities and remembered Astor not only with the bicentennial of Astoria in 2011, but also with the celebration of Astor's 250th birthday in 2013. The city of Walldorf, Germany, and the Walldorf History Club ("Vereinigung Walldorfer Heimatfreunde") remember John Jacob Astor and his family regularly. An important part of this memory remains the museum in the Astorhaus on Johann Jakob Astor Street. Here one can find some items belonging to the Astor family. The Astorhaus is also the home of the Astor Foundation, which the multimillionaire donated in his will to support the sick, children and old people of Walldorf.[172]

Many other items, such as cigarettes, cinemas, hotels, fashion and cosmetic products, use the name Astor. It suggests luxury, elegance and style. None of these products, however, remind us of the life of John Jacob Astor as a skillful businessman or as a previously poor immigrant. The memory is reduced only to the fabulous wealth and the elegant world of the rich.

7

Astor Revisited — Afterthoughts

John Jacob Astor's fortune and wealth were so exceptional in the early republic that his career set a new benchmark for success in North America. It was outstanding to an extent that it provoked his contemporaries to integrate tales of it into the public founding myths of the United States of America. Written and oral accounts, hearsay and true stories, melted together over the years, and Astor found admirers as well as critics.

However, he never kept company with dreamers. He was a man of deeds, relentless in the pursuit of wealth. Since his difficult childhood he was a lonely man and it was hard for him to establish connections with other people or even friendship. The fact that he was always on his own made him a more daring and more intuitive merchant than his contemporaries ever could be. He embraced business techniques and trading strategies far in advance of his time.

Public opinion about Astor was torn. Some admired his business-mindedness, economic foresight, and courage to follow his instincts with all measures he thought reasonable. Others saw in him nothing but a greedy capitalist without any sense of the moral obligations of a republican citizen. Envy was as widespread as true mistrust in Astor's republican attitude. Astor was caught in the middle of the big debate between liberalism and republicanism in the Jacksonian democracy. In the first decades of the 19th century public opinion in the United States was still largely influenced by the ideas of Jeffersonian democracy. The young republic was built on land ownership of individual citizens, as in the early years of the Roman republic. In that way, the landowners were the backbone of the society. In the Jacksonian years the government took a much less property-centered approach to good citizenship. All male citizens, without regard to their property, were to participate actively in governing the United States. Considering the fact that John Jacob Astor was not just an individual landowner, but a landlord who possessed property equivalent to that of thousands of individual landowners, he again does not fit into the picture of republican ideas and ideals.

It is easy to see why a negative image of Astor developed in the 1850s and soon became the dominant master narrative of Astor's biography. However, a close reading of the actual sources in the archives shows a man who simply worked hard to make his way from poverty to luxury, someone who was always enthusiastic about his projects and tried new roads, untaken before him, in order to advance socially, territorially and economically. There is much more to find than a hard-hearted, greedy millionaire.

Astor had excellent business instincts and social skills, invested in projects with a high turnover at a limited risk, and followed his visions without any compromise, but he was not reckless. He diversified his portfolio when this concept was far from being an established entrepreneurial principle. However, this is what he did right from the beginning of his life as businessman. He never relied on a single good, so even failures meant nothing but a small setback or even the opportunity and impulse to turn his engagement to new endeavors. Among his fellow citizens in the United States, he always aimed at being an integrated and valuable member of society. Also he built reliable networks in economy, society and politics and had access to presidents, governors, senators and mayors.

Astor's business practices were a raw model for the American economy of later periods. He focused on sales of high-end consumer goods and real estate development rather than production, keeping his investments low and the turnover high. Unlike economic giants of later decades like Cornelius Vanderbilt and John D. Rockefeller, Astor never invested in metal or mining resources like copper or gold. His broad portfolio of trading goods with tea, silk, furs, instruments and real estate made him virtually independent of economic trends, lacking deliveries due to harvesting problems, or changes of consumer preferences. If the profit of one of the trading goods fell, he simply added a new one.

Astor's success soon became an important pull factor among German immigrants. The myth that spread among Germans was the tale of the poor little boy who became the richest American. The newspapers that targeted those ready to leave Germany were full of stories about Astor's life and fortune. Every time the economic situation in Germany worsened, his example was printed over and over again and motivated many to follow their American dream. After their arrival in New York, many realized that the Astors were truly rich, but also exceptional and not representative of the common immigrant. Most of the newcomers who dreamed of being millionaires were stranded as dishwashers.

When Astor arrived in the United States the country was still so young that the opportunities were truly unlimited. Astor developed innovative business ideas and had hardly any competitors. He was not a thinker or economic theoretician who formulated his business strategies and published them.

Growing up helping his father in his business, Astor had a hands-on approach to business. His attitude was, "Don't talk about it, just do it." His most important skills were to observe, evaluate and improve. Therefore he never developed ideas from scratch but adapted and perfected existing business models. As soon as he saw others succeed in a certain industry, he took a closer look; and when he saw a niche to optimize the business, he acted upon his impulse, made it his own business, and thrived to dominate the market.

Astor traded fur with the Native Americans at a time when the economy of the former colonies was still mostly agricultural. He sold luxury items when New York's elite had just begun to spend on recreational activities again and the years of boycott during the War of 1812 had left a lack of high-end products. So the demand for them was increasing and Astor could satisfy it. When merchants were happily trading tobacco within the United States, he traded overseas with Old Europe and the new markets in Asia; and when the United States slowly expanded west, he did not wait for the infrastructure to be established, but was the first to actually send ships to build the first American city on the Pacific Coast. He was the one who bought real estate beyond the New York city limits when no one else believed the city would ever grow so far north as to ever encompass these regions, and he rented or sold them when more and more immigrants poured into New York. Astor did not cause any of these developments. It is safe to say he was responsible neither for the westward expansion that led to the establishment of the states west of the Appalachians, nor for the economic crises in Europe that pushed so many away from their home on a search for a better life.

What Astor did was to make the most of what he observed as trends of his time and to have an excellent business understanding as to which directions the developments would likely be heading. Astor advanced on the social ladder in a time when the United States moved from the aftermath of the American Revolution to the early beginnings of the industrial revolution. He constantly adapted to the economic changes of this phase, and in some cases he even caused these changes. Probably his most important skill was to know when it was enough and when to let a certain business go.

His decision to leave Germany was almost entirely economically motivated, which is one of the few similarities between him and his fellow German immigrants. While most of the immigrants in the 1840s came straight from their home countries and with little or no knowledge of English, Astor had already acquired English in London, where he spent the first years after he had left Germany with his brother George, who had established a company that traded and produced high-end instruments. Also many of the immigrants had been farmers and low-level craftsmen. Astor had learned much about trading, not only with his brother in London but also with his father in Walldorf. Trade was his talent. So Astor was prepared for the life in the United States in many more ways than his fellow immigrants. He came with a business plan and even a startup selection of goods and an established supply chain with his brother George. London was the decisive milestone in Astor's acculturation process. With the help of his brother, he learned English and how to do business and administration in English. In London he also found his way in a metropolis and used his social skills to make new friends.

Marrying Sarah Todd was another factor that accelerated Astor's integration and acculturation in New York. English became the first language in the family and Astor had easy access to New York's established elite through his wife's family. Sarah was related to merchants, ship owners and other members of the commercial elite of New York. These were the networks Astor could use his business skills in order to lay a foundation for his future fortune. His children were not treated as children of a first-generation immigrant, but as children of an American couple.

When Astor was a senior citizen, and the numbers of German immigrants speedily increased due to the economic crises in Europe, he engaged in establishing an office to support the new arrivals. He became president of the German Society of the City of New York and provided help for the immigrants to help themselves. Instead of providing financial help only, he followed again a hands-on approach to support those who came from Germany to North America — some of them might have read about his success in migration magazines and followed his example. Just donating money to the new immigrants would lead them to spend it and ask for more. The immigrants needed more than a handout. They needed support and information for all circumstances, because the reality in North America was different from what they might have read in Germany. Additionally, they had to work hard to overcome the first obstacles in the new country. He led the German Society for four years and made a donation in his will, so that a permanent office for German immigrants could be established.

New York and Astor's home Walldorf did not really have much in common. The American commercial center rapidly recovered from the War of Independence. Astor was able to follow the rise of the city from the partially destroyed battleground to the international commercial metropolis. Right from the beginning of his career as a businessman, Astor chose New York's rich elite as the target group of his goods. This had two advantages: first, he developed a customer base that could afford his trading goods. Second, he gained access to the most important social, economic, and political circles of his new home. Due to his marriage with Sarah Todd, his economic and private networks overlapped, and he could make use of the synergies.

When more and more stocks were traded in New York, Astor started trading in stocks in 1792. At the trading places like the Tontine Coffee House he met with his fellow merchants and could further expand his networks. Probably the most important network of Astor's early years in New York was his Freemason's lodge, Holland Lodge No. 8, that belonged to the New York Great Lodge. Here he met his close friend DeWitt Clinton, the future mayor of New York.

John Jacob Astor was not only an excellent networker, he also provided social spaces where networks could meet and relationships be established. He had soon realized that in order to optimize the information he could get, he needed to be in the middle of the action. Therefore he bought the Park Theatre on Broadway, where the rich New Yorkers met for a play, or rather the businessmen let their wives watch a play while they retreated to the smoking room to do business. Being the owner of the place also secured Astor the prime spot in the theater. In 1828 he added the City Hotel to his portfolio of hot spots, and in 1836 he opened his own hotel on Broadway, the Astor House, which was the first in a long series of hotels owned by the Astor family. It was so luxurious and equipped with state-of-the-art technique that the name Astor was soon synonymous with indescribable luxury. This trend was even enforced when Astor donated the Astor Library, New York's first public library.

But besides being a good networker, Astor had difficulties in establishing close relationships with people. It must have taken him a long time until he trusted someone. The early losses of his life, the death of his mother and the emigration of his brothers, formed his character significantly. Shaped by his experiences, he was never so emotionally bound to any group of persons that he could not leave them behind. In these terms it was easier for him than for an average immigrant to leave Walldorf behind. He cut the connection, and was finally so distant that he may have not even visited Walldorf on one of his European trips. Again, after finding a new home and life in London, it was easy for him to leave that life behind him when he immigrated to the United States. The same pattern can be observed in the fact that he could leave his fur trade business and the American Fur Company without any regret almost overnight and engage himself into new businesses. Moreover, he was also able to spend most of the time between 1819 and 1834 in Europe, far away from his wife and children. All those examples show that Astor was not a man of strong connections to other people surrounding him.

Astor was a pre-industrial merchant using all the trading possibilities of his time. He could make his enormous profit through the free market, and he guided many other traders, merchants, and immigrants by his vision. In many ways John Jacob Astor can be considered the Founding Father of the American business model of the United States of America — no matter in which light one sees him.

Chapter Notes

Preface
1. He was baptized with the name of Johann Jakob. During his years in London, from about 1780 to 1783, he anglicized his first names to John Jacob. See chapter 2.

Introduction
1. Allan Nevins, ed., *The Diary of Philip Hone, 1828–1851* (New York: Dodd, Mead and Company, 1969), 847; *New York Tribune*, March 30, 1848.
2. http://www.nytimes.com/ref/business/20070715_GILDED_GRAPHIC.html, last visited on May 27, 2012.
3. The term "American Dream" was first introduced by James T. Adams in 1931. James T. Adams, *The Epic of America* (New York: Boston, Little, Brown, 1931). A critical analysis of the American Dream can be found in Jim Cullen, *The American Dream: A Short History of an Idea that Shaped a Nation* (New York: Oxford University Press, 2003).
4. Ludwig M. Goldberger, *Das Land der unbegrenzten Möglichkeiten. Beobachtungen über das Wirtschaftsleben der Vereinigten Staaten von Amerika* (Berlin: F. Fontane, 1903), 17.
5. See "Millionaire," in *Oxford English Dictionary*, vol. 6 (Oxford: Oxford University Press 1933), 450. In 1845 Peter G. Stuyvesant and John Jacob Astor were the only two inhabitants of New York City who had possessed over a million dollars. See Edwin G. Burrows and Mike Wallace, *Gotham: A History of New York City to 1898* (New York: Oxford University Press, 1999), 712.
6. Louie Crew, "Charles Dickens as a Critic of the United States," *Midwest Quarterly* 16.1 (1974): 42.
7. Nevins, *Hone*, 589.
8. *New York True Sun*, March 30, 1848.
9. *New York Tribune*, April 3, 1848.
10. *New York True Sun*, March 30, 1848.
11. *New York Herald*, March 31, 1848.
12. Ibid.
13. Horace Mann, *A Few Thoughts for a Young Man* (Syracuse: Mills, Hopkins, 1853), 61.
14. James Gordon Bennett was born at Newmill in Banffshire, Scotland, in 1795. He immigrated to the United States when he was 24 years old. At first he worked as a teacher; later he became a journalist writing for different newspapers and publishing houses. Finally, he decided to found his own newspaper and to publish his stories at his own risk. The result was the *New York Herald*, founded May 6, 1835. After the first period, he reduced the price for his newspaper, creating the first one-cent newspaper. Through the introduction of new news categories like finance and economics, articles about personal gossip and scandal, he made the paper a great commercial success. Furthermore, he was the first to introduce many of the methods of the modern American reporter. See Oliver Carlson, *The Man Who Made News: James Gordon Bennett* (New York: Duell, Sloan and Pearce, 1942); Bernard A. Weisberger, *The American Newspaperman* (Chicago: University of Chicago Press, 1961).
15. Horace Mann, the "Father of American Education," was born in Franklin, Massachusetts, in 1796. As a politician he served in the Massachusetts House of Representatives from 1827 to 1833, then in the state Senate from 1834 up to 1837. In 1848, he was elected to the United State House of Representatives. He argued that a universal and general education was the best method to transform the children of the nation into disciplined, republican citizens. For that argument he won a widespread recognition among modernizers and reformers. Furthermore, he supported the idea of the emancipation of slaves. See Jonathan Messerli, *Horace Mann: A Biography* (New York: Alfred A. Knopf, Inc., 1972).
16. Horatio Alger Jr. was born in Revere, Massachusetts, on January 13, 1832. He became a well-known 19th-century novelist, writing

over 100 novels telling the story of people who rose from "rags to riches." His tales always told the story of young men raising themselves from poverty through hard work, braveness, and commitment. See Gary Scharnhorst, *The Lost Life of Horatio Alger Jr.* (Bloomington: Indiana University Press, 1985).

17. See Susan Schulten, "Success," in *Encyclopedia of American Cultural and Intellectual History*, ed. by Mary K. Cayton and Peter W. Williams, vol. 3 (New York: Scribner, 2001), 3–7.

18. Max Weber, *Die protestantische Ethik und der Geist des Kapitalismus* (Bodenheim: Westdeutscher Verlag, 1993).

19. The term "self-made man" was introduced by Henry Clay in a speech to the U.S. senate. See Schulten, *Success*, 5.

20. Weber, *Die Protestantische Ethik*, 14.

21. Weber, *Die Protestantische Ethik*, 14.

22. Popular works still bridge from today's business leaders to John Jacob Astor. He is the oldest and first example of the Horatio Alger myth of someone going from "rags to riches" or "from a dishwasher to a millionaire." For example, see W.H. Brands, *Masters of Enterprises: Giants of American Business from John Jacob Astor and J.P. Morgan to Bill Gates and Oprah Winfrey* (New York: Free Press, 1999); Meade Minnigerode, Certain Rich Men: Stephen Girard, John Jacob Astor, Jay Cooke, Daniel Drew, Cornelius Vanderbilt, Jay Gould, Jim Fisk (New York: G.P. Putnam's Sons, 1927); Egon Jameson, *Millionen aus dem Nichts* (Stuttgart: Hallwag, 1967).

23. A broad overview of German migration to the United States can be found in Kathleen N. Conzen, "Germans," in *Harvard Encyclopedia of American Ethnic Groups*, edited by Stephan Thernstrom (Cambridge: Harvard University Press, 1980), 405–425.

24. Joyce O. Appleby, *Capitalism and a New Social Order* (New York: New York University Press, 1984); Joyce O. Appleby, *Liberalism and Republicanism in the Historical Imagination* (Cambridge: Harvard University Press, 1992); Bernard Bailyn, ed., *The Ideological Origins of the American Revolution* (Cambridge: Harvard University Press, 1982); Lawrence F. Kohl, "Republicanism Meets the Market Revolution," *Reviews in American History* 19 (1991): 188–193; John G.A. Pocock, *The Machiavellian Moment: Florentine Political Thought and the Atlantic Republican Tradition* (Princeton: Princeton University Press, 1975); Sean Wilentz, "On Class and Politics in Jacksonian America," in *The Promise of American History: Progress and Prospects*, ed. by Stanley I. Kutler and Stanley N. Katz (Baltimore: Johns Hopkins University Press, 1982), 45–63; Sean Wilentz, "Society, Politics, and the Market Revolution, 1815–1848," in *The New American History* (1990): 51–71; Gordon S. Wood, "The Significance of the Early Republic," in *Major Problems in the Early Republic*, edited by Sean Wilentz (Lexington: University of Kentucky Press, 1992), 2–8; Gordon S. Wood, *The Creation of the American Republic, 1776–1787* (Chapel Hill: University of North Carolina Press, 1969); Gordon S. Wood, *Radicalism of the American Revolution* (New York: Vintage, 1993).

25. Francis D. Cogliano, *Revolutionary America, 1763–1815: A Political History* (New York: Routledge, 2000).

26. Wood, *Significance of the Early Republic*, 7.

27. Over the past two decades the first half of the 19th century has been reevaluated. Especially the period between the end of the War of 1812 and the end of the second two-party system is the focus of new research and analyses. This time can be considered as a market revolution preparing the United States for the industrial revolution and bringing many changes to economy, business, trade and infrastructure. See Charles Sellers, *The Market Revolution: Jacksonian America, 1815–1846* (Oxford: Oxford University Press, 1991); Paul Nolte, "Der Durchbruch der amerikanischen Marktgesellschaft. Wirtschaft, Politik und Kultur in der Frühen Republik 1790–1850," in *Historische Zeitschrift* 259 (1994): 695–716.

28. See Chapter 4, Founding the American Fur Company.

29. The model of acculturation has been studied since 1918. It has been used as a theory within many fields such as psychology, anthropology, history, and cultural studies in general, as well as sociology. Since the introduction of the term there have been numerous theories and definitions of acculturation. Despite definitions and evidence that acculturation entails a two-way process of change and exchange, research has primarily focused on the adjustments and adaptations made by minorities such as immigrants and refugees, as well as indigenous peoples in exchange with their dominant majority or host culture. More recent research focuses on different steps of acculturation and how variations in acculturation affect how well individuals adapt to their host culture. See Milton Gordon, *Assimilation in American Life: The Role of Race, Religion and National Origins* (New York: Oxford University Press, 1964).

30. Gordon, *Assimilation*, 71.

31. See Friedhelm Guttandin, *Einführung in die Protestantische Ethik* (Opladen: Westdeutscher Verlag), 22.

32. Kenneth Wiggins Porter, *John Jacob*

Astor: Business Man, 2 vols. (New York: Russel & Russel 1966); John D. Haeger, *John Jacob Astor: Business and Finance in the Early Republic* (Detroit: Wayne State University Press, 1991).

33. Bourdieu, Pierre, *Die verborgenen Mechanismen der Macht. Schriften zu Politik und Kultur* (Hamburg: VSA, 1992), 50–52.
34. Bourdieu, *Die verborgenen Mechanismen*, 63.
35. Bourdieu, *Sozialer Sinn: Kritik der theoretischen Vernunft* (Frankfurt am Main: Suhrkamp, 1987), 205–207.
36. Bourdieu, *Die verborgenen Mechanismen*, 77.
37. Elizabeth Colwill, "Subjectivity, Self-Representation and the Revealing Twitches of Biography," *French Historical Studies* 24 (2001): 423.
38. Christian Klein, ed., *Grundlagen der Biographik* (Stuttgart: J.B. Metzler Verlag, 2002), 8.
39. Hans-Ulrich Wehler, *Bismarck und der Imperialismus* (Köln: Kiepenhauer & Witsch, 1969).
40. Pathography is considered a type of biographical approach which has as a main purpose the "deconstruction" of the myth or public image of the subject, through a focus on personal or social failures.
41. Michiko Kakutani, "A Biographer Who Claims A License to Blur Reality," *New York Times*, October 2, 1999.
42. Gustavus Myers, *Geschichte der Großen Amerikanischen Vermögen*, 2 vols. (Berlin: S. Fischer Verlag, 1916); Elizabeth Louisa Gebhard, *The Life and Ventures of the Original John Jacob Astor* (New York: Bryan Pub, 1915); Arthur D. Howden-Smith, *John Jacob Astor: Landlord of New York* (New York: Blue Ribbon Books, 1929); John U. Terrell, *Furs by Astor* (New York: Morrow, 1963); Lucy Kavaler, *The Astors: An American Legend* (New York: Dodd Mead, 1968); Virginia Cowles, *The Astors* (New York: Knopf, 1979); John D. Gates, *The Astor Family: A Unique Exploration of One of America's First Families* (Garden City: Doubleday, 1981); Derek Wilson, *The Astors 1763–1992: Landscapes with Millionaires* (London: Weidenfield and Nicolson, 1993); Axel Madsen, *John Jacob Astor: America's First Multimillionaire* (New York: John Wiley & Sons, 2001).
43. David Jacques, "John Jacob Astor: A Mercantile Biography," in *Hunt's Merchant Magazine* 11 (1844): 153–159.
44. James Parton, *Life of John Jacob Astor* (New York: American News Company, 1865). The same text was also published in James Parton, "John Jacob Astor," in *Harper's New Monthly Magazine* 30 (December 1864): 308–323. Three years later Parton published the same text in a small book. See James Parton, *Famous Americans of Recent Times* (Boston: Ticknor and Fields, 1867).
45. Friedrich Kapp, *Geschichte der Deutschen Einwanderung in Amerika* (Leipzig: Quandt & Händel, 1868); Friedrich Kapp, *Die Deutschen im Staate New York während des 18. Jahrhunderts* (New York: E. Steiger, 1884); Gustav Körner, *Das deutsche Element in den Vereinigten Staaten von Nordamerika, 1818–1848* (Cincinnati: Verlag Wilde, 1880); Franz von Löher, *Geschichte und Zustände der Deutschen in Amerika* (Cincinnatti: Verlag von Eggers und Wulkop, 1847); Wolfgang Menzel, *Geschichte der Deutschen bis auf die neuesten Tage*, vol. 5 (Stuttgart: Cotta, 1856).
46. Besides Astor, the socialist Myers accused Jay Gould, J.P. Morgan, Cornelius Vanderbilt and several other American tycoons. For Myers, only Andrew Carnegie was an example of philanthropy. See Myers, *Amerikanische Vermögen*, vol. 2, 677.
47. Gebhard, *The Life and Ventures*. After Myers's portrayal of Astor as a bad and greedy man, the German-American writer, Elizabeth Gebhard, tried to write a positive story of Astor's life.
48. George Bryce, *The Remarkable History of the Hudson's Bay Company. Including that of the French Traders of North-Western Canada and of the North-West, XY, and Astor Fur Companies* (London: S. Low, Marston & Company, 1910).
49. See Howden-Smith, *Landlord of New York*. He argued that Astor's German heritage was the reason for his greed and immorality. Moreover, he used popular myths about Astor and took them for granted without researching their origin.
50. Porter, *Business Man*.
51. The second volume concentrates almost completely on Astor's business practices as well as the policy of the American Fur Company.
52. Calvin I. Hoy, *John Jacob Astor: An Unwritten Chapter* (Boston: Meader Publishing Company, 1936).
53. Cowles, *The Astors*; Gates, *The Astor Family*; Kavaler, *An American Legend*; Wilson, *Landscapes with Millionaires*.
54. German original: "Pionier der gewinn—und machtstrebenden Leidenschaft völlig entfesselter Individualität." See F. Schilling, "Johann Jakob Astor," in *Handwörterbuch des Grenz—und Auslanddeutschtums*, vol. 1 (Breslau: n.p., 1933), 161–163.
55. German original: "Der deutsche Betrachter [schaut] mit Schrecken und Trauer auf das Leben dieses Mannes, who keine Verbindung zwischen dem Geist des deutschen Volkes und diesem Manne." Ibid.

56. Emil Bode, *Deutsche Kämpfer in Nordamerika* (Leipzig: n.p., ca. 1934), 24.
57. Bode, *Deutsche Kämpfer*, 24.
58. Haeger, *Business and Finance*.
59. Madsen, *First Multimillionaire*.
60. Ronda, *Astoria & Empire*.
61. *John Jacob Astor Business Records*. Baker Library Historical Collections. Harvard Business School, vols. 1–48.
62. *John Jacob Astor Letters*. Western Americana Collection, Beinecke Rare Book and Manuscript Library, Yale University; *Robert Stuart Papers*. Western Americana Collection, Beinecke Rare Book and Manuscript Library, Yale University.
63. *Astor Family Papers, 1792–1916*. The New York Public Library.
64. *The Astor Family Papers, 1807–1919*, The New York Historical Society; William Kelby, *Notes on the Astor Family*, The New York Historical Society; *The Churchbook of the German Reformed Church of the City of New York*, The New York Historical Society.
65. *Minutes of the German Society, New York 1784–1853*, German Society of the City of New York; *Protocols of the German Society of the City of New York*, German Society of the City of New York.
66. *John Jacob Astor: Business Letters, 1813–1828*, edited by Valery Chaldize (Benson: Chaldize Publications, 1991).
67. Daniel Preston, et. al., eds., *The Papers of James Monroe* (Westport: Greenwood Press, 2003).
68. J.C.A. Stagg, ed., *The Papers of James Madison Digital Edition* (Charlottesville: University of Virginia Press, Rotunda, 2010).
69. Julian P. Boyd et al., eds., *The Papers of Thomas Jefferson* (Princeton: Princeton University Press, 1950).
70. James F. Hopkins et al., eds., *The Papers of Henry Clay* (Lexington: University of Kentucky Press, 1959–1992).
71. Holly C. Shulman, ed., The Papers of Dolley Madison Digital Edition (Charlottesville: University of Virginia Press, Rotunda, 2008).
72. Washington Irving, *Astoria; or, Anecdotes of an Enterprise Beyond the Rocky Mountains*. 2 vols. (Philadelphia: J.B. Lippincott, 1961).
73. Moses Yale Beach, *The Wealth and Biography of the Wealthy Citizens of the City of New York* (New York: Sun Office, 1846); Philip A. Rollins, ed., *The Discovery of the Oregon Trail: Robert Stuart's Narratives of His Overland Trip Eastward from Astoria in 1812–13* (Lincoln: University of Nebraska Press, 1995).
74. Nevins, *Hone*.
75. James Bryce, ed., *A Great Peacemaker: The Diary of James Gallatin, Secretary to Albert Gallatin 1813–1827* (New York: Charles Scribner's Sons, 1915).
76. William Waldorf Astor, "John Jacob Astor," *Pall Mall Magazine* (June 1899): 171–184.
77. Robert Baird, ed., *Memoir of Mrs. Eliza Astor Rumpff, and of the Duchess de Broglie, Daughter of Madame de Stael* (New York: American Tract Society, n.d.).
78. Joseph A. Scoville, *The Old Merchants of New York City*, 5 vols. (New York: Carlton, 1870).
79. Carl W.F.L. Stocker, *Chronik von Walldorf* (Bruchsal: n.p., 1888).
80. Wilhelm Oertel von Horn, *Johann Jakob Astor* (Wiesbaden: Kreidel und Niedner, 1854). For his 1862 work on Astor, James Parton used a German source, which may have been Horn's work: "The principal source is a small biography of Astor published in Germany about ten years ago, written by a native of Baden, a Lutheran clergyman, who gathered his material in Waldorf": see Parton, *Life of John Jacob Astor*, 24.
81. Horn mentions Valentin Christoph Kamm; see Horn, *Astor*, 9. Kamm was born on January 11, 1763, in Walldorf and died on December 3, 1852. See *Walldorf Church Book*, no. 2, Archiv der evangelischen Landeskirche in Baden, 79. Valentin Kamm and John Jacob Astor celebrated the ritual of confirmation together in 1777. See *Walldorf Church Book*, no. 2, 215.
82. *Walldorf Church Book*, no. 2, June 27, 1700 to January 1, 1788, Archiv der evangelischen Landeskirche in Baden; *Walldorf Church Book*, no. 3, 1789 to 1818, Archiv der evangelischen Landeskirche in Baden.

Chapter 1

1. Every biography of Astor claimed that Walldorf was part of the Duchy of Baden. Because Baden had an important school reform, some historians believed Astor was well educated. In fact, Walldorf belonged to the old Palatinate.
2. About Prince Elector Karl Theodor, see Günther Ebersold, *Rokoko, Reform und Revolution: Ein politisches Lebensbild des Kurfürsten Karl Theodor* (Frankfurt am Main: Lang, 1985); Hans Rall, *Kurfürst Karl Theodor: Regierender Herr in sieben Ländern* (Mannheim: Bibliographisches Institut, 1993).
3. See Rall, *Karl Theodor*, 117ff.
4. Karl Moersch, *Geschichte der Pfalz: Von den Anfängen bis ins 19. Jahrhundert* (Bad Dürkheim: Pfälzische Verlagsanstalt, 1987), 427.

5. Meinrad Schaab, *Geschichte der Kurpfalz*, vol. 2 (Stuttgart: Kohlhammer, 1992), 181–210.
6. Ibid., 181.
7. Friedrich-Wilhelm Henning, *Landwirtschaft und ländliche Gesellschaft in Deutschland, 1750–1976* (Paderborn: Schöningh, 1978), 313; Petrus Han, *Soziologie der Migration* (Stuttgart: UTB, 2000), 19.
8. See Hans-Jürgen Grabbe, *Vor der großen Flut* (Stuttgart: Steiner Verlag, 2001).
9. Ibid., 220.
10. Schaab, *Geschichte der Kurpfalz*, vol. 2, 97.
11. *Walldorf Church Book*, no. 2, 80.
12. Johann Jacob Astor the elder was born on July 7, 1724, in Walldorf. See *Walldorf Church Book*, no. 2, 28.
13. Horn, *Astor*, 7.
14. See Generallandesarchiv Karlsruhe 229/109 619–229/109 761.
15. *Walldorf Church Book*, no. 2, 103.
16. Generallandesarchiv Karlsruhe 229/109 619.
17. *Walldorf Church Book*, no. 2, 62. Peter Astor died in 1752 at the age of two years. See *Walldorf Church Book*, no. 2, 146.
18. *Walldorf Church Book*, no. 2, 80.
19. *Walldorf Church Book*, no. 2, 187.
20. See Thomas Nipperdey, *Deutsche Geschichte: Bürgerwelt und Starker Staat* (München: C.H. Beck, 1983), 116.
21. Ibid.
22. Klaus Ronellenfitsch, *Walldorfer Familienbuch 1650–1900* (Walldorf: Beltz, 1993), 20.
23. Ibid.
24. Horn, *Astor*, 17.
25. Howden-Smith, *Landlord of New York*, 14.
26. Thomas F. DeVoe, *The Market Book. Containing a Historical Account of the Public Markets in the Cities of New York, Boston, Philadelphia and Brooklyn* (New York: Burt Frankling, 1862), 185.
27. Frank Kidson and H.G. Farmer, "Astor & Co.," in *The New Grove Dictionary of Music and Musicians*, edited by Stanley Sadie (London: Macmillan), 662.
28. Archive of the Moravian Community, Neuwied.
29. Scoville, *The Old Merchants*, vol. 1, 165.
30. Scoville, *The Old Merchants*, vol. 1, 165.
31. Gebhard, *The Life and Ventures*, 44.
32. Stocker, *Chronik von Walldorf*, 13.
33. Schaab, *Geschichte der Kurpfalz*, 232.
34. See Madsen, *First Multimillionaire*, 13; Porter, *Business Man*, vol. 1, 4ff.
35. See Nipperdey, *Deutsche Geschichte*, 11; Schaab, *Geschichte der Kurpfalz*, vol. 2, 250ff
36. Generallandesarchiv Karlsruhe 229/109646.
37. Stocker, *Chronik von Walldorf*, 42.
38. Generallandesarchiv Karlsruhe 229/109646.
39. Stocker, *Chronik von Walldorf*, 40.
40. Horn, *Astor*, 11.
41. *Walldorf Church Book*, no. 2, 215.
42. Horn, *Astor*, 12.
43. Gebhardt, *The Life and Ventures*, 21.
44. See Han, *Soziologie*, 13–14; J.A. Jackson, *Migration* (London: Longman, 1986), 13–16.
45. *Walldorf Church Book*, no. 2, 187.
46. Horn, *Astor*, 20.
47. Horn, *Astor*, 12. Translated from the German original quotation: "Horn bezog sich auf die Aussagen von Zeitzeugen und suggerierte somit, dass sich Briefe der Brüder in Walldorf befinden. Diese Briefe sind allerdings nicht überliefert. Weder im Archiv der Stadt Walldorf noch im Heimatmuseum im Astorhaus sind derartige Archivalien erhalten."
48. Horn, *Astor*, 12.
49. DeVoe, *The Market Book*, 185.
50. Horn, *Astor*, 21ff.
51. *New York True Sun*, March 30, 1848.
52. Parton, *John Jacob Astor*, 24.
53. Ibid.
54. Translated from the German original quotation: "Als Astor im Begriff stand, in die Ferne zu gehen, beschloß er immer rechtschaffen auf fleißig zu sein und insbesondere niemals zu spielen," in Wilhelm Stricker, *Germania: Archiv zur Kenntniß des deutschen Elements in allen Ländern der Erde* (Frankfurt am Main: H.L. Brönner, 1847), 468.

Chapter 2

1. E.A. Wrigley, "A Simple Model of London's Importance in Changing English Society and Economy 1650–1750," in *Past and Present* 37 (1967): 44.
2. Stephen Inwood, *A History of London* (London: Macmillan, 1998), 317.
3. Peter Ackroyd, *London:Die Biographie* (München: Albrecht Knaus Verlag, 2002), 318.
4. Horn, *Astor*, 20.
5. Ibid.
6. Joseph G. Cogswell, "The Astor Library and its Founder," in *United States Magazine of Science, Art, Manufactures, Agriculture, Commerce and Trade* 2 (1855): 137ff
7. "John Jacob Astor," in *The Belfast News-Letter*, March 1, 1890.
8. Walldorf Church Book, no. 2.
9. Kidson and Farmer, *Astor & Co.*, 662.
10. Cogliano, *Revolutionary America*, 85.
11. See Richard B. Morris, *The Peacemakers: The Great Powers and American Independence* (New York: Harper & Row, 1965).

12. Cogliano, *Revolutionary America*, 85.
13. Letter of John Jacob Astor to Washington Irving, November 25, 1836, in Porter, *Business Man*, vol. 1, 351.
14. "Founder of the Astor Fortune Twice Escapes Shipwrecked," *New York Times*, April 21, 1912.
15. Ibid.
16. *Scioto Gazette*, April 19, 1848; Beach, *Wealthy Citizens*, 4; Parton, "John Jacob Astor," 311.
17. Gebhard, *The Life and Ventures*, 45.
18. Jacques, *Mercantile Biography*, 155.
19. Parton, *John Jacob Astor*, 30.
20. Letter of John Jacob Astor to Washington Irving, November 25, 1836, in Porter, *Business Man*, vol. 2, 351.
21. A good overview of the legend is provided by Willis L. Brown, *The Legend of John Nickolas Emerick*, http://freepages.genealogy.rootsweb.ancestry.com/~dlemrick/JohnNick.htm, last visited on July 14, 2012, and http://freepages.genealogy.rootsweb.ancestry.com/~dlemrick/JNickfacts.htm, last visited on July 14, 2012.
22. *New York Times*, May 28, 1928.
23. Letter of John Jacob Astor to Washington Irving, November 25, 1836.
24. "Founder of the Astor Fortune Twice Escapes Shipwrecked," *New York Times*, April 21, 1912.
25. Letter of John Jacob Astor to Washington Irving, November 25, 1836.
26. Ibid.

Chapter 3

1. Burrows and Wallace, *Gotham*, 270.
2. Burrows and Wallace, *Gotham*, 266.
3. Agnes Bretting, "Deutsche Siedlungsviertel in New York City, 1830–1930," in *Von Deutschland nach Amerika: Zur Sozialgeschichte der Auswanderung im 19. und 20. Jahrhundert*, edited by Günter Moltmann (Stuttgart: Steiner Verlag, 1992), 59.
4. Alexander Emmerich, "The German Society of the City of New York," in *Germany and the Americas: Culture, History and Politics*, edited by Thomas Adam and Will Kaufman (Santa Barbara: ABC Clio, 2005), 430–432; Klaus Wust, *Guardians on the Hudson: The German Society of the City of New York, 1784–1984* (New York: The Society, 1984).
5. See Richard Brookisher, *Alexander Hamilton: American* (New York: Schuster & Schuster, 1999).
6. Stanley Elkins and Eric McKitrick, *The Age of Federalism* (New York: Oxford University Press, 1995); Joyce O. Appleby, *Thomas Jefferson* (New York: Times Books, 2003).
7. Burrows and Wallace, *Gotham*, 304.
8. Axel Madsen puts Astor's arrival on July 17, 1784, his 21st birthday. See Madsen, *First Mulimillionaire*, 26. But this account cannot be considered trustworthy.
9. Letter of John Jacob Astor to Washington Irving, November 25, 1836.
10. See DeVoe, *The Market Book*, 159.
11. DeVoe, *The Market Book*, 159.
12. Ibid., 184.
13. *The New York Directory and Register for the Year 1789*, 7.
14. *The New York Directory and Register for the Year 1793*, 6.
15. Scoville, *The Old Merchants*, vol. 1, 165ff, 285ff.
16. *Churchbook of the German Reformed Church of New York* (New York Historical Society).
17. *Minutes of the German Society, New York 1784–1853* (German Society of the City of New York).
18. Ibid.
19. Ibid.
20. See Gordon, *Assimilation*, 51ff.
21. Gebhard, *The Life and Ventures*, 58.
22. Ibid., 58.
23. William Armstrong, *The Aristocracy of New York*, (New York: New York Publishing, 1848), 3.
24. Scoville, *The Old Merchants*, vol. 2, 125; vol. 4, 235.
25. *New York Packet*, September 20, 1784.
26. *New York Packet*, January 27, 1785.
27. "John Jacob Astor," in *The Belfast News-Letter*, March 1, 1890.
28. Ibid.
29. *New York Genealogical and Biographical Record*, vol. 22 (New York: New York Genealogical and Biographical Society, 1891), 118; Scoville, *The Old Merchants*, vol. 3, 308ff.
30. Porter, *Business Man*, vol. 2, 1034.
31. To read more about the Astor family, see Chapter 3, Family and Social Networks.
32. Stocker, *Chronik von Walldorf*, 14. Original version: "Mit einer Amerikanerin verheiratet und selbst so Amerikaner geworden."
33. *New York Genealogical and Biographical Record*, 118; Scoville, *The Old Merchants*, vol. 3, 308ff.
34. Scoville, *The Old Merchants*, vol. 1, 421.
35. Kelby, *Notes on the Astor Family*.
36. *New York Packet*, May 22, 1786.
37. *New York Packet*, July 27, 1787.
38. See Bob Pierce and Larry Ashley, eds., *Pierce Piano Atlas* (Long Beach: Pierce Piano Atlas, 2003).
39. *New York Packet*, April 29, 1788.
40. Astor, *John Jacob Astor*, 177.
41. John Jacob Astor Business Records, vol.

42, Folder 5, agreement between John Jacob Astor and Philipp H. Liebert, August 25, 1792.
  42. Gebhard, *The Life and Ventures*, 61.
  43. Astor, *John Jacob Astor*, 176–77.
  44. Gebhard, *The Life and Ventures*, 61.
  45. See Madsen, *First Multimillionaire*, 23.
  46. Porter, *Business Man*, vol. 1, 28.
  47. Wayne Mahood, *General Wadsworth: The Life and Times of Brevet Major General James S. Wadsworth* (Cambridge, MA: Da Capo Press, 2003).
  48. Parton, *John Jacob Astor*, 48.
  49. Astor, *John Jacob Astor*, 177.
  50. Myers, *Amerikanische Vermögen*, vol. 1, 71.
  51. Ibid.
  52. Madsen, *First Multimillionaire*, 23. For further information on Baden, Baden-Baden, and the old Palatinate, see Schaab, *Geschichte der Kurpfalz*, vol. 2, 250ff.
  53. *Astor Family Papers*, Box 1, Folder 2, John Jacob Astor to Peter Smith, October 5, 1794; John Jacob Astor to Peter Smith, September 10, 1795; John Jacob Astor to Peter Smith, New York, July 5, 1796.
  54. Ronda, *Astoria*, 25.
  55. Ibid.
  56. Scoville, *The Old Merchants*, vol. 1, 421.
  57. *New York Packet*, October 28, 1788.
  58. *Astor Family Papers*, Box 1, Folder 2, 1792–1799.
  59. Cogliano, *Revolutionary America*, 153–5.
  60. Beach, *Wealthy Citizens*, 2.
  61. Nevins, *Hone*, 374.
  62. Nevins, *Hone*, 374.
  63. See *Memoir of Mrs. Eliza Astor Rumpff*, 3.
  64. Porter, *Business Man*, vol. 1, 39.
  65. Ibid.
  66. The New York Historical Society holds a publication listing all real estate and buildings Astor owned.
  67. *New York Directory and Register for the Year 1790*.
  68. Ibid.
  69. *New York Gazette and General Advertiser*, August 4, 1797.
  70. *New York Gazette and General Advertiser*, June 1, 1798.
  71. *New York Gazette and General Advertiser*, November 15, 1798.
  72. *New York Directory and Register for the Year 1794*.
  73. Charles von Bokor, *Winkelmaß und Zirkel: Die Geschichte der Freimaurer* (Wien: Moewig Sachbuch, 1980), 131ff.
  74. *National Freemason*, October 13, 1866; *The New York Directory and Register for the Year 1793*; *The New York Directory and Register for the Year 1794*.
  75. http://www.hollandlodgeno8.org/about.php, last visited on March 8, 2011.
  76. http://www.hollandlodgeno8.org/about.php, last visited on March 8, 2011.
  77. *National Freemason*, October 13, 1866.
  78. Burrows and Wallace, *Gotham*.
  79. Scoville, *The Old Merchants*, vol. 4, 212–227.
  80. Ibid.
  81. About the Louisiana Purchase, see Wilson E. Lyon, *Louisiana in French Diplomacy, 1759–1804* (Oklahoma City: University of Oklahoma Press, 1974); Thomas J. Fleming, *The Louisiana Purchase* (Hoboken: J. Wiley, 2003).
  82. Scoville, *The Old Merchants*, vol. 3, 37.
  83. Scoville, *The Old Merchants*, vol. 4, 37; vol. 3, 21.

Chapter 4

  1. Appleby, *Capitalism and a New Social Order*; Bailyn, *Ideological Origins*; James T. Kloppenberg, "The Virtues of Liberalism: Christianity, Republicanism, and Ethics in Early American Political Discourse," in *Journal of American History* 74 (1987): 9–33; Pocock, *Machiavellian Moment*; Wood, *The Creation of the American Republic*.
  2. Robert E. Shalhope, "Republicanism," in *The Blackwell Encyclopedia of the American Revolution*, edited by Jack P. Greene and J.R. Pole (Oxford: Blackwell Publishers, 1991), 657.
  3. Appleby, *Liberalism*, 321–338.
  4. Hans-Christoph Schröder, *Die Amerikanische Revolution: Eine Einführung* (München: C.H. Beck, 1982), 152.
  5. An Analysis about property can be found in Dirk Hoerder, "Vom korporativen Eigentumsbegriff: Ein Element der amerikanischen Revolution," in *200 Jahre Amerikanische Revolution und moderne Revolutionsforschung*, edited by Hans-Ulrich Wehler (Göttingen: Vandenhoeck und Ruprecht, 1976), 76–100.
  6. See Jan Lewis, "Happiness," in *The Ideological Origins of the American Revolution*, edited by Bernard Bailyn (Cambridge, MA: Harvard University Press, 1982), 642.
  7. Ibid.
  8. *John Jacob Astor Business Records*, vol. 45, Folder 5, letter of John Jacob Astor to James Madison, July 13, 1807.
  9. Burrows and Wallace, *Gotham*, 275.
  10. Burrows and Wallace, *Gotham*, 275.
  11. Foster R. Dulles, *The Old China Trade* (New York: AMS Press, 1970), 51ff.
  12. See *New York Gazette and General Advertiser*, July 5, 1799.
  13. Porter, *Astor*, vol. 2, 589.

14. *John Jacob Astor Business Records*, vol. 45, Folder 5, letter of John Jacob Astor to James Madison, July 13, 1807.
15. See Porter, *Business Man*, vol. 1, 132.
16. Scoville, *The Old Merchants*, vol. 1, 416–421.
17. Scoville, *The Old Merchants*, vol. 1, 416–421.
18. See *New York Gazette and General Advertiser*, July 5, 1799.
19. Kenneth W. Porter, "Myths after Astor," in *Bulletin of the Business Historical Society* 10 (1936): 6.
20. Vivian Joseph, *A History of the British East India Company* (Tallis: Cheddar, 1987).
21. Manifest of the Cargo of the Ship *Severn*, John Cowman, Master, May 25, 1804, in Porter, *Business Man*, vol. 1, 406.
22. *Daily Advertiser*, April 29, 1800.
23. *New York Gazette and General Advertiser*, April 29, 1801.
24. *New York Gazette and General Advertiser*, May 11, 1801.
25. Porter, *Business Man*, vol. 1, 135.
26. *John Jacob Astor Business Records*, vol. 45, Folder 5, letter of John Jacob Astor to James Madison, July 13, 1807.
27. New York Custom House, *Manuscript Book*, New York Register, No. 199, May 7, 1805; *John Jacob Astor Business Records*, vol. 20.
28. Porter, *Business Man*, vol. 1, 155.
29. Scoville, *The Old Merchants*, vol. 1, 416–421.
30. *John Jacob Astor Business Records*, vol. 20.
31. Cogliano, *Revolutionary America*, 174; Eugene M. Wait, *America and the War of 1812* (Commack, NY: Kroshka, 1999).
32. New York Custom Records, freighter *Young Factor*, December 2, 1807.
33. *John Jacob Astor Business Records*, Letterbook I.
34. *John Jacob Astor Business Records*, vol. 20.
35. About Albert Gallatin, see Edwin G. Burrows, *Albert Gallatin and the Political Economy of Republicanism, 1761–1800* (New York: Garland, 1986).
36. *Thomas Jefferson Papers*, Albert Gallatin to Thomas Jefferson, August 3, 1808.
37. Samuel Latham Mitchill to Thomas Jefferson, July 12, 1808, in Porter, *Business Man*, vol. 1, 420.
38. Letter of Thomas Jefferson to Albert Gallatin, July 25, 1808, in Porter, *Business Man*, vol. 1, 421.
39. Letter of Albert Gallatin to Captain William Jones, August 17, 1808, in Porter, *Business Man*, vol. 1, 426.
40. *Commercial Advertiser*, August 17, 1808.
41. Burrows and Wallace, *Gotham*, 275.
42. Porter, *Business Man*, vol. 2, 913.
43. Ibid., 928.
44. Porter, *Business Man*, vol. 2, 928.
45. See Myers, *Amerikanische Vermögen*, vol. 1, 94, 98.
46. *Leeds Mercury*, September 14, 1844.
47. Parton, "John Jacob Astor," 315.
48. Burrows and Wallace, *Gotham*, 452.
49. Ibid.
50. Porter, *Business Man*, vol. 2, 989.
51. Nevins, *Hone*, 52.
52. Mary C. Henderson, *The City and the Theatre: The History of New York Playhouses* (New York: Back Stage Books, 2004), 49–52.
53. Frances Trollope, *Domestic Manners of the Americans* (New York: Vintage, 1949), 263.
54. Ibid., 264.
55. Nevins, *Hone*, 52.
56. See Stevens, Wayne E., "The Organization of the British Fur Trade, 1760–1800," in *Mississippi Valley Historical Review* 3 (1916), 172–202. About the rivalry of the two Canadian fur companies, see Ann Carlos, "The Causes and Origins of the North American Fur Trade Rivalry, 1804–1810," in *JEH* 41 (1981): 777–794.
57. Bryce, *The Hudson's Bay Company*, 117.
58. Ibid., 12.
59. Ibid., 119.
60. *Thomas Jefferson Papers*, letter of Thomas Jefferson to Meriwether Lewis, June 20, 1803.
61. *Thomas Jefferson Papers*, letter of Thomas Jefferson to Meriwether Lewis, June 20, 1803.
62. Ibid.
63. *Articles of Incorporation of the American Fur Company*, April 6, 1808, in Porter, *Business Man*, vol. 1, 413ff.
64. Letter of Albert Gallatin to John Jacob Astor, August 5, 1835. John Jacob Astor Collection, Missouri History Museum Archives, St. Louis. In Gallatin's letter it becomes clear that Astor had always hoped for military support from the government during the War of 1812.
65. Columbia University Library, *DeWitt Clinton Papers*, letter of John Jacob Astor to DeWitt Clinton, January 25, 1808.
66. Astor to DeWitt Clinton, New York, January 25, 1808, Clinton Papers, 4:5–6, Butler Library.
67. *Thomas Jefferson Papers*, letter of Thomas Jefferson to John Jacob Astor, April 13, 1808.
68. *Thomas Jefferson Papers*, letter of John Jacob Astor to Thomas Jefferson, January 27, 1808.
69. Ibid.
70. Letter of Albert Gallatin to John Jacob Astor, August 5, 1835. John Jacob Astor Collection, Missouri History Museum Archives, St. Louis.

Notes — Chapter 4

71. Ronda, *Astoria & Empire*, 45.
72. Letter of John Jacob Astor to Thomas Jefferson, March 14, 1812, in Porter, *Business Man*, vol. 1, 508.
73. Columbia University Library, *DeWitt Clinton Papers*, letter of John Jacob Astor to DeWitt Clinton, January 25, 1808.
74. *Articles of Incorporation of the American Fur Company*, April 6, 1808.
75. *Thomas Jefferson Papers*, letter of Henry Dearborn to Thomas Jefferson, April 8, 1808.
76. *Thomas Jefferson Papers*, letter of Thomas Jefferson to John Jacob Astor, April 13, 1808.
77. Ibid.
78. *Articles of Incorporation of the American Fur Company*, April 6, 1808.
79. Irving, *Astoria*, vol. 1, 16.
80. *Thomas Jefferson Papers*, letter of Thomas Jefferson to Meriwether Lewis, July 17, 1808.
81. James P. Ronda, "Dreams and Discoveries. Exploring the American West, 1760–1815," in *William and Mary Quarterly* 46 (1989): 149.
82. Cogliano, *Revolutionary America*, 175.
83. Letter of John Jacob Astor to James Madison, without date, in *The Papers of James Madison*, vol. 3, 400.
84. *Astor Business Records*, Letterbook I, John Jacob Astor to John Wright, February 14, 1814.
85. *Astor Business Records*, Letterbook II, William B. Astor to Elizabeth Astor, April 7, 1834; December 7, 1837.
86. *John Jacob Astor Business Records*, vol. 20, contract of January 11, 1809.
87. *Letters and Accounts, North West Company*, Alexander Henry to William Edgar, March 5, 1786. Toronto Public Reference Library.
88. *Thomas Jefferson Papers*, John Jacob Astor to Thomas Jefferson, August 20, 1813.
89. Frederick Merk, "The Genesis of the Oregon Question," *Mississippi Valley Historical Review* 36 (1950): 588.
90. *John Jacob Astor Business Records*, vol. 45, Folder 5, John Jacob Astor to James Monroe, February 18, 1813.
91. James Madison to Albert Gallatin, September 12, 1810, in *The James Madison Papers*, vol. 4, 536.
92. Alexander Baranoff to John Jacob Astor, July 27, 1810, in Porter, *Business Man*, vol. 1, 442.
93. James Madison to Albert Gallatin, September 12, 1810, in *The James Madison Papers*, Vol. 4, 536.
94. Ibid.
95. John Jacob Astor to Thomas Jefferson, March 14, 1812, in Porter, *Business Man*, vol. 1, 508.
96. *John Jacob Astor Business Records*, letter of Andrew Daschkoff to John Jacob Astor, November 7, 1809.
97. Porter, *Business Man*, vol. 1, 172.
98. Letter of John Jacob Astor to John Ebbets, November 13, 1809, in Porter, *Business Man*, vol. 1, 429.
99. *New York Gazette and General Advertiser*, November 16, 1809.
100. Porter, *Business Man*, vol. 1, 173.
101. Letter of John Jacob Astor to Thomas Jefferson, March 14, 1812, in Porter, *Business Man*, vol. 1, 508.
102. Account of Sales of Ship Enterprise by John Ebbets for Astor's Account, in Porter, *Business Man*, vol. 1, 432.
103. David Lavender, "Some Characteristics of the American Fur Company," *Minnesota History* 40 (Winter 1969): 181.
104. Ibid.
105. Grace Flandrau, *Astor and the Oregon Country* (St. Paul: Great Northern Railway, 1926), 9.
106. *Articles of Association of the Pacific Fur Company*. Astorians Collection, Missouri History Museum Archives, St. Louis.
107. Letter of John Jacob Astor to John Quincy Adams, January 4, 1823. *A Century of Lawmaking for a New Nation: U.S. Congressional Documents and Debates, 1774–1875*. The Library of Congress.
108. Ibid.
109. Lavener, 181.
110. Irving, *Astoria*, vol. 1, 105.
111. Ibid., 110.
112. Irving, *Astoria*, vol. 1, 111.
113. Ibid., 28.
114. Quoted after Porter, *Business Man*, vol. 1, 186.
115. Porter, *Business Man*, vol. 1, 187.
116. Irving, *Astoria*, vol. 1, 36ff.
117. Porter, *Business Man*, vol. 1, 189.
118. Letter of John Jacob Astor to John Quincy Adams, January 4, 1823. *A Century of Lawmaking*.
119. Irving, *Astoria*, vol. 1, 70.
120. Ronda, *Astoria*, 1.
121. Thomas Jefferson to John Jacob Astor, May 24, 1812. *Papers of Thomas Jefferson*. The Library of Congress.
122. Irving, *Astoria*, vol. 1, 71.
123. Ibid., 91.
124. Gabriel Franchère, *Narrative of a Voyage to the Northwest Coast of America, in the Years 1811, 1812, 1813, and 1814, Or, The First American Settlement on the Pacific* (New York: Redfield, 1854), 80–85.
125. Irving, *Astoria*, vol. 1, 90.
126. Irving, *Astoria*, vol. 1, 71.
127. *Astor Business Records*, vol. 20, John

Jacob Astor to Alexander Baranoff, October 16, 1811.

128. Irving, *Astoria*, vol. 2, 313.
129. Irving, *Astoria*, vol. 1, 93.
130. Thomas Hart Benton, *Speech in the Senate of the United States, in March, 1825, on the bill for the Occupation of the Columbia River* (St. Louis: Missourian Office, 1844), 25.
131. *John Jacob Astor Business Records*, vol. 20, John Jacob Astor to Andrew Daschkoff, April 13, 1811.
132. Cogliano, *Revolutionary America*, 176.
133. Letter of John Jacob Astor to Thomas Jefferson, March 14, 1812, in Porter, *Business Man*, vol. 1, 508.
134. Cogliano, *Revolutionary America*, 132.
135. Ibid.
136. See Cogliano, *Revolutionary America*, 179; Wait, *The War of 1812*, 235ff.
137. *Papers of James Madison*, vol. 2, 526, 536; Ibid., vol. 3, 100; *Papers of James Monroe*, passim; *The Dolley Madison Digital Edition*, John Jacob Astor to Dolley Payne, various.
138. See Christof Mauch, "Grande Dame der jungen Republik: Dolley Madison 1768–1849," in *Mrs. Präsident: Von Martha Washington bis Hillary Clinton*, edited by Philipp Gassert and Christof Mauch (Stuttgart: DVA, 2000), 54–65.
139. *The Dolley Madison Digital Edition*, John Jacob Astor to Dolley Payne Todd Madison, February 6, 1817.
140. *The Dolley Madison Digital Edition*, John Jacob Astor to Dolley Payne Todd Madison, February 12, 1815.
141. James Madison to Albert Gallatin, September 12, 1812, in *Papers of James Madison*, vol. 2, 536.
142. Ronda, *Astoria & Empire*, 1.
143. Ibid.
144. Irving, *Astoria*, vol. 1, 74ff.
145. Ramsay Crooks to the Pacific Fur Company, June 29, 1812. Astorians Collection, Missouri History Museum Archives, St. Louis.
146. Agreement of Wilson P. Hunt, Duncan McDougall, David Stuart, Robert Stuart, John Clarke and Donald McKenzie, June 27, 1812. Astorians Collection, Missouri History Museum Archives, St. Louis.
147. *Missouri Gazette*, May 8, 1813.
148. *New York Herald*, June 26, 1813.
149. Ibid.
150. *New York Herald*, June 26, 1813.
151. *John Jacob Astor Business Records*, vol. 45, Folder 5, John Jacob Astor to James Monroe, March 22, 1813.
152. *John Jacob Astor Business Records*, vol. 45, Folder 5, John Jacob Astor to James Monroe, February 1813.
153. Ibid.
154. *John Jacob Astor Business Records*, vol. 45, Folder 5, John Jacob Astor to James Monroe, March 22, 1813.
155. *John Jacob Astor Business Records*, Letterbook I, John Jacob Astor to Major Harrison, May 26, 1814.
156. Letter of John Jacob Astor to the Department of State, April 4, 1813, in Porter, *Business Man*, vol. 1, 524.
157. The Library of Congress, *Thomas Jefferson Papers*, John Jacob Astor to Thomas Jefferson, October 18, 1813.
158. Ibid.
159. Porter, *Business Man*, vol. 1, 220.
160. Irving, *Astoria*, vol. 2, 389.
161. Clyde A. Milner II, "National Initiatives," in *The Oxford History of the American West*, edited by Clyde A. Milner II, Carol A. O'Connor, Martha A. Sandweiss (New York: Oxford University Press, 1994), 159.
162. Letter of John Jacob Astor to James Monroe, August 17, 1815, in Porter, *Business Man*, vol. 1, 585.
163. Letter of John Jacob Astor to James Monroe, August 17, 1815, in Porter, *Business Man*, vol. 1, 585.
164. Irving, *Astoria*, vol. 2, 425.
165. *John Jacob Astor Business Records*, vol. 45, Folder 5, John Jacob Astor to James Monroe, March 28, 1813; *John Jacob Astor Business Records*, vol. 20, William Pigot to John Ebbets, March 22, 1814.
166. Irving, *Astoria*, vol. 2, 428.
167. *National Freemason*, October 13, 1866.
168. Ibid.
169. Ibid.
170. Treaty of Ghent, Article 1, December 24, 1814, in *Treaties and Other International Acts of the United States of America*, vol. 2, edited by Hunter Miller (Washington, D.C.: U.S. Government Printing Office, 1935), 574ff.
171. Letter of James Monroe an John Quincy Adams and Albert Gallatin, March 22, 1814, in *American State Papers: Foreign Relations*, vol. 3 (Washington, D.C.: U.S. Government Printing Office, 1815), 731.
172. *John Jacob Astor Business Records*, Letterbook I, John Jacob Astor to George Ehninger, New York, March 6, 1815.
173. *John Jacob Astor Business Records*, vol. 45, Folder 5, letter of John Jacob Astor to James Monroe, February 20, 1815; *John Jacob Astor Business Records*, vol. 45, Folder 5, letter of John Jacob Astor to James Monroe, February 21, 1815.
174. John Jacob Astor to James Monroe, July 22, 1814, in Porter, *Business Man*, vol. 1, 558.
175. *John Jacob Astor Business Records*, letters of John Jacob Astor to James Monroe, July 22, 1814; September 2, 1814; September 22, 1814.

176. *John Jacob Astor Business Records*, letters of John Jacob Astor to James Monroe, September 22, 1814.
177. *Papers of Albert Gallatin*, John Jacob Astor to Albert Gallatin, October 6, 1815; October 9, 1815; October 10, 1815.
178. Miller, *Treaties*, vol. 2, 574ff.
179. Johannes Eue, *Die Oregon-Frage: Amerikansiche Expansionspolitik Und Der Pazifische Nordwesten, 1814-1848* (Munster: LIT Verlag, 1995), 24ff.
180. Miller, *Treaties*, vol. 2, 574ff.
181. Merk, *The Genesis of the Oregon Question*, 590.
182. Eue, *Die Oregon-Frage*, 30.
183. Quoted after Parton, "John Jacob Astor," 319.
184. Letter of Albert Gallatin to John Jacob Astor, August 5, 1835, John Jacob Astor Collection, Missouri History Museum Archives, St. Louis.
185. Letter of John Jacob Astor to James Monroe, August 17, 1815, in Porter, *Business Man*, vol. 1, 585.
186. Eue, *Die Oregon-Frage*, 33.
187. Haeger, *Business and Finance*, 188.
188. *John Jacob Astor Business Records*, Letterbook I, John Jacob Astor to James Monroe, December 16, 1816.
189. Eue, *Die Oregon-Frage*, 25.
190. Thomas Hart Benton, *Speech on the Oregon Question*.
191. *John Jacob Astor Business Records*, Letterbook III, letters of John Jacob Astor send by William B. Astor to Thomas Hart Benton.

Chapter 5

1. Sean Wilentz, "The Market Revolution, 1815-1848," in *Major Problems in the Early Republic, 1787-1848*, edited by Sean Wilentz (Lexington: Wadsworth Publishing, 1992), 8-14.
2. See Wood, "The Significance of the Early Republic," 5.
3. Wilentz, *The Market Revolution*, 11ff.
4. Alexis de Tocqueville, *Democracy in America* (New York: Harper Perennial Modern Classics, 2000), 661.
5. Wood, "The Significance of the Early Republic," 7.
6. Letter of John Jacob Astor to Henry Payson, February 2, 1814, in Porter, *Business Man*, vol. 1, 549.
7. Robert E. Wright, *The Wealth of Nations Rediscovered: Integration and Expansion in American Financial Markets, 1780-1850* (Cambridge: Cambridge University Press, 2002).
8. Cogliano, *Revolutionary America*, 137-141.
9. Cogliano, *Revolutionary America*, 140.
10. George R. Taylor, "A Brief History of the Second Bank of the United States," in *Jackson versus Biddle: The Struggle over the Second Bank of the United States*, edited by George R. Taylor (Boston: D.C. Heath, 1949), 3.
11. *Papers of James Madison*, Letter of Albert Gallatin to James Madison, January 5, 1811.
12. *David Parish Letterbooks*, Letters of Stephen Girard and David Parish to Albert Gallatin, April 6, 1813; April 8, 1813. New York Historical Society.
13. Raymond Walters Jr., "The Origins of the Second Bank of the United States," in *JEH* 53 (1945): 117.
14. *John Jacob Astor Business Records*, vol. 45, Folder 8, Letter of James Madison to James Monroe, May 19, 1814.
15. Kenneth Brown, "Stephen Girard: Promoter of the Second Bank of the United States," in: *JEH* 2 (1942): 132.
16. *John Jacob Astor Business Records*, vol. 45, Folder 8, Letter of James Madison to James Monroe, May 19, 1814.
17. Letter of John Jacob Astor to Stephen Girard, August 15, 1814, in Porter, *Business Man*, vol. 1, 562.
18. Letter of John Jacob Astor to David Parish, May 17, 1814, in Porter, *Business Man*, vol. 1, 526; Letter of John Jacob Astor to David Parish, May 27, 1814, in Porter, *Business Man*, vol. 1, 527.
19. *Journal of the Senate of the United States of America, 1789-1873*, January 31, 1815. The Library of Congress.
20. Letter of John Jacob Astor to Stephen Girard, August 15, 1814, in Porter, *Business Man*, vol. 1, 562.
21. Letter of John Jacob Astor to John C. Calhoun, November 23, 1814, in Porter, *Business Man*, vol. 1, 575ff.
22. *John Jacob Astor Business Records*, vol. 45, Folder 9, Albert Gallatin to James Madison, January 5, 1811.
23. Paul Johnson, *A History of the American People* (New York: Harper Collins, 1997), 291.
24. Letter of John Smith to Albert Gallatin, April 5, 1816, in *James Madison Papers*.
25. *Journal of the Executive Proceedings of the Senate of the United States of America, 1815-1829*, April 23, 1816, Washington, D.C. The Library of Congress.
26. *John Jacob Astor Business Records*, Letterbook I, John Jacob Astor to William Jones, December 12, 1816.
27. Taylor, *The Second Bank of the United States*, 3.
28. Letter of Albert Gallatin to John Jacob Astor, August 5, 1835, John Jacob Astor Col-

lection, Missouri History Museum Archives, St. Louis.
29. *New York Gazette and General Advertiser*, March 15, 1815.
30. Haeger, *Business and Finance*, 174.
31. Ibid., 173–177.
32. Letter of John Jacob Astor to James Monroe, May 27, 1816, in Porter, *Business Man*, vol. 2, 1145.
33. Letter of John Jacob Astor to Ramsay Crooks, January 27, 1823, in Porter, *Business Man*, vol. 2, 1171ff; Letter of John Jacob Astor to Ramsay Crooks, February 16, 1824, in Porter, *Business Man*, vol. 2, 1173.
34. In his diary James Gallatin wrote that he was happy and relieved when his father declined Astor's offer. See *The Diary of James Gallatin*, 80.
35. Kelby, *Notes on the Astor Family*.
36. *Astor Business Records*, vol. 43, Folder 3, letter of John Jacob Astor, Geneva, March 19, 1824; Papers of Albert Gallatin, letter of William Backhouse Astor to Albert Gallatin, December 23, 1813, Göttingen.
37. Kelby, *Notes on the Astor Family*.
38. *The Dolley Madison Digital Edition*, John Jacob Astor to Dolley Payne Todd Madison, February 12, 1815.
39. Kelby, *Notes on the Astor Family*.
40. The Papers of Albert Gallatin: Letters, letter of John Jacob Astor to Albert Gallatin, March 14, 1818.
41. Letter of John Jacob Astor to Peter Smith, March 16, New York, in Porter, *Business Man*, vol. 2, 1160.
42. The Papers of Albert Gallatin: Letters, letter of John Jacob Astor to Albert Gallatin, March 14, 1818.
43. Porter, *Business Man*, vol. 2, 1099.
44. *John Jacob Astor Business Records*, vol. 43, Folder 3, letter of John Jacob Astor, Geneva, March 19; Papers of Albert Gallatin: Letters, letter of William Backhouse Astor to Albert Gallatin, December 23, 1813.
45. *John Jacob Astor Business Records*, vol. 43, Folder 3, letter of John Jacob Astor to an unknown person, Geneva, March 19, 1824.
46. *John Jacob Astor Business Records*, vol. 44, Folder 16, Memorandum of John Jacob Astor, September 12, 1818; Memorandum of John Jacob Astor to William Backhouse Astor, 1819, in: Porter, *Business Man*, vol. 2, 1163.
47. *John Jacob Astor Business Records*, vol. 44, Folder 17, letter of John Jacob Astor to James Monroe, April 5, 1820, Rome.
48. Letter of John Jacob Astor to Ramsay Crooks, July 5, 1825, in Schintznach, *John Jacob Astor: Business Letters, 1813–1828*, 114.
49. *The Diary of James Gallatin*, 179.
50. Eugene L. Didier, ed., *The Life and Letters of Madame Bonaparte* (New York: Charles Scriber's Sons, 1879), 66.
51. Ibid., 162–163.
52. *The Diary of James Gallatin*, 179.
53. Letter of Elizabeth Patterson Bonaparte to Mr. Patterson, December 11, 1823, in *The Life and Letters of Madame Bonaparte*, 162.
54. Ibid., 66.
55. *John Jacob Astor Business Records*, vol. 44, Folder 17, letter of John Jacob Astor to James Monroe, April 5, 1820, Rome.
56. *John Jacob Astor Business Records*, vol. 44, Folder 12, letter of John Jacob Astor to James Monroe, September 5, 1820, Frankfurt am Main.
57. *Walldorf Churchbook*, no. 3, 350.
58. Horn, *Astor*, 98. German original: "War denn bei seiner treuen, tiefgemüthlichen Pfälzernatur das Heimathgefühl, die Heimathliebe, ganz erstorben? Dachte er nicht einmal daran, die Heimath wiederzusehen? Gewiß, Astor war einmal in seinem Heimathorte und genoß die Freude, die Seinen, und die Genossen und Freunde seiner trüben Jugend noch am Leben zu finden und mit ihnen froh zu sein."
59. *Memoir of Mrs. Eliza Astor Rumpff*, 4.
60. Archive of the Moravian Community, Neuwied.
61. Archive of the Moravian Community, Neuwied.
62. *Memoirs of Mrs. Eliza Astor Rumpff*, 4ff.
63. *Raleigh Register*, April 29, 1848.
64. *John Jacob Astor Business Records*, vol. 44, folder 17, Letter of John Jacob Astor to James Monroe, April 5, 1820, Rome.
65. *John Jacob Astor Business Records*, vol. 44, folder 17, Letter of John Jacob Astor to James Monroe, April 5, 1820, Rome.
66. *John Jacob Astor Business Records*, vol. 44, folder 17, Letter of John Jacob Astor to James Monroe, April 5, 1820, Rome.
67. *The Papers of Henry Clay*, vol. 2, letter of John Jacob Astor to Henry Clay, May 20, 1820, Florence, 863.
68. *The Papers of Henry Clay*, vol. 2, letter of John Jacob Astor to Henry Clay, May 20, 1820, Florence, 863.
69. *Astor Family Papers*, Box 1, Folder 5, 1821–1829, Ramsay Crooks to John Jacob Astor, Liverpool, April 18, 1821.
70. *New York Gazette and General Advertiser*, April 29, 1822.
71. *New York Gazette and General Advertiser*, June 3, 1823.
72. *The Papers of Albert Gallatin*, letter of John Jacob Astor to Albert Gallatin, October 18, 1822.
73. *Family Papers*, Box 1, Folder 5, 1821–1829; *John Jacob Astor Business Records*, vol. 43, letter of John Jacob Astor to an unknown per-

son, April 17, 1824; *John Jacob Astor Business Records*, vol. 43, letter of John Jacob Astor to Ramsay Crooks, September 21, 1824.
74. Letter of John Jacob Astor to Ramsay Crooks, August 20, 1825, in Porter, *Business Man*, vol. 2, 1179.
75. *Memoir of Mrs. Eliza Astor Rumpff*, 5.
76. Ibid., 7.
77. Letter of Elizabeth Patterson Bonaparte to Mr. Patterson, January 23, 1826, in *The Life and Letters of Madame Bonaparte*, 188.
78. *New York Gazette and General Advertiser*, April 10, 1826.
79. About the causes and effects of the alcohol trade with the Native Americans, see Peter C. Mancall, *Deadly Medicine: Indians and Alcohol in Early America* (Ithaca: Cornell University Press, 1995).
80. William E. Unrau, *White Man's Wicked Water: The Alcohol Trade and Prohibition in Indian Country, 1802–1892* (Lawrence, KS: University Press of Kansas, 1996), 120.
81. Hiram M. Chittenden, *The American Fur Trade of the Far West*, vol. 1 (Lincoln: University of Nebraska Press, 1935), 347.
82. Unrau, *White Man's Wicked Water*, 120.
83. Alexander Ross, *The Fur Hunters of the Far West*, vol. 1 (London: Smith, Elder & Co, 1855), 15.
84. Porter, *Business Man*, vol. 2, 797.
85. Letter of John Jacob Astor to William H. Ashley, April 22, 1822, in Madsen, *First Multimillionaire*, 200.
86. *American State Papers, Indian Affairs*, vol. 2 (Washington, D.C.: U.S. Government Printing Office, 1826), 659ff.
87. Letter of John Jacob Astor to William H. Ashley, April 22, 1822, in Madsen, *First Multimillionaire*, 200.
88. Porter, *Business Man*, vol. 2, 792ff.
89. Letter of John Jacob Astor to William H. Ashley, April 22, 1822, in Madsen, *First Multimillionaire*, 200.
90. Porter, *Business Man*, vol. 2, 803.
91. Letter of William Backhouse Astor to John C. Calhoun, November 13, 1824, in Porter, *Business Man*, vol. 2, 804.
92. Letter of Albert Gallatin to James Barbour, June 30, 1826, in Porter, *Business Man*, vol. 2, 1184.
93. *John Jacob Astor Business Records*, Letterbook II, letter of John Jacob Astor to James Keith, December 15, 1829, New York.
94. Ibid.
95. John S. Galbraith, "British-American Competition in the Border Fur Trade of the 1820s," *Minnesota History* 36 (September 1959): 248.
96. *John Jacob Astor Business Records*, Letterbook II, Letter of John Jacob Astor to James Keith, December 15, 1829.
97. Bryce, *The Hudson's Bay Company*, 270.
98. Galbraith, "British-American Competition," 241ff.
99. Haeger, *Business and Finance*, 215.
100. John Jacob Astor to Ramsay Crooks, January 27, 1827, in Porter, *Business Man*, vol. 2, 1172.
101. Haeger, *Business and Finance*, 225.
102. *Papers Relating to the Trade with China*, Parliament of Great Britain, House of Lords, vol. 262, London 1829, 43.
103. Haeger, *Business and Finance*, 231.
104. Ibid.
105. Burrows and Wallace, *Gotham*, 563–586.
106. *Astor Family Papers*, Box 1, John Jacob Astor to Gerrit Smith, April 14, 1828.
107. Ibid.
108. Frank W. Stevens, *The Beginnings of the New York Central Railroad* (New York: G.P. Putman, 1926), 14ff.
109. Ibid.
110. *New York Gazette and General Advertiser*, May 30, 1828.
111. *Astor Family Papers*, Box 1, Letter of John Jacob Astor to Gerrit Smith, April 14, 1828, New York.
112. Stevens, *The New York Central Railroad*, 398.
113. *Astor Family Papers*, Box 1, Letter of John Jacob Astor to William Backhouse Astor, October 15, 1832, Paris.
114. Ibid.
115. *John Jacob Astor Business Records*, vol. 44, Folder 12, letter of John Jacob Astor, August 1832.
116. *John Jacob Astor Business Records*, Letterbook II, William B. Astor to Wilson P. Hunt, December 31, 1833; *John Jacob Astor Business Records*, Letterbook II, William B. Astor to Vincent Rumpff, January 7, 1834.
117. Henry Astor died mid–April 1833. See Nevins, *Hone*, 91.
118. Ibid.
119. Nevins, *Hone*, 121. *John Jacob Astor Business Records*, vol. 44, Folder 12.
120. *John Jacob Astor Business Records*, vol. 44, Folder 12, letter of William B. Astor to B. Pratte, August 26, 1833; *John Jacob Astor Business Records*, vol. 44, Folder 12, letter of William B. Astor to the Office of the American Fur Company, November 1, 1833.

Chapter 6

1. Burrows and Wallace, *Gotham*, 712.
2. Ibid.

3. Nevins, *Hone*, 91.
4. Jefferson Williamson, *The American Hotel: An Anecdotal History* (New York: A.A. Knopf, 1930), 31.
5. *New York Journal and State Gazette*, April 25, 1833.
6. Nevins, *Hone*, 91.
7. *John Jacob Astor Business Records*, vol. 44, Folder 12.
8. Henry died in April 1833. See Nevins, *Hone*, 91.
9. Porter, *Business Man*, vol. 2, 1035.
10. Nevins, *Hone*, 121.
11. Ibid.
12. Ibid.
13. Nevins, *Hone*, 126.
14. Irving, *Astoria*, vol. 1, 14.
15. *Astor Business Records*, vol. 43, Folder 3.
16. Williamson, *The American Hotel*, 29.
17. *John Jacob Astor Business Records*, Letterbook II, William B. Astor to John Dorr, November 2, 1833.
18. *John Jacob Astor Business Records*, vol. 43, Folder 3.
19. Nevins, *Hone*, 121.
20. Williamson, *The American Hotel*, 32.
21. Six years before the Croton Water System was developed. *John Jacob Astor Business Records*, vol. 43, Folder 3.
22. Ibid.
23. Ibid.
24. *John Jacob Astor Business Records*, Letterbook II, letter of John Jacob Astor written by William Backhouse Astor to John Dorr, April 13, 1836.
25. *John Jacob Astor Business Records*, Letterbook II, letter of John Jacob Astor written by William Backhouse Astor to John Dorr, November 2, 1833.
26. Nevins, *Hone*, 288, 301, 577.
27. Williamson, *The American Hotel*, 85.
28. About the history of the Waldorf=Astoria, see Frank Crowninshield, *The Unofficial Palace of New York: A Tribute to the Waldorf=Astoria* (New York: Waldorf=Astoria Co., 1939).
29. Today it would be at the corner of 88th Street and 2nd Avenue.
30. http://astoriaqueens.com, last visited March 10, 2011.
31. Baker Library, *Astor Business Records*, vol. 43, Folder 4.
32. "Here Astor once lived," *New York Times*, February 16, 1896.
33. Nevins, *Hone*, 182.
34. Ibid., 183.
35. Ibid., 182.
36. *Daily Herald and Gazette*, December 28, 1837.
37. *John Jacob Astor Business Records*, Testament.
38. Scoville, *The Old Merchants*, vol. 1, 314.
39. *John Jacob Astor Business Records*, Letterbook II, letters of John Jacob Astor to John Jacob Astor Ebbets, January 19, July 19, 1832.
40. *John Jacob Astor Business Records*, Letterbook II, letter of John Jacob Astor written by William B. Astor to J.J. Janeway, June 27, 1835.
41. *John Jacob Astor Business Records*, Letterbook III, letters of John Jacob Astor to John S. Giles, April 2, 1846, December 30, 1846.
42. *John Jacob Astor Business Records*, Testament.
43. Wayne R. Kime, *Pierre M. Irving and Washington Irving: A Collaboration in Life and Letters* (Waterloo: Wilfrid Laurier University Press, 1977) 32.
44. Irving, *Astoria*, vol. 1, xiv.
45. Franchère, *Narrative of a Voyage*.
46. Ross Cox, *Adventures on the Columbia River* (New York: J & J Harper, 1832).
47. Alexander Ross, *Adventures of the first settlers on the Oregon or Columbia River. Being a narrative of the expedition fitted out by John Jacob Astor, to establish the Pacific Fur Company* (London: Smith, Elder & Co, 1849).
48. W.F.A. Zimmermann, *Astoria oder Reisen und Abenteuer der Astorexpeditionen* (Leipzig: Payne, 1858).
49. Irving, *Life and Letters of Washington Irving*, vol. 2, 268.
50. In the introduction of *Astoria*, Washington Irving stated: "The trouble of rummaging among business papers, and of collecting and collating facts from amidst tedious and common-place details, was spared me by my nephew, Pierre M. Irving, who acted as my pioneer, and to whom I am greatly indebted for smoothing my path and lightening my labors." Irving, *Astoria*, vol. 1, xiv–xv.
51. Irving, *Life and Letters of Washington Irving*, vol. 3, 64.
52. Charles Astor Bristed was John Jacob Astor's grandson. His mother was Magdalen Astor. He was born in 1820 and came to live with his grandfather after the death of his mother.
53. *New York Daily Express*, November 1, 1836.
54. Nevins, *Hone*, 229.
55. Franchère, *Narrative of a Voyage*, 180.
56. Letter of Washington Irving to Pierre Irving, December 12, 1836, in *Life and Letters of Washington Irving*, vol. 3, edited by Pierre Irving (New York: G.P. Putnam, 1868), 92.
57. *The Examiner*, October 23, 1836.
58. Nevins, *Hone*, 229.
59. Letter of Washington Irving to Pierre Irving, December 12, 1836, in *Life and Letters of Washington Irving*, vol. 3, 92.

60. Porter, *Business Man*, vol. 2, 1094.
61. *North American and Daily Advertiser*, January 29, 1842.
62. Porter, *Business Man*, vol. 2, 1094.
63. *Astor Business Records*, Letterbook III.
64. *Minutes of the German Society, New York 1784–1853*, German Society of the City of New York.
65. Ibid.
66. Nevins, *Hone*, 121.
67. Ibid., 125.
68. *Astor Business Records*, Letterbook III, letter of William B. Astor to Robert Borell, December 29, 1845, New York.
69. Nevins, *Hone*, 716ff.
70. *Astor Business Records*, Letterbook II, William Backhouse Astor to Henry Brevort, July 3, 1837, New York.
71. Nevins, *Hone*, 178, 672.
72. Letter of Washington Irving to Peter Irving, September 26, 1835, in *Life and Letters of Washington Irving*, vol. 3, 78.
73. *North American and Daily Advertiser*, January 29, 1842.
74. *North American and Daily Advertiser*, January 29, 1842.
75. Ibid.
76. *Pensacola Gazette*, April 18, 1846.
77. "Here Astor once lived," *New York Times*, February 16, 1896.
78. Porter, *Business Man*, vol. 2, 1120.
79. *Astor Business Records*, Letterbook III, William Backhouse Astor to Vincent Rumpff, February 24, 1848, New York.
80. *New York Herald*, March 30, 1848.
81. Nevins, *Hone*, 848.
82. *North Wales Chronicle*, May 2, 1848.
83. *New York Tribune*, April 1, 1848.
84. Nevins, *Hone*, 848.
85. *New York Tribune*, April 1, 1848.
86. *National Freemason*, October 13, 1866.
87. *New York Herald*, April 9, 1848.
88. Herman Melville, *Bartleby the Scrivener* (New York: Melville House, 2004), 7.
89. Kelby, *Notes on the Astor Family*.
90. Kelby, *Notes on the Astor Family*.
91. *John Jacob Astor Business Records*, Letterbook II, William B. Astor to John Bristed, October 18, 1833, New York.
92. *The Papers of Charles Astor Bristed*, Western Americana Collection, Beinecke Rare Book and Manuscript Library, Yale University.
93. *John Jacob Astor Business Records*, Testament.
94. *The Letters of Washington Irving to Henry Breevort*, vol. 2, edited by George S. Hellman (New York: G.P. Putnam, 1915), 162–163.
95. *John Jacob Astor Business Records*, Testament.
96. *John Jacob Astor Business Records*, vol. 44, Folder 16, Memorandum of John Jacob Astor, September 12, 1818.
97. *John Jacob Astor Business Records*, Testament.
98. *John Jacob Astor Business Records*, Letterbook III, William B. Astor to Samuel Ward, June 6, 1846; August 20, 1846; August 31, 1846; June 5, 1847.
99. *John Jacob Astor Business Records*, Testament.
100. Kelby, *Notes on the Astor Family*.
101. *John Jacob Astor Business Records*, Testament.
102. George Astor's testament dates on December 6, 1813. See PRO, *Testament von George Astor*. John Jacob Astor got the news of the death of his older brother on December 17, 1813. See *John Jacob Astor Business Records*, Letterbook I, John Jacob Astor to John Wright, February 14, 1814.
103. *John Jacob Astor Business Records*, Letterbook II, William B. Astor to Elizabeth Astor, April 7, 1834, December 7, 1837.
104. *John Jacob Astor Business Records*, Testament.
105. *John Jacob Astor Business Records*, Letterbook I, John Jacob Astor to George Astor Jr., May 21, 1814; May 27, 1814; September 14, 1814; October 19, 1814.
106. *John Jacob Astor Business Records*, Testament.
107. *John Jacob Astor Business Records*, Letterbook I, Letter of John Jacob Astor an Elisabeth Astor, October 15, 1815, New York.
108. Porter, *Business Man*, vol. 2, 1028.
109. *John Jacob Astor Business Records*, Letterbook II, John Jacob Astor to Mary Reynell, October 3, 1834.
110. *Longworth's American Almanack, New York Register, and City Directory, 1835–36*.
111. *John Jacob Astor Business Records*, Testament.
112. Porter, *Business Man*, vol. 2, 1028.
113. Ibid.
114. Nevins, *Hone*, 92.
115. *John Jacob Astor Business Records*, Testament.
116. *John Jacob Astor Business Records*, Testament.
117. *The Dolley Madison Digital Edition*, John Jacob Astor to Dolley Payne Todd Madison, February 12, 1815.
118. *John Jacob Astor Business Records*, Testament.
119. *John Jacob Astor Business Records*, Letterbook I, John Jacob Astor to George Ehninger, November 10, 1813.
120. *New York Herald*, April 9, 1848.
121. According to Assmann it is clear that

"memory" is part of several disciplines. See Assmann, *Das kulturelle Gedächtnis*, 16.
122. The French sociologist Maurice Halbwachs researched collective memories already in 1925. See Maurice Halbwachs, *Les Cadres Sociaux de la Mémoire* (Paris: Les Presses universitaires de France, 1925). A new impulse came from Pierre Nora in the 1980s. See Pierre Nora, *Les Lieux de Mémoire*, vols. 1–3 (Paris: Gallimard, 1984, 1986, 1992).
123. Assmann, *Das kulturelle Gedächtnis*.
124. Hagen Schulze and Francois Etienne, *Deutsche Erinnerungsorte*, vol. 1 (München: C.H. Beck Verlag, 2001), 13.
125. Jacques, *Mercantile Biography*.
126. Beach, *Wealthy Citizens*.
127. Franchère, *Narrative of a Voyage*.
128. Cox, *Adventures on the Columbia River*.
129. Ross, *Adventures of the first settlers on the Oregon or Columbia River*.
130. Irving, *Life and Letters of Washington Irving*, vol. 2, 601.
131. Haeger, *Business and Finance*, 15.
132. Nevins, *Hone*, 847.
133. Untitled newspaper, April 15, 1848.
134. Parton, "John Jacob Astor," 319.
135. Mario D'Avanzo, "Melville's Bartleby and John Jacob Astor," *New England Quartterly* 41 (1968): 259–264.
136. Melville, *Bartleby*, 7.
137. Horace Greeley was born in Amherst, New Hampshire, in 1811. Thirty years later, in 1841, he founded the *New York Tribune*. He used his newspaper to accuse the state. But his accusations were partly reversed over time. During the Civil War he at first supported the cause of the Confederate States; later he claimed to be an abolitionist and supported the North. His attempts to be elected to political office, including the presidency, failed. In 1872, he lost in the presidential election against the incumbent President Ulysses Grant.
138. *New York Tribune*, April 1, 1848.
139. *New York Tribune*, March 30, 1848.
140. *New York Tribune*, April 1, 1848.
141. *New York Herald*, April 5, 1848.
142. *New York Herald*, March 31, 1848.
143. Ibid.
144. "John Jacob Astor sent to subscribe for the Herald yesterday," *New York Herald*, April 6, 1836.
145. *New York Globe*, quoted in *Daily Herald*, April 3, 1848.
146. *Daily Herald*, April 3, 1848.
147. *New York Herald*, March 31, 1848.
148. Mann, *A Few Thoughts*, 61.
149. Charles Astor Bristed, *A Letter to Horace Mann* (New York: Kernot, 1850).
150. Bristed, *A Letter*.
151. Burton Hendrick, "The Astor Fortune," *McClure's Magazine* 24 (1905), 563–578.
152. Myers, *Amerikanische Vermögen*, vol. 2.
153. Myers, *Amerikanische Vermögen*, vol. 1, 125ff.
154. Ibid., 71.
155. *The Diary of James Gallatin*.
156. Haeger, *Business and Finance*, 28.
157. Nevins, *Hone*, 580.
158. Ibid., 589.
159. See Nevins, *Hone*, 580–605.
160. Ibid., 589.
161. Ibid., 623.
162. Charles Dickens, *A Christmas Carol* (New York: 1910).
163. *Mainzer Zeitung*, August 8, 1838.
164. Löher, *Geschichte und Zustände der Deutschen in Amerika*, 394.
165. Kapp, *Geschichte der Deutschen Einwanderung in Amerika*, 358.
166. Horn, *Astor*, 4.
167. Julius Engelmann, "Johann Jakob Astor," in *Das Buch berühmter Kaufleute*, edited by Franz Otto (Leipzig: Verlag Otto Spamer, 1868), 469–488.
168. G.A. Ungerer, "Wilhelm Wundt und Heidelberg," in *Badische Heimat* 1 (March 1978), 38.
169. *Rhein-Neckar-Zeitung*, March 3, 1976.
170. Kurt-Georg Kiesinger, "200 Jahre USA: Eine Bilanz der deutsch-amerikanischen Beziehungen," in: *200 Jahre deutsch-amerikanische Beziehungen*, edited by Michael G. Eisenstadt and Dieter Oberndörfer (Bonn: Eichholz-Verlag, 1976), 26. Original: "Ich sprach von armen Einwanderern, die zu Erfolg kamen, und erinnere mich dabei, dass ich [...] zusammen mit einem Lord Astor 1963 den 200. Geburtstag jenes Johann Jakob Astor feierte. [...] Die Geschichte dieses Mannes und seiner Familie ist erstaunlich."
171. http://usa.usembassy.de/etexts/burnsham5688d.htm, last visited April 23, 2005.
172. About the history of the Astor Foundation, see Thomas Löffler, *Zu Nutzen und Gebrauch der Armen: Die Geschichte der Astor-Stiftung in Walldorf* (Walldorf: Astor-Stiftung Walldorf, 1998).

Bibliography

Primary Sources

ARCHIVE MATERIALS

Articles of Association of the Pacific Fur Company. Astorians Collection, Missouri History Museum Archives, St. Louis.
Astor Business Records, Letterbooks I–III. Baker Library Historical Collections, Harvard Business School.
Astor Family Papers, 1792–1916. The New York Public Library.
Astor Family Papers, 1807–1919. The New York Historical Society.
A Century of Lawmaking for a New Nation: U.S. Congressional Documents and Debates, 1774–1875. The Library of Congress.
Churchbook of the German Reformed Church of New York. New York Historical Society.
David Parish Letterbooks. New York Historical Society.
DeWitt Clinton Papers. 4:5–6. Rare Book and Manuscript Library, Columbia University Library.
Generallandesarchiv Karlsruhe 229/109 619–229/109 761.
John Jacob Astor Business Records. Baker Library Historical Collections, Harvard Business School, Vol. 1–48.
John Jacob Astor Collection. Missouri History Museum Archives, St. Louis.
John Jacob Astor Letters. Western Americana Collection, Beinecke Rare Book and Manuscript Library, Yale University.
Journal of the Executive Proceedings of the Senate of the United States of America, 1815–1829. Washington, D.C. The Library of Congress.
Manuscript Book, New York Register, No. 199. New York Custom House.
Materials on Astor. Archive of the Moravian Community, Neuwied, Germany.
Minutes of the German Society, New York, 1784–1853. German Society of the City of New York.
New York Directory and Register for the Year 1789. Western Americana Collection, Beinecke Rare Book and Manuscript Library, Yale University.
New York Directory and Register for the Year 1790. Western Americana Collection, Beinecke Rare Book and Manuscript Library, Yale University.
New York Directory and Register for the Year 1793. Western Americana Collection, Beinecke Rare Book and Manuscript Library, Yale University.
New York Directory and Register for the Year 1794. Western Americana Collection, Beinecke Rare Book and Manuscript Library, Yale University.
Notes on the Astor Family. The New York Historical Society.
Papers of Albert Gallatin. New York Historical Society.
Papers of Charles Astor Bristed. Western Americana Collection, Beinecke Rare Book and Manuscript Library, Yale University.
Protocols of the German Society of the City of New York. German Society of the City of New York.
Robert Stuart Papers. Western Americana Collection, Beinecke Rare Book and Manuscript Library, Yale University.
Walldorf Church Book, No. 2, Archiv der evangelischen Landeskirche in Baden.
Walldorf Church Book, No. 3, 1789 to 1818, Archiv der evangelischen Landeskirche in Baden.

NEWSPAPERS

"The Astor Fortune," *McClure's Magazine* 24 (1905): 563–578.
"A Biographer Who Claims A License to Blur Reality," *New York Times*, October 2, 1999.
Commercial Advertiser, August 17, 1808.
Daily Advertiser, April 29, 1800.
Daily Herald, April 3, 1848.
Daily Herald and Gazette, December 28, 1837.

Examiner, October 23, 1836.
"Founder of the Astor Fortune Twice Escapes Shipwrecked," *New York Times*, April 21, 1912.
"Here Astor once lived," *New York Times*, February 16, 1896.
"John Jacob Astor," *Belfast News-Letter*, March 1, 1890.
"John Jacob Astor sent to subscribe for the Herald yesterday," *New York Herald*, April 6, 1836.
Leeds Mercury, September 14, 1844.
Mainzer Zeitung, August 8, 1838.
Missouri Gazette, May 8, 1813.
National Freemason, October 13, 1866.
New York Daily Express, November 1, 1836.
New York Gazette and General Advertiser, August 4, 1797; June 1, 1798; November 15, 1798; July 5, 1799; April 29, 1801; May 11, 1801; November 16, 1809; March 15, 1815; April 29, 1822; June 3, 1823; April 10, 1826; May 30, 1828.
New York Herald, June 26, 1813; April 5, 1848; April 9, 1848; March 30, 1848; March 31, 1848.
New York Journal and State Gazette, April 25, 1833.
New York Packet, September 20, 1784; January 27, 1785; May 22, 1786; July 27, 1787; April 29, 1788; October 28, 1788.
New York Times, May 28, 1928.
New York Tribune, March 30, 1848; April 1, 1848; April 3, 1848.
North American and Daily Advertiser, January 29, 1842.
North Wales Chronicle, May 2, 1848.
Pensacola Gazette, April 18, 1846.
Raleigh Register, April 29, 1848.
Rhein-Neckar-Zeitung, March 3, 1976.
Scioto Gazette, April 19, 1848.
Untitled newspaper, April 15, 1848.

INTERNET

http://astoriaqueens.com, last visited March 10, 2011.
http://freepages.genealogy.rootsweb.ancestry.com/~dlemrick/JNickfacts.htm, last visited on July 14, 2012.
http://freepages.genealogy.rootsweb.ancestry.com/~dlemrick/JohnNick.htm, last visited on July 14, 2012.
http://www.hollandlodgeno8.org/about.php, last visited on March 8, 2011.
http://www.nytimes.com/ref/business/20070715_GILDED_GRAPHIC.html, last visited on May 27, 2012.
http://usa.usembassy.de/etexts/burnsham5688d.htm, last visited April 23, 2005.

PRINTED PRIMARY SOURCES

American State Papers, Indian Affairs, vol. 2, Washington 1826.
Armstrong, William. *The Aristocracy of New York*. New York: New York Publishing, 1848.
Baird, Robert, ed. *Memoir of Mrs. Eliza Astor Rumpff, and of the Duchess de Broglie, Daughter of Madame de Stael*. New York: American Tract Society, n.d.
Beach, Moses Yale. *The Wealth and Biography of the Wealthy Citizens of the City of New York*. New York: Sun Office, 1846.
Benton, Thomas. *Speech in the Senate of the United States, in March, 1825, on the bill for the Occupation of the Columbia River*. St. Louis: Missourian Office, 1844.
Bode, Emil. *Deutsche Kämpfer in Nordamerika*. Leipzig: n.p., ca. 1934.
Boyd, Julian P., et al., eds. *The Papers of Thomas Jefferson*. Princeton: Princeton University Press, 1950.
Bristed, Charles Astor. *A Letter to Horace Mann*. New York: Kernot, 1850.
Bryce, James, ed. *A Great Peacemaker: The Diary of James Gallatin, Secretary to Albert Gallatin 1813–1827*. New York: Charles Scribner's Sons, 1915.
Chaldize, Valery, ed. *John Jacob Astor: Business Letters, 1813–1828*. Benson: Chaldize Publications, 1991.
Cox, Ross. *Adventures on the Columbia River*. New York: J & J Harper, 1832.
Crowninshield, Frank. *The Unofficial Palace of New York: A Tribute to the Waldorf=Astoria*. New York: Waldorf=Astoria Co., 1939.
DeVoe, Thomas F. *The Market Book. Containing a Historical Account of the Public Markets in the Cities of New York, Boston, Philadelphia and Brooklyn*. New York: Burt Frankling, 1862.
Didier, Eugene L., ed. *The Life and Letters of Madame Bonaparte*. New York: Charles Scriber's Sons, 1879.
Franchère, Gabriel. *Narrative of a Voyage to the Northwest Coast of America, in the Years 1811, 1812, 1813, and 1814, Or, The First American Settlement on the Pacific*. New York: Redfield, 1854.
Hellman, George S., ed. *The Letters of Washington Irving to Henry Breevort*, vol. 2. New York: G.P. Putnam, 1915.
Hopkins, James F., et al., eds. *The Papers of Henry Clay*. Lexington: University of Kentucky Press, 1959–1992.
Horn, Wilhelm Oertel von. *Johann Jakob Astor*. Wiesbaden: Kreidel und Niedner, 1854.
Irving, Pierre. *Life and Letters of Washington Irving*, vol. 2. New York: Putnam, 1862.
Irving, Washington. *Astoria; or, Anecdotes of an Enterprise beyond the Rocky Mountains*. 2 vols. Philadelphia: J.B. Lippincott, 1961.
Kapp, Friedrich. *Die Deutschen im Staate New*

York während des 18. Jahrhunderts. New York: E. Steiger, 1884.

———. *Geschichte der Deutschen Einwanderung in Amerika*. Leipzig: Quandt & Händel, 1868.

Kiesinger, Kurt-Georg. "200 Jahr USA: Eine Bilanz der deutsch-amerikanischen Beziehungen." In *200 Jahre deutsch-amerikanische Beziehungen*, edited by Michael G. Eisenstadt and Dieter Oberndörfer. Bonn: Eichholz-Verlag, 1976.

Körner, Gustav. *Das deutsche Element in den Vereinigten Staaten von Nordamerika, 1818–1848*. Cincinnati: Verlag Wilde, 1880.

Löher, Franz von. *Geschichte und Zustände der Deutschen in Amerika*. Cincinnatti: Verlag von Eggers und Wulkop, 1847.

Mann, Horace. *A Few Thoughts for a Young Man*. Syracuse: Mills, Hopkins, 1853.

Melville, Herman. *Bartleby the Scrivener*. New York: Melville House, 2004.

Menzel, Wolfgang. *Geschichte der Deutschen bis auf die neuesten Tage*, vol. 5. Stuttgart: Cotta, 1856.

Miller, Hunter, ed. *Treaties and Other International Acts of the United States of America*, vol. 2. Washington, D.C.: U.S. Government Printing Office, 1935.

New York Genealogical and Biographical Record, vol. 22. New York: New York Genealogical and Biographical Society, 1891.

Oxford English Dictionary, vol. 6. Oxford: Oxford University Press 1933.

Papers Relating to the Trade with China, vol. 262. Parliament of Great Britain, House of Lords, London 1829.

Preston, Daniel, et. al., eds. *The Papers of James Monroe*. Westport: Greenwood Press, 2003.

Rollins, Philip A., ed. *The Discovery of the Oregon Trail: Robert Stuart's Narratives of His Overland Trip Eastward from Astoria in 1812–13*. Lincoln: University of Nebraska Press, 1995.

Ronellenfitsch, Klaus. *Walldorfer Familienbuch 1650–1900*. Walldorf: Beltz, 1991.

Ross, Alexander. *Adventures of the first settlers on the Oregon or Columbia River. Being a narrative of the expedition fitted out by John Jacob Astor, to establish the Pacific Fur Company*. London: Smith, Elder & Co., 1849.

———. *The Fur Hunters of the Far West*, vol. 1. London: Smith, Elder & Co, 1855.

Scoville, Joseph A. *The Old Merchants of New York City*. 5 vols. New York: Carlton, 1870.

Stocker, Carl W.F.L. *Chronik von Walldorf*. Bruchsal: n.p., 1888.

Stricker, Wilhelm. *Germania:Archiv zur Kenntniß des deutschen Elements in allen Ländern der Erde*. Frankfurt am Main: H.L. Brönner, 1847.

Tocqueville, Alexis de. *Democracy in America*. New York: Harper Perennial Modern Classics, 2000.

Zimmermann, W.F.A. *Astoria oder Reisen und Abenteuer der Astorexpeditionen* (Leipzig: Payne, 1858).

Secondary Sources

ARTICLES

Astor, William Waldorf. "John Jacob Astor." *Pall Mall Magazine* (June 1899): 171–184.

Bretting, Agnes. "Deutsche Siedlungsviertel in New York City, 1830–1930." In *Von Deutschland nach Amerika. Zur Sozialgeschichte der Auswanderung im 19. und 20. Jahrhundert*, edited by Günter Moltmann, 57–104. Stuttgart: Steiner Verlag, 1992.

Brown, Kenneth. "Stephen Girard, Promoter of the Second Bank of the United States." *JEH* 2 (1942): 125–148.

Carlos, Ann. "The Causes and Origins of the North American Fur Trade Rivalry. 1804–1810." *JEH* 41 (1981): 777–794.

Cogswell, Joseph G. "The Astor Library and its Founder." *United States Magazine of Science, Art, Manufactures, Agriculture, Commerce and Trade* 2 (1855): 132–144.

Colwill, Elizabeth. "Subjectivity, Self-Representation and the Revealing Twitches of Biography." *French Historical Studies* 24 (2001): 421–437.

Conzen, Kathleen N. "Germans." *Harvard Encyclopedia of American Ethnic Groups*, edited by Stephan Thernstrom. Cambridge: Harvard University Press, 1980, 405–425.

Crew, Louie. "Charles Dickens as a Critic of the United States." *Midwest Quarterly* 16.1 (1974): 42–50.

D'Avanzo, Mario. "Melville's Bartleby and John Jacob Astor." *New England Quarterly* 41 (1968): 259–264.

Emmerich, Alexander. "The German Society of the City of New York." In *Germany and the Americas: Culture, History and Politics*, edited by Thomas Adam and Will Kaufman. Santa Barbara: ABC Clio, 2005, 430–432.

Engelmann, Julius. "Johann Jakob Astor." In *Das Buch berühmter Kaufleute*, edited by Franz Otto. Leipzig: Verlag Otto Spamer, 1868, 469–488.

Galbraith, John S. "British-American Competition in the Border Fur Trade of the 1820s." *Minnesota History* 36 (September 1959): 241–248.

Hoerder, Dirk. "Vom korporativen Eigentumsbegriff. Ein Element der amerikanischen Revolution." In *200 Jahre Amerikanische*

Revolution und moderne Revolutionsforschung, edited by Hans-Ulrich Wehler. Göttingen: Vandenhoeck und Ruprecht, 1976, 76–100.

Jacques, David. "John Jacob Astor: A Mercantile Biography." *Hunt's Merchant Magazine* 11 (July 1844): 153–159.

Kidson, Frank, and H.G. Farmer. "Astor & Co." In *The New Grove Dictionary of Music and Musicians,* edited by Stanley Sadie. London: Macmillan, 1980, 662.

Kloppenberg, James T. "The Virtues of Liberalism: Christianity, Republicanism, and Ethics in Early American Political Discourse." *Journal of American History* 74 (1987): 9–33.

Kohl, Lawrence F. "Republicanism Meets the Market Revolution." *Reviews in American History* 19 (1991): 188–193.

Lavender, David. "Some Characteristics of the American Fur Company." *Minnesota History* 40 (1969): 178–187.

Lewis, Jan. "Happiness." In *The Ideological Origins of the American Revolution,* edited by Bernard Bailyn. Cambridge, MA: Harvard University Press, 1982, 641–647.

Mauch, Christof. "Grande Dame der jungen Republik. Dolley Madison 1768–1849." In *Mrs. Präsident: Von Martha Washington bis Hillary Clinton,* edited by Philipp Gassert and Christof Mauch. Stuttgart: DVA, 2000, 54–65.

Merk, Frederick. "The Genesis of the Oregon Question." *Mississippi Valley Historical Review* 36 (1950): 583–612.

"Millionaire." In *Oxford English Dictionary,* vol. 6. Oxford: Oxford University Press, 1933, 450.

Milner, Clyde A. II. "National Initiatives." In *The Oxford History of the American West,* edited by Clyde A. Milner II, Carol A. O'Connor, and Martha A. Sandweiss. New York: Oxford University Press, 1994, 156–193.

Nolte, Paul. "Der Durchbruch der amerikanischen Marktgesellschaft. Wirtschaft, Politik und Kultur in der Frühen Republik 1790–1850." *Historische Zeitschrift* 259 (1994): 695–716.

Parton, James. "John Jacob Astor." *Harper's New Monthly Magazine* 30 (December 1864): 308–323.

Porter, Kenneth W. "Myths after Astor." *Bulletin of the Business Historical Society* 10 (1936): 1–7.

Ronda, James P. "Dreams and Discoveries. Exploring the American West, 1760–1815." *William and Mary Quarterly* 46 (1989): 145–162.

Schilling, F. "Johann Jakob Astor." In *Handwörterbuch des Grenz-und Auslanddeutschtums,* vol. 1. Breslau: n.p., 1933, 161–163.

Schulten, Susan. "Success." In *Encyclopedia of American Cultural and Intellectual History,* edited by Mary K. Cayton and Peter W. Williams, vol. 3. New York: Scribner, 2001, 3–7.

Shalhope, Robert E. "Republicanism." In *The Blackwell Encyclopedia of the American Revolution,* edited by Jack P. Greene and J. R. Pole. Oxford: Blackwell, 1991, 654–660.

Stevens, Wayne E. "The Organization of the British Fur Trade, 1760–1800." *Mississippi Valley Historical Review* 3 (1916): 172–202.

Walters, Raymond, Jr. "The Origins of the Second Bank of the United States." *JEH* 53 (1945): 115–131.

Wilentz, Sean. "On Class and Politics in Jacksonian America." In *The Promise of American History: Progress and Prospects,* edited by Stanley I. Kutler and Stanley N. Katz. Baltimore: Johns Hopkins University Press, 1982, 45–63.

———. "Society, Politics, and the Market Revolution, 1815–1848." *New American History* (1990): 51–71.

Wood, Gordon S. "The Significance of the Early Republic." In *Major Problems in the Early Republic,* edited by Sean Wilentz. Lexington: University of Kentucky Press, 1992, 2–8.

Wrigley, E.A. "A Simple Model of London's Importance in Changing English Society and Economy 1650–1750." *Past and Present* 37 (1967): 44–70.

Books

Ackroyd, Peter. *London: Die Biographie.* München: Albrecht Knaus Verlag, 2002.

Adams, James T. *The Epic of America.* New York and Boston: Little, Brown, 1931.

Appleby, Joyce O. *Capitalism and a New Social Order.* New York: New York University Press, 1984.

———. *Liberalism and Republicanism in the Historical Imagination.* Cambridge: Harvard University Press, 1992.

———. *Thomas Jefferson.* New York: Times Books, 2003.

Bailyn, Bernard, ed. *The Ideological Origins of the American Revolution.* Cambridge: Harvard University Press, 1992.

Bokor, Charles von. *Winkelmaß und Zirkel: Die Geschichte der Freimaurer.* Vienna: Moewig Sachbuch, 1980.

Bourdieu, Pierre. *Sozialer Sinn: Kritik der theoretischen Vernunft.* Frankfurt am Main: Suhrkamp, 1987.

———. *Die verborgenen Mechanismen der Macht: Schriften zu Politik und Kultur.* Hamburg: VSA, 1992.

Brands, W.H. *Masters of Enterprises: Giants of American Business from John Jacob Astor and*

J.P. Morgan to Bill Gates and Oprah Winfrey. New York: Free Press, 1999.

Brookisher, Richard. *Alexander Hamilton: American*. New York: Schuster & Schuster, 1999.

Bryce, George. *The Remarkable History of the Hudson's Bay Company: Including that of the French Traders of North-Western Canada and of the North-West, XY, and Astor Fur Companies*. London: S. Low, Marston & Company, 1910.

Burrows, Edwin G. *Albert Gallatin and the Political Economy of Republicanism, 1761–1800*. New York: Garland, 1986.

Burrows, Edwin G., and Mike Wallace. *Gotham: A History of New York City to 1898*. New York: Oxford University Press, 1999.

Carlson, Oliver. *The Man Who Made News: James Gordon Bennett*. New York: Duell, Sloan and Pearce, 1942.

Chittenden, Hiram M. *The American Fur Trade of the Far West*, vol. 1. Lincoln: University of Nebraska Press, 1935.

Cogliano, Francis D. *Revolutionary America, 1763–1815: A Political History*. New York: Routledge, 2000.

Cowles, Virginia. *The Astors*. New York: Knopf, 1979.

Cullen, Jim. *The American Dream: A Short History of an Idea that Shaped a Nation*. New York: Oxford University Press, 2003.

Dulles, Foster R. *The Old China Trade*. New York: AMS Press, 1970.

Ebersold, Günther. *Rokoko, Reform und Revolution: Ein politisches Lebensbild des Kurfürsten Karl Theodor*. Frankfurt am Main: Lang, 1985.

Elkins, Stanley, and Eric McKitrick. *The Age of Federalism*. New York: Oxford University Press, 1995.

Eue, Johannes. *Die Oregon-Frage: Amerikansiche Expansionspolitik Und Der Pazifische Nordwesten, 1814–1848*. Munster: LIT Verlag, 1995.

Flandrau, Grace. *Astor and the Oregon Country*. St. Paul: Great Northern Railway, 1926.

Fleming, Thomas J. *The Louisiana Purchase*. Hoboken: J. Wiley, 2003.

Gates, John D. *The Astor Family: A Unique Exploration of One of America's First Families*. Garden City: Doubleday, 1981.

Gebhard, Elizabeth Louisa. *The Life and Ventures of the Original John Jacob Astor*. New York: Bryan, 1915.

Goldberger, Ludwig M. *Das Land der unbegrenzten Möglichkeiten: Beobachtungen über das Wirtschaftsleben der Vereinigten Staaten von Amerika*. Berlin: F. Fontane, 1903.

Gordon, Milton. *Assimilation in American Life: The Role of Race, Religion and National Origins*. New York: Oxford University Press, 1964.

Grabbe, Hans-Jürgen. *Vor der großen Flut*. Stuttgart: Steiner Verlag, 2001.

Guttandin, Friedhelm. *Einführung in die Protestantische Ethik*. Opladen: Westdeutscher Verlag, 1990.

Haeger, John D. *John Jacob Astor: Business and Finance in the Early Republic*. Detroit: Wayne State University Press, 1991.

Han, Petrus. *Soziologie der Migration*. Stuttgart: UTB, 2000.

Henderson, Mary C. *The City and the Theatre: The History of New York Playhouses*. New York: Back Stage Books, 2004.

Henning, Friedrich-Wilhelm. *Landwirtschaft und ländliche Gesellschaft in Deutschland, 1750–1976*. Paderborn: Schöningh, 1978.

Howden-Smith, Arthur D. *John Jacob Astor: Landlord of New York*. New York: Blue Ribbon Books, 1929.

Hoy, Calvin I. *John Jacob Astor: An Unwritten Chapter*. Boston: Meader Publishing Company, 1936.

Inwood, Stephen. *A History of London*. London: Macmillan, 1998.

Jackson, J.A. *Migration*. London: Longman, 1986.

Jameson, Egon. *Millionen aus dem Nichts*. Stuttgart: Hallwag, 1967.

Johnson, Paul. *A History of the American People*. New York: Harper Collins, 1997.

Joseph, Vivian. *A History of the British East India Company*. Tallis: Cheddar, 1987.

Kavaler, Lucy. *The Astors: An American Legend*. New York: Dodd Mead, 1968.

Kime, Wayne R. *Pierre M. Irving and Washington Irving: A Collaboration in Life and Letters*. Waterloo: Wilfrid Laurier University Press, 1977.

Klein, Christian, ed. *Grundlagen der Biographik*. Stuttgart: J.B. Metzler Verlag, 2002.

Löffler, Thomas. *Zu Nutzen und Gebrauch der Armen: Die Geschichte der Astor-Stiftung in Walldorf*. Walldorf, 1998.

Lyon, Wilson E. *Louisiana in French Diplomacy, 1759–1804*. Oklahoma City: University of Oklahoma Press, 1974.

Madsen, Axel. *John Jacob Astor: America's First Multimillionaire*. New York: John Wiley & Sons, 2001.

Mahood, Wayne. *General Wadsworth: The Life and Times of Brevet Major General James S. Wadsworth*. Cambridge, MA: Da Capo Press, 2003.

Mancall, Peter C. *Deadly Medicine: Indians and Alcohol in Early America*. Ithaca: Cornell University Press, 1995.

Messerli, Jonathan. *Horace Mann: A Biography*. New York: Alfred A. Knopf, 1972.

Minnigerode, Meade. *Certain Rich Men: Stephen Girard, John Jacob Astor, Jay Cooke, Daniel Drew, Cornelius Vanderbilt, Jay Gould,*

Jim Fisk. New York: G.P. Putnam's Sons, 1927.

Moersch, Karl. *Geschichte der Pfalz: Von den Anfängen bis ins 19. Jahrhundert*. Bad Dürkheim: Pfälzische Verlagsanstalt, 1987.

Morris, Richard B. *The Peacemakers: The Great Powers and American Independence*. New York: Harper & Row, 1965.

Myers, Gustavus. *Geschichte der Großen Amerikanischen Vermögen*. 2 vols. Berlin: S. Fischer Verlag, 1916.

Nevins, Allan, ed. *The Diary of Philip Hone, 1828–1851*. New York: Dodd, Mead, 1969.

Nipperdey, Thomas. *Deutsche Geschichte: Bürgerwelt und Starker Staat*. München: C.H. Beck, 1983.

Parton, James. *Famous Americans of Recent Times*. Boston: Ticknor and Fields, 1867.

_____. *Life of John Jacob Astor*. New York: The American News Company, 1865.

Pierce, Bob, and Larry Ashley, eds. *Pierce Piano Atlas*. Long Beach: Pierce Piano Atlas, 2003.

Pocock, John G.A. *The Machiavellian Moment: Florentine Political Thought and the Atlantic Republican Tradition*. Princeton: Princeton University Press, 1975.

Porter, Kenneth Wiggins. *John Jacob Astor: Business Man*. 2 vols. New York: Russel & Russel, 1966.

Rall, Hans. *Kurfürst Karl Theodor: Regierender Herr in sieben Ländern*. Mannheim: Bibliographisches Institut, 1993.

Ronda, James P. *Astoria & Empire*. Lincoln: University of Nebraska Press, 1993.

Schaab, Meinrad. *Geschichte der Kurpfalz*, vol. 2. Stuttgart: Kohlhammer, 1992.

Scharnhorst, Gary. *The Lost Life of Horatio Alger Jr*. Bloomington: Indiana University Press, 1985.

Schröder, Hans-Christoph. *Die Amerikanische Revolution: Eine Einführung*. München: C.H. Beck, 1982.

Sellers, Charles. *The Market Revolution: Jacksonian America, 1815–1846*. Oxford: Oxford University Press, 1991.

Shulman, Holly C., ed. The Papers of Dolley Madison Digital Edition. Charlottesville: University of Virginia Press, Rotunda, 2008.

Stagg, J.C.A., ed. *The Papers of James Madison Digital Edition*. Charlottesville: University of Virginia Press, Rotunda, 2010.

Stevens, Frank W. *The Beginnings of the New York Central Railroad*. New York: G.P. Putman, 1926.

Taylor, George R. *Jackson versus Biddle: The Struggle over the Second Bank of the United States*. Boston: D.C. Heath, 1949.

Terrell, John U. *Furs by Astor*. New York: Morrow, 1963.

Trollope, Frances. *Domestic Manners of the Americans*. New York: Vintage, 1949.

Unrau, William E. *White Man's Wicked Water: The Alcohol Trade and Prohibition in Indian Country, 1802–1892*. Lawrence, KS: University Press of Kansas, 1996.

Wait, Eugene M. *America and the War of 1812*. Commack, NY: Kroshka, 1999.

Weber, Max. *Die protestantische Ethik und der Geist des Kapitalismus*. Bodenheim: Westdeutscher Verlag, 1993.

Wehler, Hans-Ulrich. *Bismarck und der Imperialismus*. Cologne: Kiepenhauer & Witsch, 1969.

Weisberger, Bernard A. *The American Newspaperman*. Chicago: University of Chicago Press, 1961.

Williamson, Jefferson. *The American Hotel: An Anecdotal History*. New York: A.A. Knopf, 1930.

Wilson, Derek. *The Astors 1763–1992: Landscapes with Millionaires*. London: Weidenfield and Nicolson, 1993.

Wood, Gordon S. *The Creation of the American Republic, 1776–1787*. Chapel Hill: University of North Carolina Press, 1969.

_____. *Radicalism of the American Revolution*. New York: Vintage, 1993.

Wright, Robert E. *The Wealth of Nations Rediscovered: Integration and Expansion in American Financial Markets, 1780–1850*. Cambridge: Cambridge University Press, 2002.

Wust, Klaus. *Guardians on the Hudson: The German Society of the City of New York, 1784–1984*. New York: The Society, 1984.

Index

acculturation 6–7, 15, 32, 45, 47, 92, 170
Adams, John 61, 92
Alaska 71, 76–78
American Dream 3, 6, 152, 168
American Fur Company 11, 15–16, 67, 69–75, 77–80, 92, 100, 102–104, 106, 111–114, 116–119, 123, 132–133, 140, 157, 164, 171
Astor, Catherina 20–22, 84, 149
Astor, Christina Barbara 20–22, 108
Astor, George 20–21, 25, 27, 31, 43, 46–49, 65, 74–75, 108, 148, 169–170
Astor, Henry 20, 21, 25, 27, 42, 43, 47, 55, 122, 127, 138, 140, 146, 148–149
Astor, Johann Jakob (father) 19, 20, 23, 108
Astor, John Jacob II 54
Astor, Magdalen 54, 58, 105, 127, 134, 140, 147
Astor, Maria Magdalena 19–21, 25
Astor, Melchior 20, 21, 108, 149
Astor, Sarah Todd 15, 45–47, 48, 50, 53, 54, 64, 127, 140, 148, 170
Astor, William Backhouse 55, 104, 106, 110–111, 116–118, 122, 140–143, 144, 147–149, 159
Astor, William Waldorf Viscount 13, 49, 51–52, 129, 148
Astor Library 1, 137, 144
Astor Rumpff, Eliza 13, 55, 105, 107–109, 112, 122, 140, 148, 159
Astoria (book) 13, 16, 127, 131–135, 151
Astoria, Oregon 1, 12, 13, 15, 74–75, 82–96, 98, 100, 103, 105, 114, 117, 142, 144, 151, 157, 160, 164, 166

Baltimore 35–37, 42, 107
Beaver (ship) 64, 66, 84, 88, 101–2
Broadway 39, 56, 58, 112, 121, 124, 127, 129, 131, 142, 143, 147, 171

Canada 45, 49, 50, 52, 53, 80, 87, 89, 94
Canton 61–65, 74–75, 88, 101, 103, 120
chain migration 32
China 15, 16, 40, 43, 56, 61–67, 75, 85, 100–102, 119–120, 151

Clark, William 70, 72, 80
Clay, Henry 13, 16, 57, 86, 109–111
Clinton, DeWitt 57, 58, 66, 71, 74, 86, 102, 171
Clinton, George 71, 86
Columbia River 1, 15, 76, 78–82, 84, 88, 89–95, 103, 119, 133, 135, 141, 146, 151, 164

Daschkoff, Andrew 76–79, 87
Declaration of Independence 7, 44, 60–61
Dickens, Charles 4, 5, 159

Embargo Act 15, 65–66, 69–71, 74–75, 81, 85
Enterprise (ship) 78–79, 81–82, 90, 101
Erie Canal 58, 100, 102

Franklin, Benjamin 6, 57, 157
freemasonry 56–58
frontier 49–51, 80, 102, 113–115, 152

Gallatin, Albert 13, 65–66, 72, 77, 86–87, 92–93, 95, 98–100, 104, 106–107, 112, 117, 148, 157, 159
Geneva 15, 107, 112–113, 122, 140, 148
German Reformed Church of New York 40, 43, 47
German Society of the City of New York 9, 13, 40, 43–44, 138–139, 170
Germany 1–6, 9, 11–12, 17, 27, 31, 33, 40, 55; German-Americans 40, 43, 47, 57; immigration 17, 18, 19, 41, 48
Great Lakes 50, 53–54, 69, 80, 87, 94, 102–103, 106, 114, 119

Hamilton, Alexander 40, 41, 61, 98, 143
Hone, Philipp 13, 122, 127–128, 132, 135, 140, 143, 152, 159
Hudson's Bay Company 69–70, 95, 113–118

Irving, Washington 13, 16, 42, 73, 83, 91, 109, 127, 131, 133–137, 140, 142–143, 147, 151–152, 159

195

Index

Jackson, Andrew 57, 137, 157
Jay Treaty 54
Jefferson, Thomas 13, 15, 40, 41, 48, 57, 58, 61, 65–66, 70–78, 82, 84–86, 89–90, 94, 97, 115, 157, 164
Jeune, Johann Valentin 22–24, 25, 27, 57

Lewis, Meriwether 70, 73
liberalism 5, 60–61, 77, 156, 163, 167
Little Germany 40, 43, 139
London 15, 21, 25, 30, 31, 32, 36, 45, 49, 56, 62–65, 69, 74, 89, 91, 101, 108–109, 120, 141, 162, 169–171
Louisiana 58, 59
Louisiana Purchase 59, 64, 70, 72, 74, 76; Louisiana Territory 70
luxury 1, 8, 9, 13, 33, 35, 54, 105, 124, 126, 128–129, 136, 163, 166, 168–171

Madison, Dolley 13, 86–87
Madison, James 13, 57, 72, 74, 77–79, 82, 85–87, 89, 91–92, 94, 98–100, 104, 105, 109, 115
Mann, Horace 5, 156
market revolution 7, 97, 100
Mohawk & Hudson Railroad Company 15, 120–121
Monroe, James 13, 16, 48, 57, 86, 89, 91–92, 94, 99, 107, 109–111, 115
Montreal 36, 49–55, 69–70, 76, 79–80

New York Public Library 1, 13, 145; *see also* Astor Library
North Carolina (ship) 34–37
Northwest Company 69, 70, 78–80, 88–91, 93–94, 118

Oregon 74–79, 81–82, 88–89, 91–96, 144, 151, 164

Pacific Fur Company 79–83, 87–88, 90, 94
Palatinate 14, 17, 19, 22, 52
Paris 15, 30, 33, 42, 95, 99, 104, 106–107, 109–112, 122, 142, 148
Park Theatre 68, 150, 171
Peace Treaty of Paris (1783) 33
Polk, James Knox 48
pull-factors 25
pursuit of happiness 44, 61, 146, 156
push-factors 25

republicanism 5, 60, 156, 167
Revolutionary War 7, 33, 40, 42, 48, 57, 61, 162
Russian-American Company 78–79

St. Louis 72, 79–80, 88, 102–103, 106, 112, 140
Shudi & Broadwood 32, 46
Steiner, Johann Philip 22, 24–25
success 3, 5–6, 8, 10–12, 15, 27, 31–33, 37, 40–44, 50, 54–56, 60, 62–65, 70, 144, 146, 148–151, 158, 160, 162, 164, 167–168, 170

Theodor, Carl 17, 19
Titanic 2, 35, 37, 148
Tonquin (ship) 80–84, 91, 134

Waldorf-Astoria 1, 2, 129, 131, 148, 163
Walldorf, Germany 1, 2, 3, 6, 14, 17, 19, 22, 23, 25, 44, 47, 57, 63, 84, 107–109, 144–146, 149–150, 152, 157, 162, 166, 170–171